A Special Issue of
Cognitive Neuropsychiatry

The Cognitive Neuropsychiatry of Emotion and Emotional Disorders

Edited by

André Aleman
University of Groningen, The Netherlands

Nick Medford
Institute of Psychiatry and GKT School of Medicine, UK

Anthony S. David
Institute of Psychiatry and GKT School of Medicine, UK

Psychology Press
Taylor & Francis Group
HOVE AND NEW YORK

First published in 2006 by Psychology Press Ltd
27 Church Road, Hove, East Sussex BN3 2FA

Simultaneously published in the USA and Canada
by Psychology Press
711 Third Avenue, New York, NY 10017

First issued in paperback 2015

Psychology Press is an imprint of the Taylor & Francis Group, an informa business

British Library Cataloguing in Publication Data
A catalogue record for this book is available from the British Library

ISBN 13: 978-1-138-87325-4 (pbk)
ISBN 13: 978-1-8416-9990-5 (hbk)

ISSN 1354 6805

Typeset DP Photosetting, Aylesbury, Bucks

Contents*

* This book is also a special issue of the journal *Cognitive Neuropsychiatry*, and forms
issue 3 of Volume 11 (2006). The page numbers are taken from the journal and so begin
with p. 193.

COGNITIVE NEUROPSYCHIATRY
2006, 11 (3), 193–197

Dissecting the cognitive and neural basis of emotional abnormalities

André Aleman

University of Groningen, The Netherlands

Nick Medford and Anthony S. David

Institute of Psychiatry, London, UK

The experimental investigation of emotion and its disorders was largely ignored for much of the 20th century. In contrast, the last decades have witnessed an explosion of research in this field. With the demise of black-box behaviourism, previously neglected mental phenomena and processes were promoted to the forefront of research. While the initial emphasis here was on studying cognitive function in isolation from emotion, the need to combine such study with a scientific approach to emotion has become increasingly evident. As awareness of the importance of emotion in influencing cognition and shaping behaviour has increased, many researchers have heeded this growing imperative, and eloquent accounts of the neural underpinnings of emotion by leading researchers, such as Damasio (1994) and LeDoux (1996), have taken many of the major themes to a large and receptive readership beyond the usual confines of academia. Significant contributions of emotional systems were shown not only in, for example, signalling acute danger and prioritising adaptive action, but to extend to such higher order functions as human strategic decision making (Bechara, Damasio, Tranel, & Damasio, 1997; Van't Wout, Kahn, Sanfey, & Aleman, 2006). In addition, methods of investigating different aspects of emotion, ranging from autonomic responses through regional brain activation to cognitive appraisal, have become increasingly refined over the last decades. In particular, novel and sophisticated tasks have been developed to target the neural basis of phenomena, such as affective states, previously regarded as too elusive to be amenable to scientific study.

Emotional dysfunction has long claimed a central place in most psychiatric disorders, including those conditions not normally considered as affective

Correspondence concerning this article should be addressed to André Aleman, BCN Neuroimaging Center, University Medical Center Groningen, University of Groningen, A. Deusinglaan 2, 9713 AW, Groningen, The Netherlands

http://www.psypress.com/cogneuropsychiatry   DOI:10.1080/13546800600630542

disorders (Aleman & Kahn, 2005; Phillips, Phillips, Drevels, Rauch, & Lane, 2003; Sierra, Senior et al., 2003). Biologically minded psychiatric researchers have approached the topic largely from the perspectives of psychopharmacology and psychophysiology. The potency of antidepressant medication, with its implication for neurotransmitter theories, are rightly influential. Changes in markers of stress responses paralleling fluctuations in depression and anxiety have also chimed with common sense notions of the nature of affective illnesses. However, novel insights regarding the emotional implications of neurological conditions and lesions are accumulating (e.g., Adolphs, Gosselin et al., 2005; Anderson & Phelps 2001; Scott, Young et al., 1997; Shaw, Brierley, & David, 2005) introducing the notion of that apparently static brain damage can lead to variations in affect and can modulate affective reactions. The above scheme would appear to lack a cognitive component. This situation existed up until the pioneering work of Beck (1976) whose cognitive theories gave primacy to thinking (beliefs, appraisals, assumptions, worries, etc.). These, according to Beck, drive emotions – rather than the other way round. Either way, these accounts appear to bypass the organ of thinking. The cognitive neuropsychiatric approach seeks to link all these perspectives: from phenomenology, through cognition, to physiology and ultimately, brain function and structure. While much cognitive neuropsychiatric research has been concerned with psychotic symptoms, the move to consider in this Special Issue of the journal, emotion and its disorders, and hence universal experiences, is only natural and to be encouraged.

Emotion can best be thought of as a multicomponent process (Scherer, 2004). That is, emotion involves several components, each of which fulfils a specific function in the adaptation to the situation that has triggered the emotion process (cf. Frijda, 1986). Scherer (2004) proposed that three hypothetical types of central representation can be distinguished in the emotion process: (1) unconscious reflection and regulation (involving cognitive appraisal, physiological symptoms, motor expression and action tendencies); (2) conscious representation and regulation (involving feelings); and (3) verbalisation and communication of emotional experience. Emotional processes at all three levels will be discussed in the current issue.

OVERVIEW

The first paper, by Strange and Dolan, presents a review of research into the role of the medial temporal lobe in memory for novel and emotional material. Emotional memory has been the focus of much study in recent years. Here, the findings to date are reviewed and synthesised to provide a detailed model of a key interaction between emotion and cognition, and an illustration of the importance of integrating the study of emotion into cognitive science if studies are to have relevance to real-world function and dysfunction. Tranel et al. report novel and intriguing findings in a study regarding emotional experience in a rare neurological patient with complete bilateral amygdala damage. Two experienced clinical psychologists conducted interviews with the patient, with a special eye towards her emotional phenomenology, while they were not aware of her neuropsychological background information. All investigators agreed that the patient lacked some of the deepest negative emotions from her phenomenology of life. The conclusion reached by the authors is that bilateral lesions of the amygdala may not only affect emotional perception, but also emotional experience.

The paper by Phillips is a state-of-the-art review of studies into the neural basis of mood dysregulation in bipolar disorder. The author not only reviews empirical findings from the neuroimaging literature, but integrates these findings into a testable theoretical framework. More specifically, she suggests that findings from neuroimaging studies investigating the brain response to emotional stimuli in bipolar disorder indicate increased subcortical responses and decreased reponse in a dorsomedial prefrontal cortical region during sadness. The hypothesis is advanced that the affective instability in the disorder may result from a combination of increased activity within subcortical and limbic regions implicated in the initial appraisal of emotive stimuli, resulting in increased activity in regions associated with mood generation and decisions about emotional material, and reduced activity within regions implicated in the regulation of these responses and attentional processes.

Although schizophrenia is often regarded as a nonaffective psychosis, Kohler and Martin provide an overview of studies that investigated emotional processing in schizophrenia. An introductory historical survey is followed by a brief discussion of the neurobiology of emotional processing. The main part of the paper is devoted to a review of research into disturbance of emotional experience, facial expression, and recognition of facial emotional expressions in patients with schizophrenia. The weight of evidence favours the hypothesis that emotional experience, expression, and perception are altered in schizophrenia. In the paper that follows, Van't Wout et al. extend these findings by reporting an original investigation of memory for object-locations in schizophrenia. Specifically, they compared spatial memory for threat-related vs. nonthreatening symbolic stimuli (schematic pictures). Their results reveal an attentional bias for threat-related stimuli in schizophrenia patients relative to healthy age- and education-matched control participants.

Moving on to personality disorders, Schutter and Van Honk propose a model for understanding the neurobiology of primary psychopathy, an emotional disorder characterised by a lack of fear and empathy. According to this framework, defective emotional processing in primary psychopathy is largely a result of hormone-mediated imbalances at the level of the amygdala, prefrontal cortex, and subcortical-cortical communication. Van Honk & Hermans discuss putative distortions in emotional processing and corresponding neural systems in social phobia, and put forward the suggestion that particular patterns of fear processing in early life pave the way for development of social phobia in later life. Psychological and biological evidence for this idea is discussed within a framework based on evolutionary theory. Finally, Bermond et al. present a review of the neuropsychological basis of alexithymia, a personality trait that implies deficient emotion regulation. The authors provide a comprehensive review of different brain areas implicated in different aspects of alexithymia, and their interactions. Notably, the authors advance an interesting and testable hypothesis regarding different emotional personality types, which can potentially guide future research into the neurocognitive basis of alexithymia.

CONCLUSION

Given the upsurge in emotion research within psychiatry and neurology over the last decades, it seemed an appropriate moment to take stock of research and theory. This Special Issue combines a range of timely reviews with new empirical papers regarding the cognitive and neural basis of emotional processing. After dissecting the cognitive and neural components that underpin emotional processes in health and disease, it is necessary to integrate and resynthesise the elements of these phenomena to specify the nature and importance of the components and their interactions in natural contexts.

REFERENCES

Adolphs, R., Gosselin, F., Buchanan, T. W., Tranel, D., Schyns, P., & Damasio, A. R. (2005). A mechanism for impaired fear recognition after amygdala damage. *Nature, 433*, 68–72.

Aleman, A., & Kahn, R. S. (2005). Strange feelings: Do amygdala abnormalities dysregulate the emotional brain in schizophrenia? *Progress in Neurobiology, 77*, 283–298.

Anderson, A. K., & Phelps, E. A. (2001). Lesions of the human amygdala impair enhanced perception of emotionally salient events. *Nature, 411*, 305–309.

Bechara, A., Damasio, H., Tranel, D., & Damasio, A. R. (1997). Deciding advantageously before knowing the advantageous strategy. *Science, 275*, 1293–1295.

Beck, A. T. (1976). *Cognitive therapy and the emotional disorders.* New York: Meridian

Brierley, B., Medford, N., Shaw, P., & David, A. S. (2004). Emotional memory and perception in temporal lobectomy patients with amygdala damage. *Journal of Neurology, Neurosurgery and Psychiatry, 75*, 593–599.

Damasio, A.R. (1994). *Descartes'error: Emotion, reason and the human brain.* New York: Putnam.

Frijda, N. H. (1986). *The emotions.* Cambridge, UK: Cambridge University Press.

LeDoux, J. (1996). *The emotional brain: The mysterious underpinnings of emotional life.* New York: Simon & Schuster.

Phillips, M. L., Drevets, W. C., Rauch, S. L., & Lane, R. D. (2003). Neurobiology of emotion perception: II. Implications for major psychiatric disorders. *Biological Psychiatry, 54*, 515–528.

Scherer, K. R. (2004). Feelings integrate the central representation of appraisal-driven response organisation in emotion. In S. R. Manstead, N. Frijda, & A. Fischer (Eds.), *Feelings and emotions: The Amsterdam symposium.* Cambridge, UK: Cambridge University Press.

Scott, S. K., Young, A. W., Calder, A. J., Hellawell, D. J., Aggleton, J. P., & Johnson, M. (1997). Impaired auditory recognition of fear and anger following bilateral amygdala lesions. *Nature*, *385*, 254–257.

Shaw, P., Brierley, B., & David, A. S. (2005). A critical period for the impact of amygdala damage on the emotional enhancement of memory? *Neurology*, *65*, 326–328.

Sierra, M., Senior, C., Dalton, J., McDonough, M., Bond, A., Phillips, M. L., O'Dwyer, A. M., & David, A. S. (2002). Autonomic response in depersonalization disorder. *Archives of General Psychiatry*, *59*, 833–838.

Van't Wout, M., Kahn, R. S., Sanfey, A. G., & Aleman, A. (2006). Affective state and decision-making in the Ultimatum Game. *Experimental Brain Research*, *169*, 564–568.

COGNITIVE NEUROPSYCHIATRY
2006, 11 (3), 198–218

Anterior medial temporal lobe in human cognition: Memory for fear and the unexpected

Bryan A. Strange and Raymond J. Dolan

Institute of Neurology, London, UK

Introduction. To survive, an organism must remember occurrences of value in its environment. These include those that pose a threat to survival, novel or unexpected stimuli, or a general class of stimuli that represent punishment or reward. There is substantial evidence that memory for novel and emotionally salient events is enhanced relative to familiar or emotionally neutral events.
Methods. We present human functional magnetic resonance imaging (fMRI) experiments that address the neurobiological processes underlying upregulation of memory for novel or emotional events.
Results. Enhanced memory for novel or unexpected stimuli is mediated by anterior hippocampus, whereas increased memory for emotional stimuli is mediated by a β-adrenergic-dependent modulation of amygdala-hippocampal interactions. We introduce a hypothesis that medial temporal connectivity with autonomic control centres may be central to this memory enhancement.
Conclusion. Enhanced memory for stimuli that are of adaptive importance to survival is mediated by the anterior medial temporal lobe and effected via connections with the autonomic system.

Stimuli that deviate from their prevailing context along some dimension (i.e., contextually novel) are better remembered than those that determine a context. This well-known memory enhancement, referred to as the von Restorff effect (von Restorff, 1933), suggests that unexpected stimuli have preferential access to episodic memory. Episodic memory is also enhanced for emotionally arousing compared to neutral events (Bradley, Greenwald, Petry, & Lang, 1992; Cahill & McGaugh, 1998). In humans, long-term memory for events or episodes that is accessible to conscious recollection is dependent on the medial temporal lobes (Scoville & Milner, 1957). It follows, therefore, that the human medial temporal memory system should be functionally specialised for detecting and encoding novel or emotionally salient stimuli.

Correspondence should be addressed to Bryan A. Strange, Wellcome Department of Imaging Neuroscience, Functioning Imaging Laboratory, 12 Queen Square, London WC1N 3BG, UK; e-mail: bstrange@fil.ion.ucl.ac.uk

http://www.psypress.com/cogneuropsychiatry   DOI:10.1080/13546800500305096

The medial temporal lobe consists of the amygdala and hippocampus (used here to refer to dentate gyrus, CA subfields, and subiculum), as well as more superficial surrounding cortical areas, namely, entorhinal, perirhinal, and para-hippocampal cortices. Based on detailed studies of cortical connectivity, it has been proposed that within the neocortex, information from all sensory modalities is processed through a sequence of hierarchically arranged projections. During transfer from primary areas, via secondary and tertiary unimodal association areas, towards multimodal association areas, information processing becomes more elaborated or complex (Pandya & Seltzer, 1982; Van Essen & Maunsell, 1983). Since the medial temporal cortical regions are strongly interconnected with most multimodal areas, this cortical area can be viewed as supramodal cortex where all sensory cortical channels converge. This convergence is taken one step further in the hippocampus (Witter et al., 1989) and amygdala (Swanson & Petrovich, 1998), where there are dominant interactions with subcortical and brainstem modulatory inputs.

Both hippocampus and amygdala receive information not only about the external world through sensory inputs but also interoceptive information, from subcortical and brainstem systems, regarding the internal state, including the motivational state, of the organism. We will present data from human neuroimaging and animal studies that provide evidence for anterior hippocampal and amygdala roles in enhancing memory for unexpected or novel stimuli and emotional stimuli, respectively. The prevailing theory is that episodic memory enhancement for emotional stimuli is mediated by amygdala-hippocampal interactions and we will present data suggesting that this interaction is primarily with anterior hippocampus. The role of the β-adrenergic system in mediating these effects will be discussed, and a possible role for medial temporal interactions with autonomic centres in memory enhancement will be introduced.

HIPPOCAMPUS

Hippocampal damage produces the amnesic syndrome, a deficit in declarative memory (Scoville & Milner, 1957; Squire & Zola-Morgan, 1991). The inability to acquire new episodic memories suggests a hippocampal role in processing novel information. A human hippocampal role in novelty detection has been demonstrated using electrophysiological recordings and functional imaging. Single unit recordings show that hippocampal responses decrease as stimuli are presented repeatedly (Fried, MacDonald, & Wilson, 1997). Furthermore, epilepsy patients with hippocampal sclerosis demonstrate attenuated anterior medial temporal lobe event-related potentials (ERPs) for novel visually presented words while responses to repetitive presentations are unaffected (Grunwald, Lehnertz, Heinze, Helmstaedter, & Elger, 1998). Functional imaging studies have consistently demonstrated that hippocampal responses to novel stimuli are greater than responses to stimuli that subjects have been familiarised

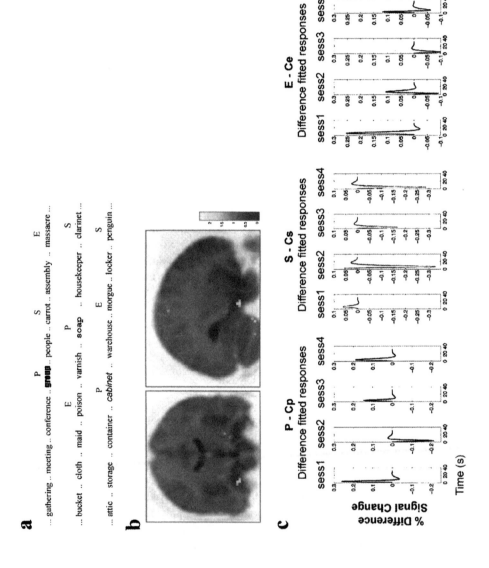

200

with previously (Constable et al., 2000; Dolan & Fletcher, 1997; Haxby et al., 1996; Martin, Wiggs, & Weisberg, 1997; Rombouts et al., 1997; Saykin et al., 1999; Stern et al., 1996; Tulving, Markowitsch, Craik, Habib, & Houle, 1996).

The majority of functional imaging studies of novelty demonstrate activation of anterior hippocampus (Constable et al., 2000; Dolan & Fletcher, 1997; Fischer, Furmark, Wik, & Fredrikson, 2000; Haxby et al., 1996; Martin et al., 1997; Saykin et al., 1999; Sperling et al., 2001; Tulving et al., 1996). Although some studies report posterior hippocampal responses to novelty (Rombouts et al., 1997; Stern et al., 1996), the majority of novelty-evoked activations in posterior medial temporal lobe occur in parahippocampal gyrus (for a review, see Schacter & Wagner, 1999). In an early study, we demonstrated that semantic, behaviourally relevant novelty, as well as physical, behaviourally irrelevant, novel stimuli evoke anterior hippocampal responses (Strange, Fletcher, Henson, Friston, & Dolan, 1999). The anterior locus of these effects was confirmed by a double dissociation showing posterior hippocampal responses as subjects became more familiar with the behaviourally relevant aspects of stimuli (Strange et al., 1999). That both forms of novelty engaged anterior hippocampus led to a suggestion that novelty responses in this region reflect a more generic function in the processing mismatches between expectation or predictions and experience.

The brain mechanisms for detecting violations of expectation have been studied extensively in "oddball" paradigms, where the oddball stimulus deviates in some dimension from the prevailing context. Evidence from intracranial recordings (Halgren et al., 1980) and scalp recordings of oddball-evoked ERPs in patients with hippocampal lesions (Knight, 1996) suggests a critical role for the hippocampus in oddball detection. However, functional neuroimaging experiments of oddball detection have generally failed to find activation of the medial temporal lobes in response to visual (Downar, Crawley, Mikolis, & Davis, 2000; Linden et al., 1999; McCarthy, Luby, Gore, & Goldman-Rokic, 1997; Strange, Henson, Friston, & Dolan, 2000), auditory (Downar et al., 2000; Higashima et al., 1996; Linden et al., 1999; Opitz, Mecklinger, Friederici, & von Cramon, 1999) or tactile (Downar et al., 2000) oddball stimuli.

Figure 1 (opposite). (a) Examples of presented nouns. (b) Left anterior hippocampus is activated by all oddball types and this response adapts across the experiment. The Statistical Parametric Map (SPM) is superimposed on a coronal section of the mean functional image at $y = -12$ and on a saggital section at $x = -30$ to demonstrate left anterior hippocampal activation. (c) The fitted responses for each oddball type minus their respective control, averaged across all individuals, are plotted for the four sessions and demonstrate the adaptive hippocampal response common to all oddball types. Abbreviations: P, perceptual oddball; S, semantic oddball; E, emotional oddball; Cp, control noun for perceptual oddball; Cs, control noun for semantic oddball; Ce, control noun for emotional oddball.

We addressed the issue of oddball-induced hippocampal activity using functional magnetic resonance imaging (fMRI) to measure hippocampal responses to three types of oddballs: perceptual, semantic, and emotional (Strange & Dolan, 2001). Figure 1a gives examples of the stimuli which were presented over four sequential scanning sessions. As the first oddball is completely unexpected, we hypothesised that the response indexing mismatch, or surprise, would be greatest to the first oddball encountered (e.g., the presentation of "group" in a novel font; see Figure 1a). Consequently, we predicted that decreasing mismatch between expectation and outcome to subsequent oddballs would be reflected in an adaptation in anterior hippocampal responses expressed across successive presentations of oddballs. As predicted, adaptive activation was expressed in left anterior hippocampus for all oddball types (Figure 1b and c). Critically, this anterior hippocampal response adapted following presentation of multiple oddballs. This adaptive hippocampal response profile is consistent with this region being engaged by mismatches between expectancy and experience (Strange et al., 1999; Ploghaus et al., 2000), and has been subsequently replicated using standard oddball stimuli (Yamaguchi, Hale, D'Esposito, & Knight, 2004). The initial presentations of oddballs are unexpected but this breach of expectancy diminishes as subjects are exposed to more and more oddballs, reflected in an adapting anterior hippocampal response.

Animal cellular recording demonstrate novelty sensitive cells in medial temporal cortex (Brown & Xiang, 1998) as well as hippocampus (Vinogradova, 1975). Medial temporal cortical responses are typically stimulus-specific, responding differentially to the relative familiarity of certain stimuli and not others (Young, Otto, Fox, & Eichenbaum, 1997), and are thought to possess firing properties that enable recognition memory for simple visual stimuli (Brown & Xiang, 1998). Responses in hippocampus, however, do not show this stimulus-selectivity (Otto & Eichenbaum, 1992; Rolls, Cahusac, Feigenbaum, & Miyashita, 1993; Vinogradova, 1975; Wiebe & Saubli, 1999) suggesting that the hippocampus mediates abstracted, stimulus-general mismatch detection. In agreement with this proposal is the observation that hippocampal responses to oddballs show adaptation expressed across successive presentations of *different* oddballs that deviate from context along the same dimension (Strange & Dolan, 2001).

Thus, the general finding that the hippocampus is sensitive to recency of prior occurrence raises the possibility that the process underlying hippocampal novelty responses is the detection of mismatch between expectation and experience. The engagement of mismatch detection in response to an unpredictable stimulus may be the physiological basis for awarding this stimulus preferential access to storage in long-term memory. This proposal is supported by the observation that patients with hippocampal lesions fail to demonstrate enhanced memory for oddball stimuli (Kishiyama, Yonelinas, & Lazzara, 2004).

AMYGDALA

The amygdala is important for emotional learning in humans (Bechara et al., 1995; Damasio, 1995). Particular aspects of emotional learning, such as the development of phobias or fear conditioning, are dependent on the amygdala and are intact following hippocampal lesions (Bechara et al., 1995). Selective amygdala damage does not, however, produce impairments in declarative memory (Bechara et al., 1995), providing a double dissociation between amygdala and hippocampal roles in emotional and declarative learning, respectively. The amygdala is, however, thought to exert modulatory effects on other memory systems (Cahill & McGaugh, 1998). Normal subjects show enhanced long-term episodic memory for emotionally arousing material relative to memory for a neutral story. Patients with selective amygdala lesions do not demonstrate this enhancement (Cahil, Babinsky, Markowitsch, & McGaugh, 1995). The β-adrenergic antagonist propranolol also selectively abolishes this memory enhancement for emotionally aversive parts of a story (Cahill, Prins, Weber, & McGaugh, 1994), suggesting that this functional role of the amygdala is mediated via engagement of β-adrenergic receptors.

We recently extended these findings by demonstrating that memory enhancements for emotional words, tested by free recall after a 30 s distractor task, is also abolished by propranolol and absent in patients with amygdala lesions (Strange, Hurleman, & Dolan, 2003). These emotional nouns were presented in a neutral context (i.e., they were emotional "oddballs"). To control for the memory enhancement for oddballs (the von Restorff effect; see above), we also presented nouns in a novel font (perceptual oddballs). Critically, memory enhancement for perceptual oddballs was not modulated by β-adrenergic blockade or amygdala lesions (Figure 2). A further interesting finding in this study (Strange et al., 2003) was that neutral nouns before the emotional noun (E-1 and E-2 nouns) were recalled less well than other neutral nouns. This emotion-induced amnesia effect was also reversed by propranolol and amygdala lesions, suggesting that amygdala-dependent modulation of memory mediated by the adrenergic system can both enhance and impair memory. The direction of memory modulation depends on the stage of encoding or consolidation of the stimulus. Adrenergic efflux at the time of encoding enhances memory whereas aderenergic input 3 s into encoding/consolidation disrupts it.

In a separate fMRI experiment, we employed a subsequent memory design to investigate the neuroanatomical correlates of adrenergic-dependent memory enhancement for emotional stimuli (Strange & Dolan, 2004). Activation during encoding for subsequently remembered items was compared to that evoked by forgotten nouns (Figure 3a). Using the same verbal stimuli from our previous experiment (Strange et al., 2003) we demonstrated that amygdala responses predict memory for emotional vs. neutral stimuli (Figure 3b). This replicated previous findings using emotionally aversive film (Cahill et al., 1996) and

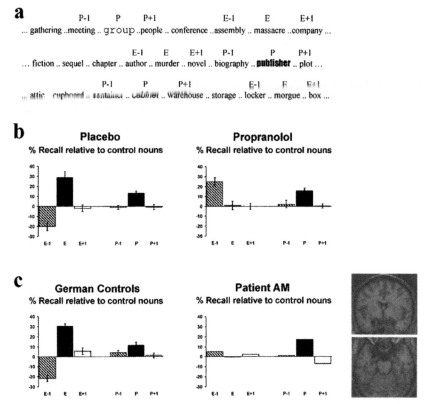

Figure 2.   (a) Examples of presented nouns. Note that these are identical to Figure 1 except for the absence of a semantic oddball. Abbreviations: E, emotional oddball; P, perceptual oddball; E-1, E+1, P-1, P+1, nouns presented before and after emotional and perceptual oddballs. (b) Emotion-induced memory impairment is β-adrenergic-dependent. Recall performance ($\pm$SE) relative to control nouns (%) is plotted following shallow encoding for placebo and propranolol groups. Memory for control nouns was not significantly different between groups. (c) Emotion-induced memory impairment is amygdala-dependent. Recall performance relative to control nouns (%) is plotted following shallow encoding for the German control group and patient AM. Coronal and transverse sections of patient AM's structural T1 image demonstrate selective bilateral amygdala lesions secondary to Urbach-Wiete disease. Recall of control nouns was not significantly different between patient and controls.

pictorial (Canli, Zhao, Brewer, Gabrieli, & Cahill, 2000; Hamann et al., 1999) stimuli. We extended these findings by showing that the presence of propranolol at encoding abolishes this amygdala response, suggesting that successful encoding of emotional stimuli is mediated by adrenergic upregulation of amygdala processing, an observation that has been recently replicated using pictures (van Stegeren et al., 2005).

We also measured neuronal activity while participants were engaged in the recognition task 10 hours after the administration of placebo/propranolol

(Strange & Dolan, 2004). For the placebo group, successful recognition of emotional nouns evoked greater hippocampal responses than recognition of neutral nouns. This effect was not present in participants who were administered propranolol prior to encoding, even though propranolol was no longer present at recognition (Figure 3c). The most influential theory of the role of the amygdala in declarative memory proposes that it mediates the enhancement of memories evoked by emotional arousal by augmenting encoding-evoked hippocampal processing (Cahill & McGaugh, 1998). Our data therefore provide direct support for the hypothesis that this is mediated through modulation of hippocampal encoding by amygdala-mediated engagement of a β-adrenergic system (Cahill & McGaugh, 1998).

The above experiment combined a pharmacological manipulation with fMRI to probe hippocampal-amygdala coupling underlying the effects of emotion on memory. In a further study we combined fMRI with human medial temporal lesion data to probe this coupling. We measured encoding-evoked medial temporal responses in epilepsy patients with varying degrees of sclerotic damage either limited to the hippocampus or to both hippocampus and amygdala (Richardson, Strange, & Dolan, 2004). Using voxel-based morphometry (hippocampus) and T2 relaxation parameters (amygdala) of structural magnetic resonance images, we demonstrated that the severity of left hippocampal pathology predicted recognition of neutral and emotional items alike, whereas the severity of amygdala pathology predicted memory performance for emotional items alone. Encoding-related hippocampal activity, measured with fMRI, for successfully remembered emotional items correlated with the degree of left amygdala pathology. Conversely, amygdala-evoked activity with respect to subsequently remembered emotional items correlated with the degree of left hippocampal pathology. We therefore demonstrated a reciprocal dependence between amygdala and hippocampus during the encoding of emotional memories.

Emotional noun encoding-evoked hippocampal activation in this experiment (Richardson et al., 2004) was present in anterior hippocampus. Dolcos et al. (2004) demonstrated that successful encoding activity in the amygdala and hippocampus was greater and more strongly correlated for emotional than for neutral pictures. Critically, a double dissociation was found along the longitudinal axis of the medial temporal lobe with activity in anterior regions predicting memory for emotional items, whereas activity in posterior regions predicted memory for neutral items. This suggests that anterior hippocampus is more involved in emotional memory processes than posterior hippocampus and that the reciprocal amygdala-hippocampal functional dependence is primarily with anterior hippocampus.

The anatomical connectivity between amygdala and hippocampus supports the anterior-posterior dissociation in amygdala-hippocampal interplay. Much of the characterisation of hippocampal connectivity has been done in the rat. Rat

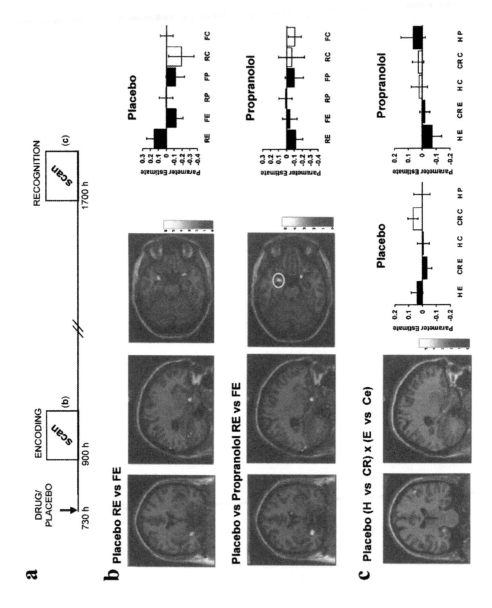

hippocampal connectivity is largely homologous to that observed in the monkey and, by extension, to that in humans. The orientation of the rat hippocampus is, however, different to that in primates, with primate posterior hippocampus corresponding to rat dorsal hippocampus and anterior hippocampus corresponding to rat ventral hippocampus (Rosene & Van Hoesen, 1987). Both ventral (anterior) CA1 (van Groen & Wyss, 1990) and ventral subiculum (Canteras & Swanson, 1992) project to the amygdala. The reciprocal projections from amygdala to CA1 and subiculum terminate preferentially in the ventral third of these subfields and amygdala-entorhinal projections terminate primarily in medial entorhinal cortex, which projects to ventral (anterior) dentate gyrus (Krettek & Price, 1977).

The strong connectivity between amygdala and anterior hippocampus raises a number of hypotheses regarding possible functional similarities between the two regions. First, lesions of anterior hippocampus should, like amygdala lesions, abolish enhanced memory for emotional stimuli. We have confirmed this prediction in epilepsy patients with sclerotic lesions of anterior hippocampus and normal amygdala (Richardson et al., 2004). Second, the functional specialisation of anterior hippocampus for novelty detection and the strong anterior hippocampal-amygdala connectivity may suggest an amygdala role in novelty detection. Differential amygdala electrophysiological responses to novelty have been demonstrated in monkey (Rolls & Wilson, 1993) and humans (Halgren et al., 1980). Functional imaging studies have also demonstrated enhanced amygdala responses to novel vs familiar stimuli. There are reports of decreasing

---

Figure 3 (opposite).   (a) Experimental time-line for the fMRI scanning experiment. Drug/placebo was administered in the morning with the encoding scanning session coinciding with propranolol's peak plasma concentration. The recognition session was scanned 10 h later so that recognition-related neuronal responses were not contaminated by the presence of drug. (b) Encoding-related neuronal responses during successful encoding of emotional nouns. Activation in left amygdala was greater for subsequently remembered vs. forgotten emotional oddballs in the placebo group. The activation is overlaid on coronal ($y = 2$), sagittal ($x = -26$) and transverse ($z = -20$) T1 sections. This region was also significant in the interaction of subsequently remembered vs. forgotten emotional vs. control nouns. The same left amygdala region was present when successful encoding activation for emotional oddballs was compared between placebo and drug groups. The parameter estimates for this activation (circled) are plotted ($\pm$ SE) for both groups. The transverse sections also demonstrate a right-lateralised activation located anterior to the amygdala in the uncus. Abbreviations: confidently subsequently recognised (R) and forgotten (F); E, emotional oddball; P, perceptual oddball; C, control noun. (c) Recognition-related neuronal responses during successful retrieval of emotional nouns. In the placebo group, left hippocampal body is more active for correct confident emotional hits vs. correct rejections of emotional foils relative to correct confident control hits vs. correct neutral rejections. The activation is overlaid on coronal ($y = -22$) and sagittal ($x = -18$) sections of the T1 image. Activation in this region was present in the three-way interaction of (placebo vs. drug) $\times$ (correct hit vs. correct rejection) $\times$ (emotion vs. neutral). Abbreviations: confident correct hits (H) and correct rejections (CR); E, emotional oddball/emotional foils; C, control noun/neutral foils; P, perceptual oddball.

amygdala responses during repeated exposure to unpleasant visual stimuli (Liberzon et al., 2000), fearful faces (Breiter et al., 1996), and complex visual stimuli (Fischer et al., 2000). Thus, although anterior hippocampal responses to novelty have been observed more frequently, there is evidence that the amygdala plays a role in novelty detection.

Given the amygdala role in processing fearful stimuli, a third, critical hypothesis, is that anterior hippocampus is also involved in fear processing. As mentioned above, fear conditioning is thought to be mediated by the amygdala and independent of the hippocampus. The hippocampus is, however, necessary for the conditioning of fear to contextual information, an observation reflecting the well established hippocampal role in spatial processing (Maguire et al., 1998; Morris, & Garrud, Rawlins, & O'Keefe, 1982; O'Keefe & Nadel, 1978). Critically, Kjelstrup et al. (2002) extended this fear processing role by demonstrating that the hippocampus is also necessary for unconditioned fear, and that the involved circuitry is at the ventral pole of the hippocampus (i.e., anterior hippocampus). Rats with selective hippocampal lesions fail to avoid open arms in an elevated plus-maze and have decreased neuroendocrine stress responses during confinement to a brightly lit chamber. These effects are reproduced by lesions of the ventral half of the hippocampus, but not by damage to the dorsal three quarters of the hippocampus or the amygdala. Ventral lesions failed to impair contextual fear conditioning or spatial navigation, suggesting that the ventral hippocampus may specifically influence some types of defensive fear-related behaviour (Kjelstrup et al., 2002).

A ventral (anterior) hippocampal role in unconditioned fear responses is relevant to the proposal that anterior hippocampus mediates novelty detection. Stimulus novelty is thought to elicit two states within an animal, curiosity or fear, with the ensuing behaviour considered a result of competition between these two states (Montgomery, 1955). The dominant behavioural response to curiosity is exploration, while the response to fear is either withdrawal or freezing. Indeed, mild electrical stimulation of the hippocampus evokes an alerting, or arrest, reaction (Bland & Vanderwolf, 1972; Kaada, Jansen, & Anderson, 1953; MacLean, 1957) during stimulation. This is followed by a period of active exploration. Hippocampal application of cholinergic agonists can also elicit this alerted state (Grant & Jarrard, 1968) and local application of anticholinergic drugs leads to a decrease in exploratory behaviour (Van Abeelen, Gilissen, Hanssen, & Lenders, 1972). The alerting response is associated with cortical desynchronisation, respiratory acceleration, and heart rate increases (Kaada, Feldman, & Langfeldt, 1971).

There is evidence that stimulus novelty evokes similar autonomic responses. Johnson & Moberg (1980) demonstrated that rats exposed to a novel environment exhibited a marked rise of plasma corticosterone in response to the initial exposure. Following their first exposure to a novel environment, animals with bilateral lesions in the dentate gyrus had plasma corticosterone concentrations which were significantly lower than those observed for the control animals. Whereas the control groups demonstrated a significant decrease in their adrenal response following 18 exposures (habituation), there was no decrease of the adrenocortical response to novelty stress within the dentate-lesioned group between trials 1 and 18. The effect of the dentate lesions appeared to be specific to the behavioural stress in that dentate lesions failed to alter resting levels, or the animal's adrenal responses to laparotomy stress and ether inhalation (Johnson & Moberg, 1980). Importantly, basic autonomic and endocrine functions appear to be intact in animals with hippocampal lesions. Basal metabolic rate (Kim, 1960), heart rate (Jarrard & Korn, 1969), and galvanic skin responses (Bagshaw, Kimble, & Pribram, 1965) are all normal. Thus, the role of the hippocampus in modulating autonomic and neuroendocrine responses is restricted to situations of stress evoked by fear or novelty. Anterior hippocampal responses to unpredictable or novel stimuli may therefore reflect an evolutionary adaptive mechanism whereby novel stimuli evoke an autonomic response.

HIPPOCAMPUS AND THE AUTONOMIC SYSTEM

That hippocampal stimulation, either electrically or pharmacologically, evokes autonomic changes suggests that the novelty response may by mediated by strong reciprocal connectivity between anterior hippocampus and autonomic centres. That hippocampal lesions decrease neuroendocrine responses to fear-evoking situations also suggests hippocampal-hypothalamic interactions in mediating fear responses. These interactions are mediated via hippocampal projections to the lateral septum. Critically, hippocampal subcortical connections, which exit the hippocampal circuit through the fimbria/fornix, are topographically organised along the anterior-posterior axis. In the rat, dorsal, intermediate, and ventral hippocampal regions project to cytoarchitectonically different sectors of the lateral septum. The dorsal half of hippocampus and subiculum give rise to only meagre projections to the most dorsomedial portion of the lateral septal nucleus. Progressively heavier, topographically organised projections to more ventral levels of lateral septal nucleus originate from more ventral levels of CA1 and subiculum (Risold & Swanson, 1996, 1997; Swanson & Cowan, 1977; van Groen & Wyss, 1990). Each of these sectors of lateral septal nucleus, in turn, innervates specific sets of nuclei in the hypothalamic region (Risold & Swanson, 1996, 1997).

The ventral tip of field CA1 and subiculum project to ventral lateral septum which in turn innervates heavily the periventricular zone (Risold & Swanson, 1997). This suggests that the most ventral part of the hippocampus preferentially influences hypothalamic nuclei involved in endocrine and autonomic responses (and ingestion behaviour). Ventral (anterior) subiculum also projects to hypothalamus and nucleus accumbens whereas dorsal subiculum projects to the mammilary bodies (Canteras & Swanson, 1992; Krettek & Price, 1977; Swanson & Cowan, 1977). Both ventral CA1 (van Groen & Wyss, 1990) and ventral subiculum (Canteras & Swanson, 1992) project to the amygdala. The strong efferent connections of the ventral hippocampus with hypothalamus and amygdala (Canteras & Swanson, 1992; Risold & Swanson, 1996, 1997; Witter et al., 1989) suggests that anterior hippocampus may contribute to aspects of autonomic, endocrine, defensive, or emotional control. An intermediate region of CA1/subiculum, occupying all but the ventral tip of the ventral half of these fields, projects to parts of the rostral lateral septum that are in turn heavily connected with hypothalamic medial zone nuclei (Risold & Swanson, 1997). This zone plays an important role in expressing defensive behaviour (Canteras, Chiavegatto, Valle, & Swanson, 1997). The medial hypothalamic defensive behaviour system receives a covergent input from the amygdala (see below). In addition to the direct projections back to the lateral septum and amygdala, the hypothalamus defensive behaviour subsystem projects to the thalamus and to the orbitomedial prefrontal cortex (Risold & Swanson, 1997).

In rodents, CA1 and subiculum project to, and receives afferents from, the orbitomedial prefrontal cortex (PFC) (Jay, Glowinski, & Thierry, 1989; Jay & Witter, 1990), an area characterised as viscerosensory and visceromotor (Neafsey, 1990); 70% of this projection arises from the anterior third of the hippocampus (Cavada, Company, Tejedor, Cruz-Rizzolo, & Reinoso-Suarez, 2000). Similar connectivity is observed with the primate analogue, the orbitofrontal cortex (Barbas, 2000), a region also implicated in mismatch detection (Nobre, Coull, Frith, & Mesulam, 1999). Ventral CA1/subiculum projections to orbitomedial PFC synapse with a subset of efferent neurons projecting to the nucleus of the solitary tract (Ruit & Neafsey 1988, 1990). Like hippocampal stimulation described above, electrical stimulation of the orbitomedial PFC in rats and primates influences heart rate, respiration, and blood pressure (Anand & Dua, 1956). Importantly, Ruit and Neafsey (1988) demonstrated that orbitomedial PFC lesions block the cardiovascular depressor effects of ventral hippocampal stimulation. This raises the possibility that the medial frontal cortex may be a relay by which the hippocampus influences cardiovascular responses during stress or in response to novelty. Thus, the hippocampus detects novelty and may achieve an autonomic response by engaging the medial hypothalamic defensive behaviour system as well as directly, and indirectly, engaging the medial PFC.

Human data demonstrate that novel stimuli that evoke the P3a "novelty" ERP waveform elicit autonomic responses, indexed by skin conductance (Knight, 1996). Like the adaptive anterior hippocampal responses described above, repeated presentations of P3a-evoking stimuli result in adaptation of skin conductance responses. Patients with hippocampal lesions do not produce these autonomic responses (Knight, 1996) and it has been suggested that hippocampal-hypothalamic pathways (Risold & Swanson, 1996) subserve this peripheral autonomic orienting response (Knight, 1996). It should be noted that these patients had lesions of posterior hippocampus (Knight, 1996). As mentioned above, the hippocampal-hypothalamic projection passes posteriorly through the fornix to the septum, hence a posterior hippocampal lesion could disrupt signals to hypothalamus generated in anterior hippocampus. It remains to be determined whether anterior hippocampal lesions produce an equivalent impairment in generating autonomic signals to novel stimuli.

Reciprocal connections between hippocampus and septum enable hippocampal sensitivity to interoceptive signals as well as to effect changes in autonomic state. This raises the possibility that the anterior hippocampal responses observed with functional imaging do not reflect detection of novelty but instead index a changed physiological state, or both. Hippocampal activation is observed in paradigms with no mnemonic task that simply manipulate autonomic states, such as through the Valsalva manoeuvre (Henderson et al., 2002). In addition to novelty-evoked activations previously reported, several studies have observed anterior hippocampal activations during associative tasks (Vandenberghe et al., 1996; Martin et al., 1997; Henke, Buck, Weber, & Weiser, 1997; Henk, Weber, Kneifel, Wieser, & Buck, 1999). Hippocampal sensitivity to autonomic states raises, therefore, a possibility that a function of anterior hippocampus is to associatively encode a stimulus with the interoceptive state generated by it.

AMYGDALA AND THE AUTONOMIC SYSTEM

The central nucleus of the amygdala (CEA) is thought to modulate autonomic motor outflow. It has brainstem projections to autonomic-related centres, including the dorsal motor nucleus of the vagus nerve, nucleus of the solitary tract, and parabrachial nucleus, as well as regions of the lateral hypothalamic nucleus and periaqueductal grey, thought to modulate autonomic responses (Petrovich, Canteras, & Swanson, 2001). It also projects to a region of the pontine reticular nucleus thought to mediate reflexes, such as acoustic startle (Davis, Falls, Campean, & Kim, 1993). Importantly, the central nucleus receives inputs from the ventral (anterior) hippocampus (Canteras & Swanson, 1992). The basolateral nucleus of the amygdala, thought to mediate amygdala-evoked enhanced hippocampal processing and episodic memory for aversive stimuli, is reciprocally connected with hippocampus and exerts its noradrenergic influence via brainstem structures (McGaugh, 2000)

Lesions to the central nucleus produce autonomic deficits that are similar to that following ventral hippocampal damage. Central nucleus lesions completely abolish the immobility response normally seen after a footshock (Roozendaal, Koohaas, & Bohus, 1991). Furthermore, the magnitude of the responses of all measured hormones (epinephrine, norepinephrine, corticosterone, and prolactin) was attenuated in lesioned rats. These results suggest that the CEA plays an important and general role in the behavioural, autonomic, and hormonal output during a brief unavoidable, unconditioned footshock.

Modulation of the hypothalamic-pituitary-adrenocortical (HPA) axis by both anterior hippocampus and amygdala is relevant to their mnemonic roles. Both types of corticosteroid receptors (mineralocorticoid and glucocorticoid receptors) are found in large numbers in the hippocampus (Watzka et al., 2000). It has been demonstrated that moderate concentrations of steroids enhance hippocampal synaptic plasticity and performance on memory tasks (Kim & Yoon, 1998). Thus, one mechanism whereby amygdala and anterior hippocampus could enhance memory for fearful or unexpected stimuli is by augmenting corticosteroid release. Also relevant to the current discussion, it has been proposed that the mineralocorticoid receptors located in the hippocampus are primarily involved in this novelty detection, whereas the glucocorticoid receptors are more involved in consolidation and storage processes of memory (Kloet, Oitzl, & Joëls, 1999).

DISCUSSION

Anterior hippocampus is sensitive to unpredictable stimuli, which may be the basis for enhanced episodic memory for these stimuli. The amygdala is critical for the enhanced memory observed for fearful or aversive stimuli. There is, however, overlap of function; amygdala responds to novel stimuli and anterior hippocampus is engaged by fearful situations. This raises the possibility that an anterior hippocampal role in novelty processing is a component of a more general role in detecting any anxiety-provoking stimulus (Bannerman et al., 2004). Enhanced memory for emotional stimuli depends on amygdala-hippocampal cooperativity, mediated via a noradrenergic system and facilitated by strong, reciprocal connections between anterior hippocampus and amygdala. Amygdala and anterior hippocampus both modulate autonomic centres, providing a basis for autonomic responses evoked by unexpected or aversive stimuli.

In addition to a role in modulating hippocampal function during episodic encoding, the amygdala has been shown to influence responses in human visual cortex (Morris et al., 1998; Vuilleumier, Richardson, Armony, Driver, & Dolan, 2004) and modulate perception of emotional stimuli (Anderson & Phelps, 2001). It has been suggested that hippocampal novelty responses engage the cholinergic system, leading to enhanced cortical processing and episodic memory for the novel stimulus (Hasselmo, 1995). Hence, in addition to anterior hippocampal-amygdala cooperativity during emotional encoding, these anterior medial temporal lobe structures may share a similar functional property. Their respective roles in human cognition may both be effected by up-regulation of cortical responses. Amygdala or anterior hippocampal engagement by anxiety-provoking or novel stimuli triggers a cascade of neuromodulatory and neuroendocrine responses that enhances neuronal processing in neocortex. One possibility is that amygdala and hippocampus serve to balance the influence of bottom-up sensory inputs with top-down influences from higher cortical areas to enable efficient encoding of emotionally salient and unexpected or novel stimuli (Strange, Duggins, Penny, Dolan, & Friston, 2005), a function facilitated by extensive, divergent cortical back-projections and reciprocal connectivity with neuromodulatory nuclei.

REFERENCES

Anand, B.K., & Dua, S. (1956). Circulatory and respiratory changes induced by electrical stimulation of the limbic system (visceral brain). *Journal of Neurophysiology, 19*, 393–400.

Anderson, A. K., & Phelps, E. A. (2001). Lesions of the human amygdala impair enhanced perception of emotionally salient events. *Nature, 411*, 305–309.

Bagshaw, M. H., Kimble, D. P., & Pribram, K. H. (1965). The GSR of monkeys during orientation and habituation and after ablation of the amygdala, hippocampus, and inferotemporal cortex. *Neuropsychologia, 3*, 111–119.

Bannerman, D. M., Rawlins, J. N., McHugh, S. B., Deacon, R. M., Yee, B. K., Bast, T., Zhang, W. N., Pothuizen, H. H., & Feldon, J. (2004). Regional dissociations within the hippocampus–memory and anxiety. *Neuroscience and Biobehavioral Reviews, 28*, 273–283.

Barbas, H. (2000). Connections underlying the synthesis of cognition, memory, and emotion in primate prefrontal cortices. *Brain Research Bulletin, 52*, 319–330.

Bechara, A., Tranel, D., Damasio, H., Adolphs, R., Rockland, C., & Damasio, A. R. (1995). Double dissociation of conditioning and declarative knowledge relative to the amygdala and hippocampus in humans. *Science, 269*, 1115–1118.

Bland, B. H., & Vanderwolf, C. H. (1972). Electrical stimulation of the hippocampal formation: Behavioral and bioelectrical effects. *Brain Research, 43*, 89–106.

Bradley, M. M., Greenwald, M. K., Petry, M. C., & Lang, P. J. (1992). Remembering pictures: Pleasure and arousal in memory. *Journal of Experimental Psychology: Learning, Memory, and Cognition, 18*, 379–390.

Breiter, H. C., Etcoff, N. L., Whalen, P. J., Kennedy, W. A., Rauch, S. L., Buckner, R. L., Strauss, M. M., Hyman, S. E., & Rosen, B. R. (1996). Response and habituation of the human amygdala during visual processing of facial expression. *Neuron, 17*, 875–887.

Brown, M. W., & Xiang, J.-Z. (1998). Recognition memory: Neuronal substrates of the judgement of prior occurrence. *Progress in Neurobiology, 55*, 149–189.

Cahill, L., Babinsky, R., Markowitsch, H. J., & McGaugh, J. L. (1995). The amygdala and emotional memory. *Nature, 377*, 295–296.

Cahill, L., Haier, R. J., Fallon, J., Alkire, M. T., Tang, C., Keator, D., Wu, J., & McGaugh, J. L. (1996). Amygdala activity at encoding correlated with long-term free recall of emotional information. *Proceedings of the National Academy of Sciences USA, 93*, 8016–8021.

Cahill, L., & McGaugh, J. L. (1996). Modulation of memory storage. *Current Opinion in Neurobiology, 6*, 237–242.

Cahill, L., & McGaugh, J. L. (1998). Mechanisms of emotional arousal and lasting declarative memory. *Trends in Neuroscience, 21*, 294–299.

Cahill, L., Prins, B., Weber, M., & McGaugh, J. L. (1994). Beta-adrenergic activation and memory for emotional events. *Nature, 371*, 702–704.

Canli, T., Zhao, Z., Brewer, J., Gabrieli, J. D., & Cahill, L. (2000). Event-related activation in the human amygdala associates with later memory for individual emotional experience. *Journal of Neuroscience, 20,* RC99.

Canteras, N. S., Chiavegatto, S., Valle, L. E., & Swanson, L. W. (1997). Severe reduction of rat defensive behavior to a predator by discrete hypothalamic chemical lesions. *Brain Research Bulletin, 44,* 297–305.

Canteras, N., & Swanson, L. W. (1992). Projections of the ventral subiculum to the amygdala, septum, and hypothalamus: a PHA-L anterograde tracing study in the rat. *Journal of Comparative Neurol, 324,* 180–194.

Cavada, C., Company, T., Tejedor, J., Cruz-Rizzolo, R. J., & Reinoso-Suarez, F. (2000). The anatomical connections of the macaque monkey orbitofrontal cortex. A review. *Cerebral Cortex, 10,* 220–242.

Constable, R. T., Carpentier, A., Pugh, K., Westerveld, M., Oszunar, Y., & Spencer, D. D. (2000). Investigation of the human hippocampal formation using a randomized event-related paradigm and Z-shimmed functional MRI. *NeuroImage, 12,* 55–62.

Damasio, A. R. (1995). *Descartes' error: Emotion, reason and the human brain.* New York: Putnams.

Davis, M., Falls, W. A., Campeau, S., & Kim, M. (1993). Fear-potentiated startle: A neural and pharmacological analysis. *Behavioural Brain Research, 58,* 175–198.

Dolan, R. J., & Fletcher, P. C. (1997). Dissociating prefrontal and hippocampal function in episodic memory encoding. *Nature, 388,* 582–585.

Dolcos, F., LaBar, K. S., & Cabeza, R. (2004). Interaction between the amygdala and the medial temporal lobe memory system predicts better memory for emotional events. *Neuron, 42,* 855–863.

Downar, J., Crawley, A. P., Mikulis, D. J., & Davis, K. D. (2000). A multimodal cortical network for detecting changes in the sensory environment. *Natural Neuroscience, 3,* 277–283.

Fischer, H., Furmark, T., Wik, G., & Fredrikson, M. (2000). Brain representation of habituation to repeated complex visual stimulation studied with PET. *Neuroreport, 11,* 123–126.

Fried, I., MacDonald, K. A., & Wilson, C. L. (1997). Single neuron activity in human hippocampus and amygdala during recognition of faces and objects. *Neuron, 18,* 753–765.

Grant, L. D., & Jarrard, L. E. (1968). Functional dissociation within hippocampus. *Brain Research, 10,* 392–401.

Grunwald, T., Lehnertz, K., Heinze, H. J., Helmstaedter, C., & Elger, C. E. (1998). Verbal novelty detection within the human hippocampus proper. *Proceedings of the National Academy of Sciences USA, 95,* 3193–3197.

Halgren, E., Squires, N. K., Wilson, C. L., Rohrbaugh, J. W., Babb, T. L., & Crandall, P. H. (1980). Endogenous potentials generated in the human hippocampal formation and amygdale by infrequent events. *Science, 210,* 803–805.

Hamann, S. B., Ely, T. D., Grafton, S. T., & Kilts, C. D. (1999). Amygdala activity related to enhanced memory for pleasant and aversive stimuli. *Nature Neuroscience, 2,* 289–293.

Hasselmo, M. E. (1995). Neuromodulation and cortical function: Modeling the physiological basis of behavior. *Behavioural Brain Research, 67,* 1–27.

Haxby, J. V., Ungerleider, L., Horwitz, B., Maisog, J., Rappaport, S., & Grady, C. (1996). Face encoding and recognition in the human brain. *Proceedings of the National Academy of Sciences USA, 93,* 922–927.

Henderson, L. A., Macey, P. M., Macey, K. E., Frysinger, R. C., Woo, M. A., Harper, R. K., Alger, J. R., Yan-Go, F. L., & Harper, R. M. (2002). Brain responses associated with the Valsalva maneuver revealed by functional magnetic resonance imaging. *Journal of Neurophysiology, 88,* 3477–3486.

Henke, K., Buck, A., Weber, B., & Wieser, H. G. (1997). Human hippocampus establishes associations in memory. *Hippocampus, 7,* 249–256.

Henke, K., Weber, B., Kneifel, S., Wieser, H. G., & Buck, A. (1999). Human hippocampus associates information in memory. *Proceedings of National Academy of Sciences USA, 96,* 5884–5889.

Higashima, M., Kawasaki, Y., Urata, K., Maeda, Y., Sakai, N., Mizukoshi, C., Nagasawa, T., Kamiya, T., Yamaguchi, N., Koshino, Y., Matsuda, H., Tsuji, S., Sumiya, H., & Hisasda, K. (1996). Simultaneous observation of regional cerebral blood flow and event-related potential during performance of an auditory task. *Cognition and Brain Research, 4,* 289–296.

Jarrard, L. E., & Korn, J. H. (1969). Effects of hippocampal lesions on heart rate during habituation and passive avoidance. *Communications in Behavioral Biology, 3,* 141–150.

Jay, T. M., Glowinski, J., & Thierry, A. M. (1989). Selectivity of the hippocampal projection to the prelimbic area of the prefrontal cortex in the rat. *Brain Research, 505,* 337–340.

Jay, T. M., & Witter, M. P. (1990). Distribution of hippocampal CA1 and subicular efferents in the prefrontal cortex of the rat studied by means of anterograde transport of *Phaseolus vulgaris*-leucoagglutinin. *Journal of Comparative Neurology, 313,* 574–586.

Johnson, L. L., & Moberg, G. P. (1980). Adrenocortical response to novelty stress in rats with dentate gyrus lesions. *Neuroendocrinology, 30,* 187–192.

Kaada, B. R., Feldman, R. S., & Langfeldt, T. (1971). Failure to modulate autonomic reflex discharge by hippocampal stimulation in rabbits. *Physiology and Behavior, 7,* 225–231.

Kaada, B. R., Jansen, J. Jr., & Anderson, P. (1953). Stimulation of the hippocampus and medial cortical areas in unanesthetized cats. *Neurology, 3,* 844–857.

Kim, C. (1960) Nest building, general activity, and salt preference of rats following hippocampal ablation. *Journal of Comparative and Physiological Psychology, 53,* 11–16.

Kim, J. J., & Yoon, K. S. (1998). Stress: Metaplastic effects in the hippocampus. *Trends in Neuroscience, 21,* 505–509.

Kishiyama, M. M., Yonelinas, A. P., & Lazzara, M. M. (2004). The von Restorff effect in amnesia: The contribution of the hippocampal system to novelty-related memory enhancements. *Journal of Cognition and Neuroscience, 16,* 15–23.

Kjelstrup, K. G., Tuvnes, F. A., Steffenach, H. A., Murison, R., Moser, E. I., & Moser, M. B. (2002). Reduced fear expression after lesions of the ventral hippocampus. *Proceedings of the National Academy of Science USA, 99,* 10825–10830.

Kloet de, E. R., Oitzl, M. S., & Joëls, M. (1999). Stress and cognition: Are corticosteroids good or bad guys? *Trends in Neuroscience, 22,* 422–426.

Knight, R. T. (1996). Contribution of human hippocampal region to novelty detection. *Nature, 383,* 256–259.

Krettek, J. E., & Price, J. L. (1977). Projections from the amygdaloid complex and adjacent olfactory structures to the entorhinal cortex and to the subiculum of the rat and cat. *Journal of Comparative Neurology, 172,* 723–752.

Liberzon, I., Taylor, S. F., Fig, L. M., Decker, L. R., Koeppe, R. A., & Minoshima, S. (2000). Limbic activation and psychophysiologic responses to aversive visual stimuli: Interaction with cognitive task. *Neuropsychopharmacology, 23,* 508–516.

Linden, D. E. J., Prvulovic, D., Formisano, E., Vollinger, M., Zanella, F. E., Goebel, R., & Dierks, T. (1999). The functional neuroanatomy of target detection: An fMRI study of visual and auditory oddball tasks. *Cerebral Cortex, 9,* 815–823.

Maguire, E. A., Burgess, N., Donnett, J., Frackowiak, R. S. J., Frith, C., & O'Keefe, J. (1998). Knowing where and getting there: A human navigation network. *Science, 280,* 921–924.

Martin, A., Wiggs, C. L., & Weisberg, J. (1997). Modulation of human medial temporal lobe activity by form, meaning and experience. *Hippocampus, 7,* 587–593.

Maclean, P. D. (1957). Chemical and electrical stimulation of hippocampus in unrestrained animals. II. Behavioral findings. *AMA Archives of Neurology and Psychiatry, 78,* 128–142.

McCarthy, G., Luby, M., Gore, J., & Goldman-Rakic, P. (1997). Infrequent events transiently activate human prefrontal and parietal cortex as measured by functional MRI. *Journal of Neurophysiology, 77*, 1630–1634.

McGaugh, J. L. (2000). Memory: A century of consolidation. *Science, 287*, 248–251.

Montgomery, K. C. (1955). The relation between fear induced by novel stimulation and exploratory behaviour. *Journal of Comparative Physiology and Psychol, 48*, 254–260.

Morris, J. S., Friston, K. J., Ducchel, C., Frith, C. D., Young, A. W., Calder, A. J., & Dolan, R. J. (1998). A neuromodulatory role for the human amygdala in processing emotional facial expressions. *Brain, 121*, 47–57.

Morris, R. G. M., Garrud, P., Rawlins, J. P., & O'Keefe, J. (1982). Place navigation impaired in rats with hippocampal lesions. *Nature, 297*, 681–683.

Neafsey, E. J. (1990). Prefrontal cortical control of the autonomic nervous system: Anatomical and physiological observations. *Progress in Brain Research, 85*, 147–165.

Nobre, A. C., Coull, J. T., Frith, C. D., & Mesulam, M.-M. (1999). Orbitofrontal cortex is activated during breaches of expectation in tasks of visual attention. *Nature Neuroscience, 2*, 11–12.

O'Keefe, J., & Nadel, L. (1978). *The hippocampus as a cognitive map*. Oxford, UK: Oxford University Press.

Opitz, B., Mecklinger, A., Friederici, A. D., & von Cramon, D. Y. (1999). The functional neuroanatomy of novelty processing: Integrating ERP and fMRI results. *Cerebral Cortex, 9*, 379–391.

Otto, T., & Eichenbaum, H. (1992). Neuronal activity in the hippocampus during delayed non-match to sample performance in rats: Evidence for hippocampal processing in recognition memory. *Hippocampus, 2*, 323–334.

Pandya, D. N., & Seltzer, B. (1982). Association areas of the cerebral cortex. *Trends Neuroscience, 5*, 386–392.

Petrovich, G. D., Canteras, N. S., & Swanson, L. W. (2001). Combinatorial amygdalar inputs to hippocampal domains and hypothalamic behaviour systems. *Brain Research Brain Research Reviews, 38*, 247–289.

Ploghaus, A., Tracey, I., Clare, S., Gati, J. S., Rawlins, J. N. P., & Matthews, P. M. (2000). Learning about pain: The neural substrate of the prediction error for aversive events. *Proceedings of the National Academy of Sciences USA, 97*, 9281–9286.

Richardson, M. P., Strange, B. A., & Dolan, R. J. (2004). Encoding of emotional memories depends on amygdala and hippocampus and their interactions. *Nature Neuroscience, 7*, 278–85.

Risold, P. Y., & Swanson, L. W. (1996). Structural evidence for functional domains in the rat hippocampus. *Science, 272*, 1484–1486.

Risold, P. Y., & Swanson, L. W. (1997). Connections of the rat lateral septal complex. *Brain Research Reviews, 24*, 115–195.

Rolls, E. T., Cahusac, P. M. B., Feigenbaum, J. D., & Miyashita, Y. (1993). Responses of single neurons in the hippocampus of the macaque related to recognition memory. *Experimental Brain Research, 93*, 299–306.

Rolls, E. T., & Wilson, F. A. W. (1993). The effects of stimulus novelty and familiarity on neuronal activity in the amygdala in monkeys performing recognition memory tasks. *Experimental Brain Research, 93*, 367–382.

Rombouts, S., Machielsen, W., Witter, M., Barkhof, F., Lindeboom, J., & Scheltens, P. (1997). Visual association encoding activates the medial temporal lobe: A functional magnetic resonance imaging study. *Hippocampus, 7*, 594–601.

Roozendaal, B., Koolhaas, J. M., & Bohus, B. (1991). Attenuated cardiovascular, neuroendocrine, and behavioral responses after a single footshock in central amygdaloid lesioned male rats. *Physiology and Behavior, 50*, 771–775.

Rosene, D. L., & Van Hoesen, G. W. (1987). The hippocampal formation of the primate brain. In E. G. Jones & A. Peters (Eds.), *Cerebral cortex* (Vol. 6 pp. 345–456). New York: Plenum.

Ruit, K. G., & Neafsey, E. J. (1988). Cardiovascular and respiratory responses to electrical and chemical stimulation of the hippocampus in anesthetized and awake rats. *Brain Research, 457,* 310–321.

Ruit, K. G., & Neafsey, E. J. (1990). Hippocampal input to a "visceral motor" corticobulbar pathway: An anatomical and electrophysiological study in the rat. *Experimental Brain Research, 82,* 606–616.

Saykin, A. J., Johnson, S. C., Flashman, L. A., McAllister, T. W., Sparling, M., Darcey, T. M., Moritz, C. H., Guerin, S. J., Weaver, J., & Mamourian, A. (1999). Functional differentiation of medial temporal and frontal regions involved in processing novel and familiar words: An fMRI study. *Brain, 122,* 1963–1971.

Schacter, D. L., & Wagner, A. D. (1999). Medial temporal lobe activations in fMRI and PET studies of episodic encoding and retrieval. *Hippocampus, 9,* 7–24.

Scoville, W. B., & Milner, B. (1957). Loss of recent memory after bilateral hippocampal lesions. *Journal of Neurosurgery and Psychiatry, 20,* 11–21.

Sperling, R. A., Bates, J. F., Cocchiarella, A. J., Schacter, D. L., Rosen, B. R., & Albert, M. S. (2001). Encoding novel face-name associations: A functional MRI study. *Human Brain Mapping, 14,* 129–139.

Squire, L. R., & Zola-Morgan, S. (1991). The medial temporal lobe memory system. *Science, 253,* 1380–1386.

Stern, C. E., Corkin, S., Gonzalez, R. G., Guimaraes, A. R., Baker, J. R., Jennings, P. J., Carr, C. A., Suigura, R. M., Vedantham, V., & Rosen, B. R. (1996). The hippocampal formation participates in novel picture encoding: Evidence from functional magnetic resonance imaging. *Proceedings of the National Academy of Sciences USA, 93,* 8660–8665.

Strange, B. A., & Dolan, R. J. (2001). Adaptive anterior hippocampal responses to oddball stimuli. *Hippocampus, 11,* 690–698.

Strange, B. A., & Dolan, R. J. (2004). Beta-adrenergic modulation of emotional memory-evoked human amygdala and hippocampal responses. *Proceedings of the National Academy of Sciences USA, 101,* 11454–11458.

Strange, B. A., Duggins, A., Penny, W., Dolan, R. J., & Friston, K. J. (2005). Information theory, novelty and hippocampal responses: unpredicted or unpredictable? *Neural Networks, 18,* 225–230.

Strange, B. A., Fletcher, P. C., Henson, R. N. A., Friston, K. J., & Dolan, R. J. (1999). Segregating the functions of human hippocampus. *Proceedings of the National Academy of Sciences USA, 96,* 4034–4039.

Strange, B. A., Henson, R. N. A., Friston, K. J., & Dolan, R. J. (2000). Brain mechanisms for detecting perceptual, semantic, and emotional deviance. *NeuroImage, 12,* 425–433.

Strange, B. A., Hurlemann, R., & Dolan, R. J. (2003). An emotion-induced retrograde amnesia in humans is amygdala- and beta-adrenergic-dependent. *Proceedings of the National Academy of Science USA, 100,* 13626–13631.

Swanson, L. W., & Cowan, W. M. (1977). An autoradiographic study of the organization of the efferent connections of the hippocampal formation in the rat. *Journal of Comparative Neurology, 172,* 49–84.

Swanson, L. W., & Petrovich, G. D. (1998). What is the amygdala? *Trends in Neuroscience, 21,* 323–331.

Tulving, E., Markowitsch, M. J., Craik, F. I. M., Habib, R., & Houle, S. (1996). Novelty and familiarity activations in PET studies of memory encoding and retrieval. *Cereb Cortex, 6,* 71–79.

Van Abeelen, J., Gilissen, L., Hanssen, T., & Lenders, A. (1972). Effects of intrahippocampal injections with methylscopolamine and neostigmine upon exploratory behaviour in two inbred mouse strains. *Psychopharmacologia, 24,* 470–475.

Vandenberghe, R., Price, C., Wise, R., Josephs, O., & Frackowiak, R. S. J. (1996). Functional anatomy of a common semantic system for words and pictures. *Nature, 383,* 254–256.

Van Essen, D. C., & Maunsell, J. H. R. (1983). Hierarchical organisation and functional streams in the visual cortex. *Trends in Neuroscience, 6,* 370–374.

van Groen, T., & Wyss, J. M. (1990). Extrinsic projections from area CA1 of the rat hippocampus: Olfactory, cortical, subcortical, and bilateral hippocampal formation projections. *Journal of Comparative Neurology, 302,* 515–528.

van Stegeren, A. H., Goekoop, R., Everaerd, W., Scheltens, P., Barkhof, F., Kuijer, J. P., & Rombouts, S. A. (2005). Noradrenaline mediates amygdala activation in men and women during encoding of emotional material. *NeuroImage, 24,* 898–909.

Vinogradova, O. S. (1975). Functional organization of the limbic system in the process of registration of information: Facts and hypotheses. In R. L. Isaacson & K. H. Pribram (Eds.), *The hippocampus* (Vol. 2, pp. 3–69). New York: Plenum.

von Restorff, H. (1933). Uber die wirkung von bereichsbildungen im spurenfeld [On the effect of spheres formation in the trace field]. *Psychologie Forschung, 18,* 299–342.

Vuilleumier, P., Richardson, M. P., Armony, J. L., Driver, J., & Dolan, R. J. (2004). Distant influences of amygdala lesion on visual cortical activation during emotional face processing. *Nature Neuroscience, 7,* 1271–1278.

Watzka, M., Beyenburg, S., Blumcke, I., Elger, C. E., Bidlingmaier, F., & Stoffel-Wagner, B. (2000). Expression of mineralocorticoid and glucocorticoid receptor mRNA in the human hippocampus. *Neuroscience Letters, 290,* 121–124.

Wiebe, S. P., & Saubli, U. V. (1999). Dynamic filtering of recognition memory codes in the hippocampus. *Journal of Neuroscience, 19,* 10562–10574.

Witter, M. P., Groenewegen, H. J., Lopes da Silva, F. H., & Lohman, A. H. M. (1989). Functional organisation of the extrinsic and intrinsic circuitry of the parahippocampal region. *Progress in Neurobiology, 33,* 161–253.

Yamaguchi, S., Hale, L. A., D'Esposito, M., & Knight, R. T. (2004). Rapid prefrontal-hippocampal habituation to novel events. *Journal of Neuroscience, 24,* 5356–5363.

Young, B. J., Otto, T., Fox, G. D., & Eichenbaum, H. (1997). Memory representation within the parahippocampal region. *Journal of Neuroscience, 17,* 5183–5195.

COGNITIVE NEUROPSYCHIATRY
2006, 11 (3), 219–232

Altered experience of emotion following bilateral amygdala damage

Daniel Tranel

University of Iowa College of Medicine, Iowa City, USA

Greg Gullickson and Margaret Koch

Anderson-Arnold and Associates, Iowa City, USA

Ralph Adolphs

University of Iowa College of Medicine, Iowa City and
California Institute of Technology, Pasadena, USA

It has been well established that the amygdala is critical for processing various aspects of emotion, and in particular, for the perception of negative emotions such as fear. Perhaps the strongest evidence for this conclusion in humans comes from an extensive series of investigations in patient SM, an extremely rare neurological patient who has complete, focal bilateral amygdala damage. One question that has remained unanswered, however, is whether SM has a normal phenomenological experience of emotion, especially negative emotion. To explore this issue, we designed a study in which two experienced clinical psychologists conducted "blind" interviews of SM (the psychologists were not provided any background information regarding SM), with a special emphasis regarding the nature of her emotional experience. Both of them reached the conclusion that SM expressed a normal range of affect and emotion, and neither felt that SM warranted a DSM-IV diagnosis. However, they both noted that SM was remarkably dispassionate when relating highly emotional and traumatic life experiences, and they noted that she did not seem to have a normal sense of distrust and "danger". To the psychologists, SM came across as a "survivor", as being "resilient" and even "heroic" in the way that she had dealt with adversity in her life. In the full light of SM's neurological and neuropsychological profile, however, these observations reflect the fact that SM is missing from the experiences in her life some of the deepest

Correspondence concerning this article should be addressed to Dr Daniel Tranel. Department of Neurology, University of Iowa Hospitals and Clinics, 200 Hawkins Drive, Iowa City, Iowa 52242, USA; e-mail: daniel-tranel@uiowa.edu

Authors G.G. and M.K. contributed equally to this article.

We thank Dr. Tony Buchanan for his assistance in collecting some of the data reported in this study, and Ruth Henson for help with scheduling various assessments of the patient. Supported by Grant P01 NS19632 from NINDS, Grant R01 MH67681 from NIMH and the William T. Gimbel Discovery Fund.

http://www.psypress.com/cogneuropsychiatry   DOI:10.1080/13546800444000281

negative emotions, in a manner that parallels her defect in perceiving such emotions in external stimuli. These findings have interesting parallels with recent animal work (cf. Bauman, Lavenex, Mason, Capitanio, & Amaral, 2004a), and they provide valuable insights into the emotional life of an individual with complete bilateral amygdala damage.

It has long been established that the amygdala is important for the regulation of social and emotional behaviours, dating back to the seminal work of Kluver and Bucy (1939) on this issue. Decades of studies in monkeys have shown that lesions to the amygdala impair the ability to evaluate the social and emotional meanings of visual stimuli (Emery et al., 2001; Kling & Brothers, 1992; Meunier, Bachevalier, Murray, Malkova, & Mishkin, 1999; Rosvold, Mirsky, & Pribram, 1954; Weiskrantz, 1956; Zola-Morgan, Squire, Alvarez-Royo, & Clower, 1991). More recently, there is a consistent line of work in humans showing that bilateral amygdala damage interferes with normal processing of social and emotional signals in visual stimuli, especially facial expressions and in particular negatively valenced emotions, such as fear, anger, and sadness (Adolphs & Tranel, 1999; Adolphs, Tranel, Damasio, & Damasio, 1994, 1995; Adolphs et al., 1999; Anderson, Spencer, Fulbright, & Phelps, 2000; Broks et al., 1998; Calder et al., 1996; Schmolck & Squire, 2001; Young, Hellawell, Van de Wal, & Johnson, 1996; for a review, see Adolphs, 2002). Functional imaging studies have provided largely convergent findings (Blair, Morris, Frith, Perrett, & Dolan, 1999; Breiter et al., 1996a; Morris et al., 1996; Phillips et al., 2001; Whalen et al., 1998).

Perhaps the most compelling evidence for the role of the amygdala in processing social and emotional information in visual stimuli has come from a unique human case, known as patient SM. She has complete bilateral amygdala damage, but without significant involvement of any other neural structures, thus providing the purest known case of focal bilateral amygdala destruction. An extensive series of investigations in SM has yielded definitive evidence that her ability to process social and emotional information in visual stimuli is reliably compromised (for reviews, see Adolphs, 1999, 2002; Adolphs & Tranel, 2000). For example, she cannot recognise fear in facial expressions (Adolphs et al., 1994), and recently, a mechanism for this impairment was identified (Adolphs et al., 2005). SM has a severe defect in recognising the arousal of both lexical and nonlexical visual stimuli that denote emotions (Adolphs, Russell, & Tranel, 1999). She is remarkably deficient in her ability to judge traits such as "trustworthiness" and "approachability" in the faces of strangers in laboratory tasks (Adolphs, Tranel, & Damasio, 1998), as well as anecdotally in her everyday social interactions with others (Adolphs & Tranel, 2000). Her abnormal preference for stimuli that are judged by normal individuals to be aversive extends to other types of visual stimuli besides faces, such as landscapes and complex visual patterns (Adolphs & Tranel, 1999). It is important to underscore that all of these impairments occur in the setting of entirely intact basic visual perception. SM has intact ability to perceive stimuli—she performs normally on even the most difficult neuropsychological tests of visual perception, and she can discriminate among faint morphs of emotional expressions, including fear (Adolphs & Tranel, 2000).

Thus, it is abundantly clear that SM has impaired recognition of social and emotional information. An important question that has never been fully answered in the studies available to date is the extent to which SM has normal *experience* of emotion. We have commented on this issue briefly in previous publications (Adolphs & Tranel, 2000), pointing out that SM did not report normal experiences of strong fear when watching movie clips from films, such as *The Shining* and *The Silence of the Lambs*. She did, however, report (and exhibit) strong anger feelings when watching an anger-inducing scene from the film *Cry Freedom*; thus, overall, these observations were somewhat mixed. Furthermore, all experiments that aim to investigate the experience of emotion based on its induction through stimuli, such as pictures or films, run into a basic confound. Since, as we have reviewed above, SM fails to recognise normally the emotion in such stimuli in the first place, it remains unclear whether any abnormalities in her emotional experience to them are attributable to a defect in the ability to experience emotions as such, or merely to a defect in recognising them. A potentially richer and more definitive way to begin an investigation of SM's emotional experiences is to undertake a characterisation of her emotional life from her autobiography and presentation outside of the laboratory setting. Informally, these are the same observations on the basis of which we assign emotional lives to other people normally; formally, such observations can be made by trained professionals (e.g., clinical psychologists, psychiatrists) to diagnose deviations from normal emotional experience. We took such an approach in the present study.

To begin with, we can emphasise that in routine interactions with SM, for example, the numerous contacts with her during the course of various experiments and her frequent visits to our laboratory, she generally displays a good range of affect, albeit with a tendency to be quite positive about most people, situations, and issues. She establishes good rapport with others, and clearly can "tune in" to her examiners. However, we were concerned that these observations might provide a biased test of SM's emotional experience. There is the obvious caveat that the primary experimenters (D.T. and R.A.) are far from naïve about SM's condition. And most of this information was collected in situations that were not structured or explicitly designed to elicit controlled observations regarding SM's emotional life.

To tackle this issue head-on, we designed an experiment in which we elicited the collaboration of two experienced clinical psychologists, to investigate in detail the nature of SM's phenomenology of emotion. The collection of data was ''controlled'', in the sense that the psychologists were blind to SM's condition, and were not privy to any of her background information prior to their interactions with her. We report here the results of this experiment, providing for the first time systematic data indicating that the experiential aspects of SM's emotional life are altered subtly but reliably in much the same way that her recognition of emotional information in external stimuli is altered.

METHODS AND RESULTS

The subject

The subject of this report is patient SM. At the time of the current study, which was conducted in late 2003, SM was 38 years old. She has a rare, heritable disease known as Urbach-Wiethe disease (lipoid proteinosis). Urbach-Wiethe disease affects primarily epithelial tissue, and as one frequent manifestation (in about half the cases), creates characteristic mineralisations and atrophy of medial temporal lobe neural tissue. SM manifests this characteristic, and in her case, the process affects almost exclusively the amygdala, bilaterally, with no significant involvement of other nearby tissues. In short, she has complete, bilateral, and circumscribed destruction of the amygdala.

SM has been studied extensively in our laboratory. She was initially reported in 1990 (Tranel & Hyman, 1990), and comprehensive updates on her neuropsychological and neuroanatomical profiles were published a few years ago (Adolphs & Tranel, 2000). In brief, her cognitive profile is essentially normal. She has low average to average intellectual abilities (WAIS-R Full Scale IQ = 88), and normal performances in the areas of speech (outside of hoarseness) and linguistic functions, visuoperceptual, visuospatial, and visuoconstructional functions, and executive control functions, such as planning and decision making. Her memory is mostly intact, although she has been noted to have mild, variable defects on some visual memory tests. Her MMPI-2 profile was not indicative of any major psychopathology (see table 18.1, Adolphs & Tranel, 2000). In short, SM has no notable neuropsychological impairments on conventional testing, nor does she have notable psychopathology.

The Positive and Negative Affect Schedules (PANAS; Watson, Clark, & Tellegen, 1988) have also been administered to SM. The results have been consistent with other measurements of emotional functioning, and with our behavioural observations. Specifically, SM tends to endorse a relatively high degree of items that purportedly tap into positive affect, and a relatively low degree of items that purportedly tap into negative affect. On one recent administration, for example, SM obtained a score of 43 on the positive affect scale, and a score of 19 on the negative affect scale (raw scores).

We have always observed SM to be alert, fully oriented, and entirely cooperative with testing. She has normal attention and cognitive stamina. Her interpersonal behaviour is notable for a somewhat coquettish and disinhibited style. She tends to be friendly with her examiners, with a familiar style of interaction that goes a little beyond what is typical in conventional Midwestern culture. Of course, with those of us who know her very well (especially R.A. and D.T.), this behaviour is based on true familiarity; however, she tends to be almost as friendly and familiar with brand new experimenters, where one might expect somewhat more initial caution and distance. But she is not blatantly inappropriate, and she is entirely capable of modulating her behaviour according to the demands of the situation. She does not show any full-blown components of the classic Kluver-Bucy syndrome that is found in monkeys with relatively much larger lesions.

The experimenters

The primary experimenters were G.G. and M.K. (co-authors of this paper). They are licensed clinical psychologists in the state of Iowa, and both have full-time private practices doing conventional forms of psychological assessment and psychotherapy. G.G. and M.K. were chosen to collaborate in this investigation for several reasons: both are seasoned clinicians, having been in practice for decades; both are highly regarded in the community for their diagnostic acumen; and both have traditional Boulder model clinical training. We wanted to utilise more than one psychologist for this study, in order to establish the reliability of the results, and it was desirable to have one male and one female psychologist so that possible gender-specific effects could be factored in.

The experiment

The experiment was set up in the following manner. The two clinical psychologists were contacted by D.T., and asked to collaborate in a "controlled" investigation of the psychological status of a neurological patient. Specifically, they were told that patient SM had a rare neurological condition, and that we wanted to get a professional judgement about her psychological status. The psychologists (G.G. and M.K.) were instructed that they would have an opportunity to interview the patient, for about an hour,[1] but that they would not be provided any background information about the patient. They were told to use their professional judgement about the direction and range of the interview, but that they should make sure to gather information about SM's emotional status and emotional experiences. The psychologists were told that SM was free of any kind of thought disorder, and that this domain did not need to be explored. No further instructions were provided. The psychologists complied with these conditions.

---

[1] An hour (55–60 minutes) is the typical length of a session in the psychologists' practices. We deliberately conformed to this time-frame, to keep the experiment as "ecologically valid" as possible.

SM was instructed that she was going to be interviewed by two clinical psychologists, for the purposes of gathering additional information about her psychological status. She was told that the interviews would each be about an hour in length, and that all of the findings would be treated with the usual rules of confidentiality that govern all experimental data collected under the auspices of the research project in which she is enrolled. She provided informed consent to participate in the experiment, and agreed to all of the conditions.[2]

The findings

The psychologists were asked to generate written summaries of their interviews of SM. These summaries were prepared based solely on the interviews, without additional background information. The following impressions were extracted from these summaries. The psychologists reached remarkably congruent impressions of SM. Both of them felt that SM had a normal range of affect, with no evidence of a personality disorder, affective disorder, or thought disorder. SM came across as pleasant and friendly, and reflective and thoughtful. There was no indication of depression or anxiety. It was noted that she could exhibit empathy for others (e.g., she expressed concern for the US troops serving in the Middle East, and for their families); however, her threshold for noticing another person's pain was described as "fairly high".

The psychologists noted that SM had experienced a considerable amount of adversity in her life. She experienced alienation and hardship since early childhood, which has continued to some extent into her adult life. In her developmental years, this included teasing and shunning from schoolchildren (mostly related to her Urbach-Wiethe disease, which has left her with a very hoarse voice) and abuse from authority figures. She experienced the death of her father (who was a "hero" to her) during adolescence. She has been left pretty much on her own to cope with raising three boys, with very limited financial resources and social support. She has been left alone most of her life to deal with difficult situations.

The psychologists were struck by the fact that SM did not appear at all dysphoric when relating these major negative life experiences. She was asked specifically about her emotional reactions to these experiences, and she "denied feeling strong emotion". To both psychologists, SM impressed them as being a "survivor", as being "resilient", and as having "exceptional coping skills". Neither psychologist doubted the veracity of this presentation, or viewed it as an indication of impaired emotions; rather, they saw SM as having a practical, matter-of-fact attitude; as having dealt with adversity and moved on. They noted

---

[2] We also debriefed SM following the interviews. Specifically the first author (D.T.) spoke with SM for about 45 minutes, explaining the general purpose of the investigation and the general impressions of the two psychologists who had interviewed her. She found the feedback unsurprising and, in many respects, flattering.

that SM deals with major negative events in her life without surprise, anger, or outrage; she takes "hard times" in stride and considers them to be just part of the flow of life. She does not question why or even whether she has had a "raw deal" from life, and she does not seem interested in considering why some persons have a harder life than others. She appears to believe that major adversity is simply "the normal course of events".

It was noted that SM seemed very trusting of others, almost to the point that she would trust "anyone". She did not appear to have a normal sense of danger or distrust of others. However, neither psychologist labelled SM as pathological in this regard; rather, they were impressed that she matter-of-factly adopted an "I'm okay—you're okay" attitude, and basically felt that most people were fine, well intentioned, and positive.

In contrast to her demeanor when discussing negative experiences and events, SM displayed "strong positive affect" when relating aspects of her life that she views favourably. She was very animated and positive, for example, when talking about her sons, how they were growing up, and how one of them now had a girlfriend. SM feels that parenting her boys is one of the things that gives her life the most meaning and purpose. SM described herself as religious, and she noted that her faith has always been helpful and comforting to her. She related considerable positive self-esteem: She described herself as "hopeful" and "loving", and as having "a big heart". She has positive goals and interests for the future. She was content; in fact, when one of the psychologists asked her what she would wish for if granted three wishes, she did not identify anything that she would wish for.

The denouement

Several weeks after the interviews, we held a "debriefing session", in which the psychologists were apprised of the general nature of SM's condition. This session was very revealing: the psychologists were struck by the fact that what they perceived as "resilience" and even "heroism" was really a manifestation of missing emotions. Fear and anger were particularly missing. It was agreed that SM does not have any serious psychopathology, and that she does not warrant a DSM-IV diagnosis; moreover, her deficits are not egregious or blatant, and they have to be expertly exposed in order to be noticed and appreciated. But in retrospect, the psychologists agreed that SM has a partially truncated emotional life: Specifically, she is missing much of the "negative" side. When asked directly, the psychologists agreed that SM expressed very little negative emotion, and appeared to experience very little negative emotion. They agreed that she was not a good judge of character, and was overly trusting of others. The principal theme in this debriefing session was that in the light of the full story, the psychologists would change their attributions for many of their observations of SM: rather than being a "survivor" and having "exceptional coping skills", she has an abnormally low level of negative emotional phenomenology.

COMMENT

The findings from this study suggest that patient SM, who has focal bilateral amygdala damage and a consistent and pervasive defect in recognising negative emotions in external stimuli, has a parallel defect in terms of the experiential aspects of her emotional life. Specifically, she is missing from her phenomenology of life some of the deepest negative emotions, in a manner that parallels her defect in perceiving such emotions in external stimuli. These findings, which have interesting parallels in recent animal work (e.g., Bauman et al., 2004a), provide valuable insights into the emotional life of an individual with complete bilateral amygdala damage.

We have several brief comments about these observations. First, this report emphasizes the close link between impaired recognition of emotions, and impairments in their experience. Similar parallels between recognition and experience have been found in other studies (e.g., Adolphs, 2002; Adolphs, Tranel, & Damasio, 2003; Calder, Lawrence, & Young, 2001). Such parallels suggest that recognition and experience may be not just correlated, but causally related. At present, we can only speculate on this issue, but we consider it likely in SM's case that a primary impairment in her ability to recognise, evaluate, appraise, and judge stimuli with respect to aspects of their emotional value may in turn have resulted in her impoverished emotional experiences, at least in part. This idea may be particularly relevant in SM, as it is likely that her amygdala damage was sustained relatively early in life. A compromised ability to recognise emotions during development and adolescence could result in a truncated repertoire of emotional experiences.

A second point is that SM's basic ability to exhibit a range of emotionally and socially appropriate behaviours is remarkably intact—so much so that trained clinicians who were blind to her background and pathology did not really detect psychopathology that they would label as such. This observation is very much in line with recent studies in nonhuman primates with experimentally induced amygdala lesions: Such animals also appear to exhibit a normal range of social behaviours (Amaral et al, 2003; Bauman et al., 2004a; Bauman, Lavenex, Mason, Capitanio, & Amaral, 2004b), although the stimuli on the basis of which they do so may not be recognised normally (Prather et al., 2001). Taken together with these recent studies in monkeys, the present study thus permits a reinterpretation of the role of the amygdala in social behaviour. Unlike the conclusions drawn from the classic Kluver and Bucy studies, we conclude that the amygdala is *not* necessary for relatively normal social behaviour as such. Instead, it is necessary for linking stimuli to the appropriate elicitation of such behaviours, and to the appropriate experience of emotion. This is especially true for negative emotions. Again, we should emphasise that a similar conclusion was reached by Amaral and his colleagues, who pointed out that the amygdala "is not needed to develop fundamental aspects of social behavior and may be more related to the detection and avoidance of environmental dangers" (Bauman et al., 2004a, p. 1388).

Finally, it is instructive to situate the current findings in the broader context of literature addressing the question of whether the amygdala plays a critical role in the experience of emotion. Most of the available literature has pointed towards an affirmative answer to this question. For example, functional imaging studies have reliably demonstrated activation of the amygdala in normal individuals exposed to emotion-inducing events, especially aversive or anxiety-provoking stimuli (Lane et al., 1997; Schneider et al., 1996; Zald, Lee, Fluegel, & Pardo, 1998; Zald & Pardo, 1996). In parallel with this, it has been shown that various clinical populations demonstrate amygdala activation when confronted with anxiety-provoking stimuli (Birmbauer et al., 1998; Breiter, Rauch, Kwong, Baker, & Rosen, 1996b; Rauch et al., 1996), and may even have abnormal structural aspects of amygdala anatomy (Sheline et al., 1998). Moreover, several studies have shown that the degree of amygdala activity in functional imaging paradigms correlates positively with the intensity of subjective emotional experience (Abercrombie et al., 1998; Ketter et al., 1996). In short, there is a large corpus of convergent evidence from functional imaging studies supporting the notion that the amygdala plays a critical role in the subjective experience of emotion (for a review, see Davidson & Irwin, 1999). This conclusion is consistent with the prevailing theoretical formulations of neural underpinnings of emotional phenomenology (Damasio, 1994; LeDoux, 1996).

A notable exception to this preponderance of evidence comes from a recent lesion study, which purported to show that bilateral (and unilateral) amygdala damage did not lead to a change in the subjective experience of emotion (Anderson & Phelps, 2002). This study was based on the finding that a patient with bilateral amygdala damage (and 20 patients with unilateral amygdala damage) reported levels of positive and negative affect on the Positive and Negative Affect Schedules (PANAS; Watson et al., 1988) that did not differ from the levels reported by normal comparison participants. As pointed out by the authors, there were several caveats to this study, including the low base rate of reports of negative emotional affective states in all of the participants (especially for anxiety/fear) and the fact that the results are based entirely on introspective, self-report data. Another important consideration is that the PANAS provides a temporally narrow snapshot of the emotional landscape of an individual, given that the items are completed for how the person is feeling "at the present moment". In the light of our current report in SM, these caveats take on even more importance. SM's self report (even on the PANAS) is, in fact, not dissimilar to the reports of the bilateral patient of Anderson and Phelps; however, when funnelled through the expert analysis of clinical psychologists, and placed in the overall context of SM's background, the abnormalities of the experiential aspects of emotion in SM are clearly exposed. And it has to be noted that our basic finding here is very consistent with the numerous functional imaging studies adduced above.

Another important point is that several structures other than the amygdala have been implicated in mediating various aspects of emotional experience: for instance, somatosensory cortices in the right hemisphere, the insula (Craig, 2002), the substantia nigra (Dejjani et al., 1999), a number of pontine and brainstem nuclei involved in control of and representation of interoceptive information (Damasio et al., 2000), anterior cingulate cortex (Lane et al., 1998), and even regions of the spinal cord (Hohmann, 1966). One major open question concerns the precise role that all these different structures contribute towards emotional experience. One can think of the initial induction of an emotional state, either via perception of external stimuli (e.g., music, film clips, pictures) or via recollection of emotional material (e.g., autobiographical memories of highly emotional events). Such an emotional state would then consist of a variety of psychophysiological changes, and would in turn be represented in brain regions concerned with interoception, such as somatosensory cortices and insula (Craig, 2002). Some of these brain regions would then presumably contribute directly to the contents of a conscious experience of the emotion (Craig, 2002), according to some theories in concert with other brain regions that can represent the eliciting stimulus (Damasio, 1999). Higher order brain regions, such as the cingulate cortex could serve to bind these two components (Damasio, 1999), and could also come into play in regulating the emotional response and the subsequent experience of the feeling (Lane et al., 1997, 1998). We have proposed a theoretical framework that summarises these various components, and that assigns sets of specific neural structures to them (Adolphs, 2002). With regard to the amygdala, covariances have been found between amygdala activation and reported emotional experiences associated with recollection of memories, with the induction of emotional states, and also as a consequence of the regulation of emotional states (Ochsner et al., 2002; Schaefer et al., 2002; Siegle et al., 2002). Thus, it remains an open question exactly what component it is that the amygdala is contributing that distinguishes its contribution from those of other structures. Put concretely: What might be the consequences for emotional experience following damage to some of the other structures we have just mentioned? Might one obtain similar findings as those that we report here in SM also following focal damage to somatosensory cortices, insula, or cingulate cortex? We think it very likely that the answer is: Yes and No. Yes, some components of emotional experience would be impaired following damage to such structures, but the reasons for, and mechanisms behind, the impairment would be different. That is, similar impairments might result but for different reasons. Needless to say, this will be an important line of future investigations, ongoing in our laboratory.

In sum, this investigation indicates that SM, who has focal, bilateral amygdala damage, is missing from her phenomenology of life some of the deepest negative emotions, in a manner that parallels her defect in perceiving such emotions in external stimuli. Given SM's neuroanatomical status, it can be inferred that her impoverished emotional landscape is attributable to the bilateral amygdala damage. However, other studies will have to be conducted before a strong causal link can be made between amygdala and emotional experience. One interesting direction for future research would be to utilise a semi-quantitative method, such as the Experience Sampling Method of Myin-Germeys et al. (2001) to ascertain aspects of negative and positive affect that occur in the daily course of life. Also, it would be important to compare SM with other patients with lesions in different components of the neural circuitry subserving emotional processing, for example, anterior cingulate cortices, medial prefrontal cortices, and unilateral amygdala damage.

REFERENCES

Abercrombie, H. C., Schaefer, S. M., Larson, L. L., Oakes, T. R., Lindgren, K. A., Holden, J. E., Perlman, S. B., Turski, P. A., Kraha, D. D., Benca, R. M., & Davidson, R. J. (1998). Metabolic rate in the right amygdala predicts negative affect in depressed patients. *NeuroReport, 9*, 3301–3307.

Adolphs, R. (1999). Social cognition and the human brain. *Trends in Cognitive Sciences, 3*, 469–479.

Adolphs, R. (2002). Recognizing emotion from facial expressions: Psychological and neurological mechanisms. *Behavioral and Cognitive Neuroscience Reviews, 1*, 21–61.

Adolphs, R., Gosselin, F., Buchanan, T. W., Tranel, D., Schyns, P., & Damasio, A. R. (2005). A mechanism for impaired fear recognition after amygdala damage. *Nature, 433*, 68–72.

Adolphs, R., Russell, J. A., & Tranel, D. (1999). A role for the human amygdala in recognizing emotional arousal from unpleasant stimuli. *Psychological Science, 10*, 167–171.

Adolphs, R., & Tranel, D. (1999). Preferences for visual stimuli following amygdala damage. *Journal of Cognitive Neuroscience, 11*, 610–616.

Adolphs, R., & Tranel, D. (2000). Emotion recognition and the human amygdala. In J. P. Aggleton (Ed.), *The amygdala: A functional analysis* (pp. 587–630). New York: Oxford University Press.

Adolphs, R., Tranel, D., & Damasio, A. R. (1998). The human amygdala in social judgment. *Nature, 393*, 470–474.

Adolphs, R., Tranel, D., & Damasio, A. (2003). Dissociable neural systems for recognizing emotions. *Brain and Cognition, 52*, 61–69.

Adolphs, R., Tranel, D., Damasio, H., & Damasio, A. R. (1994). Impaired recognition of emotion in facial expressions following bilateral damage to the human amygdala. *Nature, 372*, 669–672.

Adolphs, R., Tranel, D., Damasio, H., & Damasio, A. R. (1995). Fear and the human amygdala. *Journal of Neuroscience, 15*, 5879–5892.

Adolphs, R., Tranel, D., Hamann, S., Young, A., Calder, A., Anderson, A., Phelps, E., Lee, G. P., & Damasio, A. R. (1999). Recognition of facial emotion in nine subjects with bilateral amygdala damage. *Neuropsychologia, 37*, 1111–1117.

Amaral, D. G., Bauman, M. D., Capitanio, J. P., Lavenex, P., Mason, W. A., Mauldin-Jourdain, M. L., & Mendoza, S. P. (2003). The amygdala: Is it an essential component of the neural network for social cognition? *Neuropsychologia, 41*, 517–522.

Anderson, A. K., & Phelps, E. A. (2002). Is the human amygdala critical for the subjective experience of emotion? Evidence of intact dispositional affect in patients with amygdala lesions. *Journal of Cognitive Neuroscience, 14*, 709–720.

Anderson, A. K., Spencer, D. D., Fulbright, R. K., & Phelps, E. A. (2000). Contributions of the anteromedial temporal lobes to the evaluation of facial emotion. *Neuropsychology, 14*, 526–536.

Bauman, M. D., Lavenex, P., Mason, W. A., Capitanio, J. P., & Amaral, D. G. (2004a). The development of social behavior following neonatal amygdala lesions in rhesus monkeys. *Journal of Cognitive Neuroscience, 16*, 1388–1411.

Bauman, M. D., Lavenex, P., Mason, W. A., Capitanio, J. P., & Amaral, D. G. (2004b). The development of mother-infant interactions following neonatal amygdala lesions in rhesus monkeys. *Journal of Neuroscience, 24*, 711–721.

Bejjani, B.-P., Damier, P., Arnulf, I., Thivard, L., Bonnet, A. M., Dormont, D., Cornu, P., Pidoux, B., Samson, Y., & Agid, Y. (1999). Transient acute depression induced by high-frequency deep-brain stimulation. *New England Journal of Medicine, 340*, 1476–1480.

Birbaumer, N., Grodd, W., Diedrich, O., Klose, U., Erb, M., Lotze, M., Schneider, F., Weiss, U., & Flor, H. (1998). fMRI reveals amygdala activation to human faces in social phobics. *Neuro-Report, 9*, 1223–1226.

Blair, R. J. R., Morris, J. S., Frith, C. D., Perrett, D. I., & Dolan, R. J. (1999). Dissociable neural responses to facial expressions of sadness and anger. *Brain, 122*, 883–893.

Breiter, H. C., Etcoff, N. L., Whalen, P. J., Kennedy, W. A., Rauch, S. L., Buckner, R. L., Strauss, M. M., Hyman, S. E., & Rosen, B. R. (1996a). Response and habituation of the human amygdala during visual processing of facial expression. *Neuron, 17*, 875–887.

Breiter, H. C., Rauch, M. D., Kwong, K. K., Baker, J. R., & Rosen, B. R. (1996b). Functional magnetic resonance imaging of symptom provocation in obsessive-compulsive disorder. *Archives of General Psychiatry, 53*, 595–606.

Broks, P., Young, A. W., Maratos, E. J., Coffey, P. J., Calder, A. J., Isaac, C. L., Mayes, A. R., Hodges, J. R., Montaldi, D., Cezayirli, E., Roberts, N., & Haydley, D. (1998). Face processing impairments after encephalitis: Amygdala damage and recognition of fear. *Neuropsychologia, 36*, 59–70.

Calder, A. J., Young, A. W., Rowland, D., Perrett, D., Hodges, J. R., & Etcoff, N. L. (1996). Facial emotion recognition after bilateral amygdala damage: Differentially severe impairment of fear. *Cognitive Neuropsychology, 13*, 699–745.

Craig, A. D. (2002). How do you feel? Interoception: The sense of the physiological condition of the body. *Nature Reviews Neuroscience, 3*, 655–666.

Damasio, A. R. (1994). *Descarte's error: Emotion, reason, and the human brain.* New York: Grosset/Putnam.

Damasio, A. R. (1999). *The feeling of what happens: Body and emotion in the making of consciousness.* New York: Harcourt Brace.

Damasio, A. R., Grabowski, T. J., Bechara, A., Damasio, H., Ponto, L. L., Parvzi, J., & Hichwa, R. D. (2000). Feeling emotions: Subcortical and cortical brain activity during the experience of self-generated emotions. *Nature Neuroscience, 3*, 1049-1056.

Davidson, R. J., & Irwin, W. (1999). The functional neuroanatomy of emotion and affective style. *Trends in Cognitive Sciences, 3*, 11–22.

Emery, N. J., Capitanio, J. P., Mason, W. A., Machado, C. J., Mendoza, S. P., & Amaral, D. G. (2001). The effects of bilateral lesions of the amygdala on dyadic social interactions in rhesus monkeys (Macaca mulatta). *Behavioral Neuroscience, 115*, 515–544.

Hohmann, G. W. (1966). Some effects of spinal cord lesions on experienced emotional feelings. *Psychophysiology, 3*, 143–156.

Ketter, T. A., Andreason, P. J., George, M. S., Lee, C., Gill, D. S., Parekh, P. I., Willis, M. W., Herscovitch, P., & Post, R. (1996). Anterior paralimbic mediation of procaine-induced emotional and psychosensory experiences. *Archives of General Psychiatry, 53*, 59–69.

Kling, A. S., & Brothers, L. (1992). The amygdala and social behavior. In J. P. Aggleton (Ed.), *The amygdala: Neurobiological aspects of emotion, memory and mental dysfunction* (1st ed., pp. 353–378). New York: Wiley-Liss.

Kluver, H., & Bucy, P. C. (1939). Preliminary analysis of functions of the temporal lobes in monkeys. *Archives of Neurology and Psychiatry*, *42*, 979–997.

Lane, R. D., Reiman, E. M., Bradley, M. M., Ahern, G. L., Davidson, R. J., & Schwartz, G. E. (1997). Neural activation during selective attention to subjective emotional responses. *Neuro-Report*, *8*, 3969–3972.

Lane, R. D., Reiman, E. M., Axelrod, B., Yun, L. S., Holmes, A., & Schwartz, G. E. (1998). Neural correlates of levels of emotional awareness: evidence of an interaction between emotion and attention in the anterior cingulate cortex. *Journal of Cognitive Neuroscience*, *10*, 525–535.

LeDoux, J. (1996). *The emotional brain*. New York: Simon & Schuster.

Meunier, M., Bachevalier, J., Murray, E. A., Malkova, L., & Mishkin, M. (1999). Effects of aspiration versus neurotoxic lesions of the amygdala on emotional responses in monkeys. *European Journal of Neuroscience*, *11*, 4403–4418.

Morris, J. S., Frith, C. D., Perrett, D. I., Rowland, D., Young, A. W., Calder, A. J., & Dolan, R. J. (1996). A differential neural response in the human amygdala to fearful and happy facial expressions. *Nature*, *383*, 812–815.

Myin-Germeys, I., van Os, J., Schwartz, J. E., Stone, A. A., & Delespaul, P. A. (2001). Emotional reactivity to daily life stress in psychosis. *Archives of General Psychiatry*, *58*, 1137–1144.

Ochsner, K., Bunge, S. A., Gross, J. J., & Gabrieli, J. D. (2002). Rethinking feelings: An fMRI study of the cognitive regulation of emotion. *Journal of Cognitive Neuroscience*, *14*, 1215–1229.

Phillips, M. L., Medford, N., Young, A. W., Williams, L., Williams, S. C., Bullmore, E. T., Gray, J. A., & Brammer, M. J. (2001). Time courses of left and right amygdalar responses to fearful facial expressions. *Human Brain Mapping*, *12*, 193–202.

Prather, M. D., Lavenex, P., Mauldin-Jourdain, M. L., Mason, W. A., Capitanio, J. P., Mendoza, S. P., & Amaral, D. G. (2001). Increased social fear and decreased fear of objects in monkeys with neonatal amygdala lesions. *Neuroscience*, *106*, 653–658.

Rauch, S. L., van der Kolk, B. A., Fisler, R. E., Alpert, N. M., Orr, S. P., Savage, C. R., Fischman, A. J., Jenike, M. A., & Pitman, R. K. (1996). A symptom provocation study of posttraumatic stress disorder using positron emission tomography and script-driven imagery. *Archives of General Psychiatry*, *53*, 380–397.

Rosvold, H. E., Mirsky, A. F., & Pribram, K. H. (1954). Influence of amygdalectomy on social behavior in monkeys. *Journal of Comparative and Physiological Psychology*, *47*, 173–178.

Schaefer, S. M., Jackson, D. C., Davidson, R. J., Aguirre, G. K., Kimberg, D. Y., Thomson-Schill, S. L. (2002). Modulation of amygdalar activity by the conscious regulation of negative emotion. *Journal of Cognitive Neuroscience*, *14*, 913–921.

Schmolck, H., & Squire, L. R. (2001). Impaired perception of facial emotions following bilateral damage to the anterior temporal lobe. *Neuropsychology*, *15*, 30–38.

Schneider, F., Gur, R. E., Alavi, A., Seligman, M. E. P., Mozley, L. H., Smith, R. J., Mozley, P. D., & Gur, R. C. (1996). Cerebral blood flow changes in limbic region induced by unsolvable anagram tasks. *American Journal of Psychiatry*, *153*, 206–212.

Sheline, Y. I., Gado, M. H., & Price, J. L. (1998). Amygdala core nuclei volumes are decreased in recurrent major depression. *NeuroReport*, *9*, 2023–2028.

Siegle, G. J., Steinhauser, S. R., Thase, M. E., Stenger, V. A., & Carter, C. S. (2002). Can't shake that feeling: Event-related fMRI assessment of sustained amygdala activity in response to emotional information in depressed individuals. *Biological Psychiatry*, *51*, 693–707.

Tranel, D., & Hyman, B. T. (1990). Neuropsychological correlates of bilateral amygdala damage. *Archives of Neurology*, *47*, 349–355.

Watson, D., Clark, L. A., & Tellegen, A. (1988). Development and validation of brief measures of positive and negative affect: The PANAS Scales. *Journal of Personality and Social Psychology*, *54*, 1063–1070.

Whalen, P. J., Rauch, S. L., Etcoff, N. L., McInerney, S. C., Lee, M .B., & Jenike, M. A. (1998). Masked presentations of emotional facial expressions modulate amygdala activity without explicit knowledge. *Journal of Neuroscience, 18*, 411–418.

Weiskrantz, L. (1956). Behavioral changes associated with ablations of the amygdaloid complex in monkeys. *Journal of Comparative and Physiological Psychology, 49*, 381–391.

Young, A. W., Hellawell, D. J., Van de Wal, C., & Johnson, M. (1996). Facial expression processing after amygdalotomy. *Neuropsychologia, 34*, 31–39.

Zald, D. H., Lee, J. T., Fluegel, K. W., & Pardo, J. V. (1998). Aversive gustatory stimulation activates limbic circuits in humans. *Brain, 121*, 1143–1154.

Zald, D. H., & Pardo, J. V. (1996). Emotion, olfaction, and the human amygdala: Amygdala activation during aversive olfactory stimulation. *Proceedings of the National Academy of Sciences, USA, 94*, 4119–4124.

Zola-Morgan, S., Squire, L. R., Alvarez-Royo, P., & Clower, R. P. (1991). Independence of memory functions and emotional behavior: Separate contributions of the hippocampal formation and the amygdala. *Hippocampus, 1*, 207–220.

COGNITIVE NEUROPSYCHIATRY
2006, 11 (3), 233–249

The neural basis of mood dysregulation in bipolar disorder

Mary L. Phillips

Institute of Psychiatry, London, UK

Bipolar disorder is characterised by affective instability and mood dysregulation. Understanding of the neural mechanism underlying this remains limited, however. Here, findings will be described from studies that have employed neuroimaging techniques to measure neural responses to emotionally salient stimuli in individuals with the disorder. These findings will be discussed in relation to a theoretical framework previously proposed for understanding the separate cognitive processes underlying emotion perception to allow the formulation of a postulated neural mechanism for the mood dysregulation in bipolar disorder.

Bipolar disorder affects up to 1.5% of the population (Kessler et al., 1994), with illness relapse rates estimated at between 37% and 44% per year (O'Connell, Mayo, Flatow, Cuthbertson, & O'Brien, 1991; Gitlin, Swendsen, Heller, & Hammen, 1995), a total mortality elevated by 58% (predominantly from suicide and cardiovascular disease (Angst, Stassen, Clayton, & Angst, 2002), and syndromic recovery after one year post manic or mixed episodes only at 48% (Keck et al., 1998). Whilst it is clear clinically that mood dysregulation, or affective instability, is a key symptom of the disorder, the nature of the neural mechanism underlying this abnormality remains poorly understood. Clarification of this mechanism will be crucial for the future development of effective therapeutic interventions for this common but poorly treated disorder.

Emotion perception can be understood in terms of three related processes (Phillips et al., 2003a):

1. The identification of emotionally salient information in the environment.
2. The generation of emotional experiences and behaviour in response to (1).
3. The regulation of emotional experiences and behaviour. The role of context as a determinant in the regulation of affective reactivity has been

Correspondence concerning this article should be addressed to Mary L. Phillips, Section of Neuroscience and Emotion PO69, Division of Psychological Medicine, Institute of Psychiatry, De Crespigny Park, London SE5 8AZ, UK; e-mail: m.phillips@iop.kcl.ac.uk

http://www.psypress.com/cogneuropsychiatry   DOI:10.1080/13546800444000290

emphasised by others (e.g., Davidson, Jackson, & Kalin, 2000). Component processes employed in emotion regulation may include a reappraisal of the emotionally salient information such that its impact, and resulting experience and expression of emotion are altered, and suppression of the expression of the emotional experience (Gross, 2002). Thus, emotion regulation can be defined as a reappraisal and/or suppression of processes (1) and (?), in order to ensure that the affective state and behaviour generated in response to environmental emotionally salient stimuli are contextually appropriate (see Figure 1).

A challenge for neuroimaging studies of emotion perception in healthy and psychiatric populations has been to develop tasks with the ability to engage these three processes. Whilst emotive stimuli, including facial expressions, and mood induction techniques have been employed in studies examining the neural bases of processes (1) and (2), respectively, it has been more difficult to design paradigms which have examined the neural basis of process (3).

In the following sections, findings from studies will be described in which these and other paradigms have been employed to examine the neural basis of the separate cognitive processes underlying emotion perception in individuals with bipolar disorder.

NEURAL RESPONSES TO EMOTIONALLY-SALIENT STIMULI

The accurate recognition of facial expressions is crucial for successful interpersonal function in the social environment (Darwin, 1872/1998). As such, facial expressions represent ecologically valid, emotionally salient stimuli. In healthy individuals, findings from neuroimaging studies have implicated a network of predominantly anterior limbic regions in the response to and appraisal of emotional stimuli. These regions include the amygdala, but also other areas: ventral striatum, hippocampus, and anterior insula (Calder, Lawrence, & Young, 2001; Mataix-Cols et al., 2003; Morris et al., 1996; Phillips et al., 1997; Sprengelmeyer et al., 1998; Surguladze, Rausch, Eysel, & Przuntek, 2003).

Previous studies of euthymic and remitted individuals with bipolar disorder indicate impaired fear (Yurgelun-Todd et al., 2000), and enhanced disgust recognition (Harmer, Grayson, & Goodwin, 2002) in facial expressions, or no specific deficits in recognising emotion (Venn et al., 2004) in unfamiliar others. Studies in manic individuals with the disorder have indicated both specific impairments in the recognition of fear and disgust of unfamiliar others (Lembke & Ketter, 2002), and generalised deficits in the recognition of all emotional expressions (Getz, Shear, & Strakowski, 2003). Finally, a tendency to misinterpret the faces of peers as being angry has been reported in adolescent individuals with bipolar disorder (McClure, Pope, Hoberman, Pine, & Leibenluft, 2003).

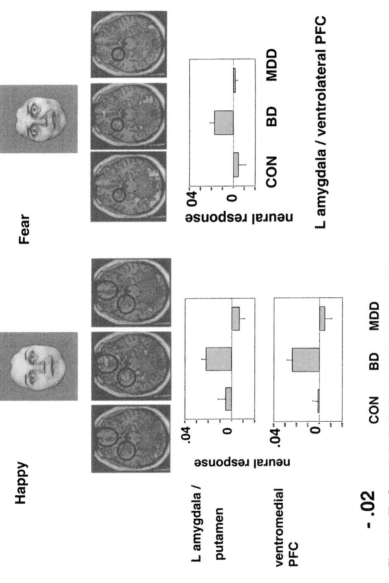

Figure 1. The figure depicts brain slices in healthy individuals (CON), individuals with bipolar disorder (BD) and individuals with major depressive disorder (MDD) in response to facial expressions of happiness (A) and fear (B) contrasted with neutral faces. The graphs demonstrate that BD compared with CON and MDD demonstrated increased activity within the left amygdala (dark grey), ventral striatum (putamen), and ventromedial prefrontal cortex (PFC; light grey) in response to happy faces, and increased activity within the left amygdala in response to fearful faces (dark grey).

235

The above findings provide some evidence for an abnormality in emotional expression identification in adult and adolescent populations with bipolar disorder. There has, however, been limited examination in these individuals of the neural mechanism underlying this abnormality in processing emotional stimuli. Regarding neural responses to emotional stimuli, our recent findings in remitted individuals with bipolar disorder, using a facial expression paradigm indicate increased activity within limbic and subcortical regions, predominantly to expressions of fear and happiness, in the absence of any deficits in facial expression recognition (Lawrence et al., 2004; Figure 1). These findings support earlier reports of increased subcortical (amygdalar) activity to fearful expressions (Yurgelun-Todd et al., 2000) in remitted individuals. Interestingly, other recent findings indicate decreased amygdalar responses to sad, but not happy, facial expressions in individuals with mania (Lennox, Jacob, Calder, Lupson, & Bullmore, 2004). Our findings also indicate subsyndromal depression-related abnormalities, namely a positive correlation between depression severity and hippocampal response to sad expressions, in remitted individuals with bipolar disorder. We also demonstrated increased ventromedial prefrontal cortical responses in these individuals, particularly in response to expressions of mild happiness.

Interestingly, studies in individuals with schizophrenia have indicated a very different pattern of decreased or absent amygdalar responses to facial expressions of fear and other emotions (e.g., Gur et al., 2002; Hempel et al., 2003; Phillips et al., 1999; Williams et al., 2004). These findings suggest that affective and nonaffective psychoses can be distinguished by patterns of amygdalar response to emotional stimuli (see Phillips et al., 2003b).

NEURAL RESPONSES DURING MOOD INDUCTION

Positive and negative mood states can be induced with specific mood induction paradigms, including the use of facial expressions and/or autobiographical memory scripts, associated with activity within the ventral striatum and ventromedial prefrontal cortex in healthy individuals (Mayberg et al., 1999), and emotive scenes from a standardised series, for example, the International Affective Picture Series (IAPS; Lang, Bradley, & Cuthbert, 1998), associated with subcortical limbic responses in healthy and anxiety-disordered populations (Mataix-Cols et al., 2003; Phillips et al., 2000). Few studies to date, however, have examined neural responses during mood induction paradigms in individuals with bipolar disorder. We have developed a mood induction paradigm involving autobiographical scripts to induce happy or sad mood, followed by presentation of emotion-congruent facial expressions (Keedwell, Andrew, Williams, Brammer, & Phillips, 2005). Using this paradigm, we have demonstrated in individuals with major depressive disorder during happy mood induction an absence of the normal increase in autonomic response (as measured by skin conductance recordings;

SCR), and increased activity within dorsomedial and ventromedial prefrontal cortex, regions associated with regulation of emotional responses (Phillips et al., 2003a). Other studies using similar mood induction paradigms have demonstrated relative decreases in activity within these regions during sad mood induction in euthymic and depressed individuals with bipolar disorder (Kruger, Seminowicz, Goldapple, Kennedy, & Mayberg, 2003). In two studies, employing emotive scenes, findings demonstrate in depressed and hypomanic individuals with bipolar disorder increased subcortical responses to positive and negative scenes during affect generation (Malhi et al., 2004a, 2004b).

PARADIGMS FOR EXAMINATION OF EMOTION REGULATION

It has been more difficult to develop paradigms for the examination of emotion regulation. Strategies for this have included the measurement of neural responses during the voluntary suppression of emotional response to emotive stimuli; studies using these paradigms have demonstrated a relative increase in response within prefrontal regions, including dorsomedial and ventromedial prefrontal cortices (e.g., Levesque et al., 2003). Another strategy has been to measure neural responses during the reappraisal of the emotional content of emotive stimuli, such as facial expressions or emotive scenes. These studies have demonstrated during overt labelling of emotional expressions compared with gender decision, a pattern of increased ventrolateral and dorsolateral prefrontal cortical response and reduced or absent amygdalar and hippocampal response (e.g., Hariri, Mattay, Tessitore, Fera, & Weinberger, 2003; Lange et al., 2003), and increased ventrolateral prefrontal cortical and reduced amygdalar responses during reappraisal compared with passive viewing of emotive scenes (Ochsner, Bunge, Gross, & Gabrieli, 2002). Another strategy has been to examine neural responses during performance of tasks examining attentional processes within emotional contexts. Such tasks involve, essentially, the examination of the influence of emotion content upon attention and decision making (i.e., indirect biases in the identification of material as emotional or neutral). These tasks include the emotional Stroop task (Lyon, Startup, & Bentall, 1999), and the affective go/no-go task, in which individuals respond to emotional target words (either happy or sad) and inhibit responses to emotional distractors (either happy or sad; Murphy et al., 1999). In summary, therefore, in healthy individuals, findings from neuroimaging studies have indicated that dorsal and ventromedial prefrontal cortical regions may be implicated in the regulation of emotional responses and behaviour, both during suppression and reappraisal processes. Further studies are required to clarify the specific roles of dorsal and ventral prefrontal cortices in emotion regulation, the role of the ventromedial prefrontal cortex in particular in the generation of affective responses and emotion regulatory processes, and the functional relationships between these prefrontal cortical regions and subcortical regions implicated in the identification and appraisal of emotionally-salient stimuli (Phillips et al., 2003a).

The majority of neuroimaging studies in individuals with bipolar disorder have focused upon the examination of neural responses during rest and performance of executive and memory tasks. Findings from these studies suggest dysfunctional prefrontal cortical-subcortical functional relationships in euthymic, in addition to symptomatic, individuals with the disorder at rest and during performance of such tasks. Reports include predominant reductions in activity in dorsal and ventral prefrontal cortical regions (Baxter et al., 1985, 1989; Blumberg et al., 1999, 2003a; Ketter et al., 2001; Martinot et al., 1990), including the dorsal region of the anterior cingulate gyrus (Gruber, Rogowska, & Yurgelun-Todd, 2004), but also increases in activity within the dorsal anterior cingulate gyrus (Berns, Martin, & Proper, 2002; Blumberg et al., 2000; Goodwin et al., 1997; Rubinsztein et al., 2001) and subcortical regions (Blumberg et al., 2000; Caligiuri et al., 2003; Strakowski, Adler, Holland, Mills, & DelBello, 2004), which have been positively correlated with mania severity (Blumberg et al., 2000, 2003a; Goodwin et al., 1997).

Of the few studies directly comparing euthymic with mood episode individuals, some reports have indicated an amelioration of abnormal neural responses in euthymic individuals during executive task performance (Baxter et al., 1989; Blumberg et al., 1999, 2000; Martinot et al., 1990), although others suggest greater impairments in prefrontal cortical activity in euthymic compared with depressed individuals with bipolar disorder (Blumberg et al., 2003a). Whilst these findings do indicate deficits in prefrontal cortical response in individuals with bipolar disorder, the studies have not focused upon the examination of the neural correlates of suppression and reappraisal processes, and thus have, largely, been unable to further understanding of the neural basis of dysfunctional emotion regulation in the disorder.

A small number of studies have measured attentional task performance within emotional contexts in individuals with bipolar disorder. These have provided further evidence for negative attentional biases in depressed individuals with bipolar disorder (Murphy et al., 1999), and both negative and positive attentional biases in manic individuals (Lyon et al., 1999; Murphy et al., 1999). These findings suggest deficits in the ability to ignore the influence of emotion when performing attentional tasks in individuals with bipolar disorder, particularly those in a low mood episode.

Of the few studies examining the neural basis of attention to and away from emotional stimuli in individuals with bipolar disorder, findings indeed suggest abnormalities in prefrontal cortical responses to targeted and distracting emotional stimuli. Functional neuroimaging studies employing an affective go/no-go paradigm, have demonstrated in manic individuals with bipolar disorder decreased ventromedial prefrontal cortical responses during semantic task versus orthographic go/no-go task performance, but increased ventrolateral prefrontal cortical responses to emotional versus neutral targets, and elevated ventral and medial prefrontal cortical responses to emotional distractors (Elliott et al., 2004). Employing this paradigm, a similar pattern of increased response within ventral anterior cingulate gyrus to sad targets, and increased ventrolateral prefrontal cortical response to sad distractors, was demonstrated in individuals with major depressive disorder (Elliott, Rubinsztein, Sahakian, & Dolan, 2002). These findings are preliminary evidence suggestive of increased attention to emotional distractors during attentional task performance in manic individuals with bipolar disorder, but also point to a more generalised abnormality in this regard in affective disorders per se. Further studies are therefore required to determine in bipolar disorder the nature of the specific and persistent dysfunction in prefrontal cortical systems important for the performance of attentional tasks within emotional contexts.

OTHER CONSIDERATIONS

Structural neural abnormalities in individuals with bipolar disorder

Findings to date in individuals with bipolar disorder regarding regions important for emotion processing, including the amygdala and hippocampus, have been variable, with studies reporting volume increases, decreases, or no abnormality within the amygdalae, and volume decreases or no abnormalities in the hippocampi (Altshuler, Bartzokis, Grieder, Curran, & Mintz, 1998; Brambilla et al., 2003; McDonald et al., 2004; Strakowski et al., 1999; Videbech & Ravnkilde, 2004). Other studies have reported increased ventral striatal (caudate nucleus and putamen) volumes (Aylward et al., 1994; Blumberg et al., 2003b; Strakowski et al., 1999), and decreased middle, superior and inferior, including subgenual and anterior cingulate gyrus, prefrontal cortical volumes (Lopez-Larson, DelBello, Zimmerman, Schwiers, & Strakowski, 2002; Sassi et al., 2004; Sax et al., 1999; Sharma et al., 2003), although yet others have reported no significant differences in prefrontal cortical volumes between individuals with bipolar disorder and healthy volunteers (Brambilla et al., 2002). Interestingly, a recent study has provided further evidence for increased gray matter volumes in bilateral thalamus, insulae, and cortical regions involved in the response to emotional stimuli and mood generation in individuals with bipolar disorder (Lochhead, Parsley, Oquendo, & Mann, 2004).

Effect of previous illness history and medication on persistent abnormalities

To date, previous studies have suggested that the magnitude of executive dysfunction within remitted individuals may be associated with longer illness duration and number of illness episodes (Cavanagh, Van Beck, Muir, &

Blackwood, 2002; Clark, Iverson, & Goodwin, 2002), particularly manic episodes (Martinez-Aran et al., 2004b; Zubieta, Huguelet, O'Neil, & Giordani, 2001), suggestive of a positive correlation between prefrontal cortical dysfunction and these clincal variables, whilst a history of psychosis has been associated with greater verbal memory impairment (Martinez-Aran et al., 2004b). Structural neuroimaging studies suggest that enlarged ventricular volumes and decreased putamen size (Ali et al., 2001; Brambilla et al., 2001; Strakowski, Adler, & DelBello, 2002) are associated with an increased number of previous episodes of illness.

There are discrepant findings regarding the effect of psychotropic medication upon neurocognitive function in individuals with bipolar disorder, however. Neuroleptic medication has been associated with attentional impairments in healthy volunteers (Mehta, Sahakian, McKenna, & Robbins, 1999), but also with no impairment in attention in individuals with psychiatric disorders (King, 1994). There are conflicting findings regarding the effect of lithium on cognitive function (Ananth, Gold, & Ghadirian, 1981; Engelsmann, Katz, Ghadirian, & Schachter, 1988; Ferrier, Stanton, Kelly, & Scott, 1999; Kessing, 1998; Kocsis et al., 1993), but little effect of other mood stabilisers (Devinsky, 1995), or antidepressants (Thompson, 1991) on cognitive function, whilst citalopram has been associated with a normalisation of the otherwise increased recognition of fear in euthymic individuals with a previous history of major depressive disorder (Bhagwagar, Cowen, Goodwin, & Harmer, 2004). The effect of psychotropic medication upon structural and functional neuroanatomy in individuals with bipolar disorder is largely unknown. Long-term use of lithium has been associated with increase in volume of the subgenual cingulate gyrus (Harrison, 2002; Manji, Moore, & Chen, 2000). Neuroleptic medication levels have been positively correlated with mean regional cerebral blood flow at rest (Silfverskiold & Risberg, 1989) and prefrontal cortical activation during decision making in manic individuals with bipolar disorder (Rubinsztein et al., 2001), whilst a relative reduction in subcortical activity has been demonstrated in manic and depressed individuals with bipolar disorder taking neuroleptic and mood stabilising medications compared with unmedicated individuals (Caligiuri et al., 2003).

Whilst findings in individuals with major depressive disorder, predominantly at rest, have indicated increased prefrontal cortical (dorsolateral and ventromedial prefrontal cortex) and decreased limbic, hippocampal and subgenual cingulate gyral responses after successful treatment with medication (Bench, Friston, Brown, Frackowiak, & Dolan, 1993; Goodwin et al., 1993; Kennedy et al., 2001; Mayberg et al., 2000), although a reversed pattern after successful cognitive behavioural (Goldapple et al., 2004) and interpersonal therapy (Brody et al., 2001; Martin, Martin, Rai, Richardson, & Royall, 2001), it remains to be determined whether similar changes in neural response to emotionally salient stimuli occur in individuals with bipolar disorder after treatment.

Predictive value of these functional neural abnormalities

Few studies have examined the extent to which neurocognitive function predicts clinical outcome in individuals with bipolar disorder. Previous studies have indicated that greater cognitive dysfunction per se (Martinez-Aran et al., 2002, 2004a), a history of psychotic symptoms associated with greater cognitive dysfunction (Tohen et al., 2000), and an increased number of white matter hyperintensities (Moore et al., 2001), may be associated with poorer clinical outcome in the disorder. There has been no examination of the extent to which patterns of abnormal neural response characterising bipolar disorder predict long-term clinical course.

CONCLUSION

Towards an understanding of the neural basis of mood dysregulation

Together, findings from studies examining neural responses to emotional facial epxressions, during mood induction and to nonfacial, emotionally salient stimuli (emotional scenes), indicate increased subcortical responses and decreased reponse in a dorsomedial prefrontal cortical region during sad mood induction. Findings from studies measuring neural responses during attention to and away from emotional sitmuli have reported in individuals with bipolar disorder increases in, predominantly, ventral regions of prefrontal cortex, both to emotional word targets and distractors. Findings from studies measuring neural responses in individuals with bipolar disorder during performance of executive tasks in nonemotional contexts have, however, demonstrated a predominant pattern of decreases in both ventral and dorsal prefrontal cortical regions. This complex pattern of decreases and increases in prefrontal cortical and subcortical repsonses requires further study. Whilst the nature of the role of the ventromedial prefrontal cortex both in the generation of affective responses and emotion regulatory processes remains to be determined, findings in individuals with bipolar disorder do point to the presence of relative decreases in activity in regions associated with mood regulation and executive function during performance of such tasks (e.g., ventro- and dorsomedial prefrontal cortices), but also increases in activity in regions associated with decision making about and affective responses to emotional material during performance of those tasks (subcortical regions, ventral anterior cingulate gyrus, ventromedial, and ventrolateral prefrontal cortices). Findings also indicate structural volume increases in subcortical, and volume decreases in prefrontal cortical, regions in individuals with the disorder.

Taken together, these findings suggest a potential neural mechanism underlying the affective instability in bipolar disorder (Phillips et al., 2003b;

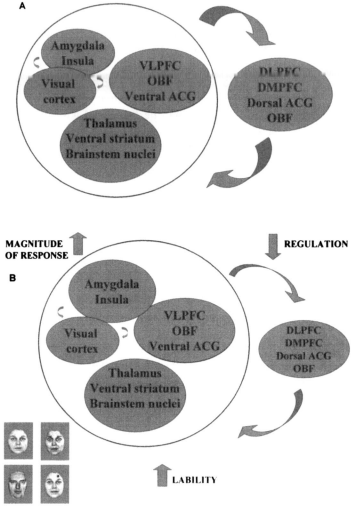

Figure 2. (A) A schematic diagram depicting neural structures important for the appraisial of emotionally salient information, mood generation, and the regulation of emotional behaviour. A predominantly ventral system is important for the identification of emotional information and the generation of affect state (depicted in dark grey), whilst a predominantly dorsal system is important for selective attention and regulation of behavioural responses to emotional stimuli (depicted in light grey). The arrows (in dark grey) represent the reciprocal functional relationship which exists between these two distinct but parallel neural systems.

(B) The figure depicts a schematic model for the neural basis of the affective instability in individuals with bipolar disorder. In individuals with the disorder, it is postulated that to emotional stimuli, including the different categories facial expression depicted here, a pattern of increased amygdalar and ventral striatal activity occurs. This, together with reduced prefrontal metabolism, leads to impaired regulation, and increased lability, of mood (represented by the reduction in size of the dark grey arrows) frequently observed in the clinical population. VLPFC, ventrolateral prefrontal cortex; DLPFC, dorsolateral prefrontal cortex; DMPFC, dorsomedial prefrontal cortex; ACG, anterior cingulate gyrus; OBF, orbitofrontal cortex.

242

Figure 2; also see Strakowski et al., 2004). Here, it has been hypothesised that the affective instability in the disorder may result from a combination of increased activity within subcortical and limbic regions implicated in the initial appraisal of emotive stimuli (amygdala ventral striatum, anterior insula), resulting in increased activity in regions associated with mood generation and decisions about emotional material (ventromedial and ventrolateral prefrontal cortices, ventral anterior cingulate gyrus), and reduced activity within regions implicated in the regulation of these responses and attentional processes (predominantly dorsomedial prefrontal cortices). Whilst these features have been demonstrated in remitted individuals with bipolar disorder, indicating the persistent nature of these abnormalities in these individuals, it remains to be determined whether these features are present before the onset of the disorder. Thus, the extent to which these abnormlaities are persistent features of the disorder rather than mood state dependent, and, furthermore, the extent to which they are specific to bipolar disorder or are common to all affective disorders remain to be determined. A small number of findings to date do suggest, however, subtle difference in patterns of neural response between manic and depressed individuals with the disorder. Whilst increased subcortical responses have been associated with both mood episode types in response to emotional stimuli (e.g., Lawrence et al., 2004; Malhi et al., 2004a, 2004b), there is emerging evidence for a relative amelioration of the abnormal pattern of decreased prefrontal cortical response in depressed compared with euthymic and manic individuals (Blumberg et al., 2003a). Similarly, findings to date suggest that the attentional biases to emotional sitmuli are demonstrated to all categories of emotional stimuli to a greater extent in maic than depressed indivuduals, who demonsrtate biases predominantly towards negative emotional sitmuli (e.g., Lyon et al., 1999; Murphy et al., 1999). One possibility, therefore is that depression in bipolar disorder may represent a relative normalisation of the abnormal pattern of emotional over-reactivity associated with mania. The extent to which medication and illness history determine patterns of abnormal neural response, and the predictive value of these abnormalities for clinical course in the disorder also remain unresolved.

Future research employing emotion processing paradigms and neuroimaging techniques in bipolar populations and those at risk of the disorder will help to clarify further the nature of the dysfunction in neural systems underlying mood regulation in bipolar disorder, and the extent to which these abnormalities are predictive of illness onset and course.

REFERENCES

Ali, S. O., Denicoff, K. D., Altshuler, L. L., Hauser, P., Li, X., Conrad, A. J., Smith-Jackson, E. E., Leverich, G. S., & Post, R. M. (2001). Relationship between prior course of illness and neuroanatomic structures in bipolar disorder: A preliminary study. *Neuropsychiatry, Neuropsychology, and Behavioral Neurology, 14*, 227–232.

Altshuler, L. L., Bartzokis, G., Grieder, T., Curran, J., & Mintz, J. (1998). Amygdala enlargement in bipolar disorder and hippocampal reduction in schizophrenia: An MRI study demonstrating neuroanatomic specificity. *Archives of General Psychiatry, 55*, 663–664.

Ananth, J., Gold, J., & Ghadirian A. M. (1981). Long term effects of lithium carbonate on cognitive functions. *Journal of Psychiatric Evaluation and Treatment, 3*, 551–555.

Angst, F., Stassen, H. H., Clayton, P. J., & Angst, J. (2002). Mortality of patients with mood disorders: Follow-up over 34–38 years. *Journal of Affective Disorders, 68*, 167–181.

Aylward, E. H., Roberts-Twillie, J. V., Barta, P. E., Kumar, A. J., Harris, G. J., Geer, M., Peyser, C. E., & Pearlson, G. D. (1994). Basal ganglia volumes and white matter hyperintensities in patients with bipolar disorder. *American Journal of Psychiatry, 151*, 687–693.

Baxter, L. R., Jr., Phelps, M. E., Mazziotta, J. C., Schwartz, J. M., Gerner, R. H., Selin, C. E., & Sumida, R. M. (1985). Cerebral metabolic rates for glucose in mood disorders. Studies with positron emission tomography and fluorodeoxyglucose F 18. *Archives of General Psychiatry, 42*, 441–447.

Baxter, L. R., Jr., Schwartz, J. M., Phelps, M. E., Mazziotta, J. C., Guze, B. H., Selin, C. E., Gerner, R. H., & Sumida, R. M. (1989). Reduction of prefrontal cortex glucose metabolism common to three types of depression. *Archives of General Psychiatry, 46*, 243–250.

Bench, C. J., Friston, K. J., Brown, R. G., Frackowiak, R. S., & Dolan, R. J. (1993). Regional cerebral blood flow in depression measured by positron emission tomography: The relationship with clinical dimensions. *Psychological Medicine, 23*, 579–590.

Berns, G. S., Martin, M., & Proper, S. M. (2002). Limbic hyperreactivity in bipolar II disorder. *American Journal of Psychiatry, 159*, 304–306.

Bhagwagar, Z., Cowen, P. J., Goodwin, G. M., & Harmer, C. J. (2004). Normalization of enhanced fear recognition by acute SSRI treatment in subjects with a previous history of depression. *American Journal of Psychiatry, 161*, 166–168.

Blumberg, H. P., Leung, H. C., Skudlarski, P., Lacadie, C. M., Fredericks, C. A., Harris, B. C., Charney, D. S., Gore, J. C., Krystal, J. H., & Peterson, B. S. (2003a). A functional magnetic resonance imaging study of bipolar disorder: State- and trait-related dysfunction in ventral prefrontal cortices. *Archives of General Psychiatry, 60*, 601–609.

Blumberg, H. P., Martin, A., Kaufman, J., Leung, H. C., Skudlarski, P., Lacadie, C., Fulbright, R. K., Gore, J. C., Charney, D. S., Krystal, J. H., & Peterson, B. S. (2003b). Frontostriatal abnormalities in adolescents with bipolar disorder: Preliminary observations from functional MRI. *American Journal of Psychiatry, 160*, 1345–1347.

Blumberg, H. P., Stern, E., Ricketts, S., Martinez, D., de Asis, J., White, T., Epstein, J., Isenberg, N., McBride, P. A., Kemperman, I., Emmerich, S., Dhawan, V., Eidelberg, D., Kocsis, J. H., & Silbersweig, D. A. (1999). Rostral and orbital prefrontal cortex dysfunction in the manic state of bipolar disorder. *American Journal of Psychiatry, 156*, 1986–1988.

Blumberg, H. P., Stern, E., Martinez, D., Ricketts, S., de Asis, J., White, T., Epstein, J., McBride, P. A., Eidelberg, D., Kocsis, J. H., & Silbersweig, D. A. (2000). Increased anterior cingulate and caudate activity in bipolar mania. *Biological Psychiatry, 48*, 1045–1052.

Brambilla, P., Harenski, K., Nicoletti, M., Mallinger, A. G., Frank, E., Kupfer, D. J., Keshavan, M. S., & Soares, J. C. (2001). Differential effects of age on brain gray matter in bipolar patients and healthy individuals. *Neuropsychobiology, 43*, 242–247.

Brambilla, P., Harenski, K., Nicoletti, M., Sassi, R. B., Mallinger, A. G., Frank, E., Kupfer, D. J., Keshavan, M. S., & Soares, J. C. (2003). MRI investigation of temporal lobe structures in bipolar patients. *Journal of Psychiatric Research, 37*, 287–295.

Brambilla, P., Nicoletti, M. A., Harenski, K., Sassi, R. B., Mallinger, A. G., Frank, E., Kupfer, D. J., Keshavan, M. S., & Soares, J. C. (2002). Anatomical MRI study of subgenual prefrontal cortex in bipolar and unipolar subjects. *Neuropsychopharmacology, 27,* 792–799.

Brody, A. L., Saxena, S., Stoessel, P., Gillies, L. A., Fairbanks, L. A., Alborzian, S., Phelps, M. E., Huang, S. C., Wu, H. M., Ho, M. L., Ho, M. K., Au, S. C., Maidment, K., & Baxter, L. R., Jr. (2001). Regional brain metabolic changes in patients with major depression treated with either paroxetine or interpersonal therapy: Preliminary findings. *Archives of General Psychiatry, 58,* 631–640.

Calder, A. J., Lawrence, A. D., & Young, A. W. (2001). Neuropsychology of fear and loathing. *Nature Reviews. Neuroscience, 2,* 352–363.

Caligiuri, M. P., Brown, G. G., Meloy, M. J., Eberson, S. C., Kindermann, S. S., Frank, L. R., Zorrilla, L. E., & Lohr, J. B. (2003). An fMRI study of affective state and medication on cortical and subcortical brain regions during motor performance in bipolar disorder. *Psychiatry Research, 123,* 171–182.

Cavanagh, J. T., Van Beck, M., Muir, W., & Blackwood, D. H. (2002). Case-control study of neurocognitive function in euthymic patients with bipolar disorder: An association with mania. *British Journal of Psychiatry, 180,* 320–326.

Clark, L., Iversen, S. D., & Goodwin, G. M. (2002). Sustained attention deficit in bipolar disorder. *British Journal of Psychiatry, 180,* 313–319.

Darwin, C. (1998). The expression of the emotions in man and animals (3rd ed.). London: Harper Collins. (Original work published 1872)

Davidson, R. J., Jackson, D. C., & Kalin, N. H. (2000). Emotion, plasticity, context, and regulation: Perspectives from affective neuroscience. *Psychological Bulletin, 126,* 890–909.

Devinsky, O. (1995). Cognitive and behavioral effects of antiepileptic drugs. *Epilepsia, 36(Suppl. 2),* S46–S65.

Elliott, R., Ogilvie, A., Rubinsztein, J. S., Calderon, G., Dolan, R. J., & Sahakian, B. J. (2004). Abnormal ventral frontal response during performance of an affective go/no go task in patients with mania. *Biological Psychiatry, 55,* 1163–1170.

Elliott, R., Rubinsztein, J. S., Sahakian, B. J., & Dolan, R. J. (2002). The neural basis of mood-congruent processing biases in depression. *Archives of General Psychiatry, 59,* 597–604.

Engelsmann, F., Katz, J., Ghadirian, A. M., & Schachter, D. (1988). Lithium and memory: A long-term follow-up study. *Journal of Clinical Psychopharmacology, 8,* 207–212.

Ferrier, I. N., Stanton, B. R., Kelly, T. P., & Scott, J. (1999). Neuropsychological function in euthymic patients with bipolar disorder. *British Journal of Psychiatry, 175,* 246–251.

Getz, G. E., Shear, P. K., & Strakowski, S. M. (2003). Facial affect recognition deficits in bipolar disorder. *Journal of International Neuropsychological Society, 9,* 623–632.

Gitlin, M. J., Swendsen, J., Heller, T. L., & Hammen, C. (1995). Relapse and impairment in bipolar disorder. *American Journal of Psychiatry, 152,* 1635–1640.

Goldapple, K., Segal, Z., Garson, C., Lau, M., Bieling, P., Kennedy, S., & Mayberg, H. (2004). Modulation of cortical-limbic pathways in major depression: Treatment-specific effects of cognitive behavior therapy. *Archives of General Psychiatry, 61,* 34–41.

Goodwin, G. M., Austin, M. P., Dougall, N., Ross, M., Murray, C., O'Carroll, R. E., Moffoot, A., Prentice, N., & Ebmeier, K. P. (1993). State changes in brain activity shown by the uptake of 99mTc-exametazime with single photon emission tomography in major depression before and after treatment. *Journal of Affective Disorders, 29,* 243–253.

Goodwin, G. M., Cavanagh, J. T., Glabus, M. F., Kehoe, R. F., O'Carroll, R. E., & Ebmeier, K. P. (1997). Uptake of 99mTc-exametazime shown by single photon emission computed tomography before and after lithium withdrawal in bipolar patients: Associations with mania. *British Journal of Psychiatry, 170,* 426–430.

Gross, J. J. (2002). Emotion regulation: Affective, cognitive, and social consequences. *Psychophysiology, 39,* 281–291.

Gruber, S. A., Rogowska, J., & Yurgelun-Todd, D. A. (2004). Decreased activation of the anterior cingulate in bipolar patients: an fMRI study. *Journal of Affective Disorders, 82,* 191–201.

Gur, R. E., McGrath, C., Chan, R. M., Schroeder, L., Turner, T., Turetsky, B. I., Kohler, C., Alsop, D., Maldjian, J., Ragland, J. D., & Gur, R. C. (2002). An fMRI study of facial emotion processing in patients with schizophrenia. *American Journal of Psychiatry, 159,* 1992–1999.

Hariri, A. R., Mattay, V. S., Tessitore, A., Fera, F., & Weinberger, D. R. (2003). Neocortical modulation of the amygdala response to fearful stimuli. *Biological Psychiatry, 53,* 494–501.

Harmer, C. J., Grayson, L., & Goodwin, G. M. (2002). Enhanced recognition of disgust in bipolar illness. *Biological Psychiatry, 51,* 298–304.

Harrison, P. J. (2002). The neuropathology of primary mood disorder. *Brain, 125,* 1428–1449.

Hempel, A., Hempel, E., Schonknecht, P., Stippich, C., & Schroder, J. (2003). Impairment in basal limbic function in schizophrenia during affect recognition. *Journal of Psychiatric Research, 122,* 115–124.

Keck, P. E., Jr., McElroy, S. L., Strakowski, S. M., West, S. A., Sax, K. W., Hawkins, J. M., Bourne, M. L., & Haggard, P. (1998). 12-month outcome of patients with bipolar disorder following hospitalization for a manic or mixed episode. *American Journal of Psychiatry, 155,* 646–652.

Keedwell, P., Andrew, C., Williams, S. C. R., Brammer, M., & Phillips, M. L. (2005). Abnormal ventromedial prefrontal cortical and subcortical responses to happy stimuli are associated with anhedonia and state anxiety in major depressive disorder. *Biological Psychiatry, 58,* 495–503.

Kennedy, S. H., Evans, K. R., Kruger, S., Mayberg, H. S., Meyer, J. H., McCann, S., Arifuzzman, A. I., Houle, S., & Vaccarino, F. J. (2001). Changes in regional brain glucose metabolism measured with positron emission tomography after paroxetine treatment of major depression. *American Journal of Psychiatry, 158,* 899–905.

Kessing, L. V. (1998). Cognitive impairment in the euthymic phase of affective disorder. *Psychological Medicine, 28,* 1027–1038.

Kessler, R. C., McGonagle, K. A., Zhao, S., Nelson, C. B., Hughes, M., Eshleman, S., Wittchen, H. U., & Kendler, K. S. (1994). Lifetime and 12-month prevalence of DSM-III-R psychiatric disorders in the United States: Results from the National Comorbidity Survey. *Archives of General Psychiatry, 51,* 8–19.

Ketter, T. A., Kimbrell, T. A., George, M. S., Dunn, R. T., Speer, A. M., Benson, B. E., Willis, M. W., Danielson, A., Frye, M. A., Herscovitch, P., & Post, R. M. (2001). Effects of mood and subtype on cerebral glucose metabolism in treatment-resistant bipolar disorder. *Biological Psychiatry, 49,* 97–109.

King, D. J. (1994). Psychomotor impairment and cognitive disturbances induced by neuroleptics. *Acta Psychiatrica Scandinavica, 380(Suppl.),* 53–58.

Kocsis, J. H., Shaw, E. D., Stokes, P. E., Wilner, P., Elliot, A. S., Sikes, C., Myers, B., Manevitz, A., & Parides, M. (1993). Neuropsychologic effects of lithium discontinuation. *Journal of Clinical Psychopharmacology, 13,* 268–275.

Kruger, S., Seminowicz, D., Goldapple, K., Kennedy, S. H., & Mayberg, H. S. (2003). State and trait influences on mood regulation in bipolar disorder: Blood flow differences with an acute mood challenge. *Biological Psychiatry, 54,* 1274–1283.

Lang, P. J., Bradley, M. M., & Cuthbert, B. N. (1998). *International affective picture system (IAPS).* NIMH Center for the Study of Emotion and Attention, University of Florida, Gainesville.

Lange, K., Williams, L. M., Young, A. W., Bullmore, E. T., Brammer, M. J., Williams, S. C. Gray, J. A., & Phillips, M. L. (2003). Task instructions modulate neural responses to fearful facial expressions. *Biological Psychiatry, 53,* 226–232.

Lawrence, N. S., Williams, A. M., Surguladze, S., Giampietro, V., Brammer, M. J., Andrew, C., Frangou, S., Ecker, C., & Phillips, M. L. (2004). Subcortical and ventral prefrontal cortical neural responses to facial expressions distinguish patients with bipolar disorder and major depression. *Biological Psychiatry, 55,* 578–587.

Lembke, A., & Ketter, T. A. (2002). Impaired recognition of facial emotion in mania. *American Journal of Psychiatry, 159*, 302–304.

Lennox, B. R., Jacob, R., Calder, A. J., Lupson, V., & Bullmore, E. T. (2004). Behavioural and neurocognitive responses to sad facial affect are attenuated in patients with mania. *Psychological Medicine, 34*, 795–802.

Levesque, J., Eugene, F., Joanette, Y., Paquette, V., Mensour, B., Beaudoin, G., Leroux, J. M., Bourgouin, P., & Beauregard, M. (2003). Neural circuitry underlying voluntary suppression of sadness. *Biological Psychiatry, 53*, 502–510.

Lochhead, R. A., Parsey, R. V., Oquendo, M. A., & Mann, J. J. (2004). Regional brain gray matter volume differences in patients with bipolar disorder as assessed by optimized voxel-based morphometry. *Biological Psychiatry, 55*, 1154–1162.

Lopez-Larson, M. P., DelBello, M. P., Zimmerman, M. E., Schwiers, M. L., & Strakowski, S. M. (2002). Regional prefrontal gray and white matter abnormalities in bipolar disorder. *Biological Psychiatry, 52*, 93–100.

Lyon, H. M., Startup, M., & Bentall, R. P. (1999). Social cognition and the manic defense: Attributions, selective attention, and self-schema in bipolar affective disorder. *Journal of Abnormal Psychology, 108*, 273–282.

Malhi, G. S., Lagopoulos, J., Sachdev, P., Mitchell, P. B., Ivanovski, B., & Parker, G. B. (2004a). Cognitive generation of affect in hypomania: An fMRI study. *Bipolar Disorders, 6*, 271–285.

Malhi, G. S., Lagopoulos, J., Ward, P. B., Kumari, V., Mitchell, P. B., Parker, G. B., Ivanovski, B., & Sachdev, P. (2004b). Cognitive generation of affect in bipolar depression: An fMRI study. *European Journal of Neuroscience, 19*, 741–754.

Manji, H. K., Moore, G. J., & Chen, G. (2000). Clinical and preclinical evidence for the neurotrophic effects of mood stabilizers: Implications for the pathophysiology and treatment of manic-depressive illness. *Biological Psychiatry, 48*, 740–754.

Martin, S. D., Martin, E., Rai, S. S., Richardson, M. A., & Royall, R. (2001). Brain blood flow changes in depressed patients treated with interpersonal psychotherapy or venlafaxine hydrochloride: preliminary findings. *Archives of General Psychiatry, 58*, 641–648.

Martinez-Aran, A., Penades, R., Vieta, E., Colom, F., Reinares, M., Benabarre, A., Salamero, M., & Gasto, C. (2002). Executive function in patients with remitted bipolar disorder and schizophrenia and its relationship with functional outcome. *Psychotherapy and Psychosomatics, 71*, 39–46.

Martinez-Aran, A., Vieta, E., Colom, F., Torrent, C., Sanchez-Moreno, J., Reinares, M., Benabarre, A., Goikolea, J. M., Brugue, E., Daban, C., & Salamero, M. (2004a). Cognitive impairment in euthymic bipolar patients: Implications for clinical and functional outcome. *Bipolar Disorders, 6*, 224–232.

Martinez-Aran, A., Vieta, E., Reinares, M., Colom, F., Torrent, C., Sanchez-Moreno, J., Benabarre, A., Goikolea, J. M., Comes, M., & Salamero, M. (2004b). Cognitive function across manic or hypomanic, depressed, and euthymic states in bipolar disorder. *American Journal of Psychiatry, 161*, 262–270.

Martinot, J. L., Hardy, P., Feline, A., Huret, J. D., Mazoyer, B., Attar-Levy, D., Pappata, S., & Syrota, A. (1990). Left prefrontal glucose hypometabolism in the depressed state: A confirmation. *American Journal of Psychiatry, 147*, 1313–1317.

Mataix-Cols, D., Cullen, S., Lange, K., Zelaya, F., Andrew, C., Amaro, E., Brammer, M. J., Williams, S. C., Speckens, A., & Phillips, M. L. (2003). Neural correlates of anxiety associated with obsessive-compulsive symptom dimensions in normal volunteers. *Biological Psychiatry, 53*, 482–493.

Mayberg, H. S., Brannan, S. K., Tekell, J. L., Silva, J. A., Mahurin, R. K., McGinnis, S., & Jerabek, P. A. (2000). Regional metabolic effects of fluoxetine in major depression: Serial changes and relationship to clinical response. *Biological Psychiatry, 48*, 830–843.

Mayberg, H. S., Liotti, M., Brannan, S. K., McGinnis, S., Mahurin, R. K., Jerabek, P. A., Silva, J. A., Tekell, J. L., Matin, C. C., Lancaster, J. L., & Fox, P. T. (1999). Reciprocal limbic-cortical function and negative mood: Converging PET findings in depression and normal sadness. *American Journal of Psychiatry, 156,* 675–682.

McClure, E. B., Pope, K., Hoberman, A. J., Pine, D. S., & Leibenluft, E. (2003). Facial expression recognition in adolescents with mood and anxiety disorders. *American Journal of Psychiatry, 160,* 1172–1174.

McDonald, C., Zanelli, J., Rabe-Hesketh, S., Ellison-Wright, I., Sham, P., Kalidindi, S., Murray, R. M., & Kennedy, N. (2004). Meta-analysis of magnetic resonance imaging brain morphometry studies in bipolar disorder. *Biological Psychiatry, 56,* 411–417.

Mehta, M. A., Sahakian, B. J., McKenna, P. J., & Robbins, T. W. (1999). Systemic sulpiride in young adult volunteers simulates the profile of cognitive deficits in Parkinson's disease. *Psychopharmacology (Berlin), 146,* 162–174.

Moore, P. B., Shepherd, D. J., Eccleston, D., Macmillan, I. C., Goswami, U., McAllister, V. L., & Ferrier, I. N. (2001). Cerebral white matter lesions in bipolar affective disorder: Relationship to outcome. *British Journal of Psychiatry, 178,* 172–176.

Morris, J. S., Frith, C. D., Perrett, D. I., Rowland, D., Young, A. W., Calder, A. J., & Dolan, R. J. (1996). A differential neural response in the human amygdala to fearful and happy facial expressions. *Nature, 383,* 812–815.

Murphy, F. C., Sahakian, B. J., Rubinsztein, J. S., Michael, A., Rogers, R. D., Robbins, T. W., & Paykel, E. S. (1999). Emotional bias and inhibitory control processes in mania and depression. *Psychological Medicine, 29,* 1307–1321.

O'Connell, R. A., Mayo, J. A., Flatow, L., Cuthbertson, B., & O'Brien, B. E. (1991). Outcome of bipolar disorder on long-term treatment with lithium. *British Journal of Psychiatry, 159,* 123–129.

Ochsner, K. N., Bunge, S. A., Gross, J. J., & Gabrieli, J. D. (2002). Rethinking feelings: An FMRI study of the cognitive regulation of emotion. *Journal of Cognitive Neuroscience, 14,* 1215–1229.

Phillips, M. L., Drevets, W. C., Rauch, S. L., & Lane, R. (2003a). Neurobiology of emotion perception: I. The neural basis of normal emotion perception. *Biological Psychiatry, 54,* 504–514.

Phillips, M. L., Drevets, W. C., Rauch, S. L., & Lane, R. (2003b). Neurobiology of emotion perception: II. Implications for major psychiatric disorders. *Biological Psychiatry, 54,* 515–528.

Phillips, M. L., Marks, I. M., Senior, C., Lythgoe, D., O'Dwyer, A. M., Meehan, O., Williams, S. C., Brammer, M. J., Bullmore, E. T., & McGuire, P. K. (2000). A differential neural response in obsessive-compulsive disorder patients with washing compared with checking symptoms to disgust. *Psychological Medicine, 30,* 1037–1050.

Phillips, M. L., Williams, L., Senior, C., Bullmore, E. T., Brammer, M. J., Andrew, C., Williams, S. C., & David, A. S. (1999). A differential neural response to threatening and non-threatening negative facial expressions in paranoid and non-paranoid schizophrenics. *Psychiatry Research, 92,* 11–31.

Phillips, M. L., Young, A. W., Senior, C., Brammer, M., Andrew, C., Calder, A. J., Bullmore, E. T., Perrett, D. I., Rowland, D., Williams, S. C., Gray, J. A., & David, A. S. (1997). A specific neural substrate for perceiving facial expressions of disgust. *Nature, 389,* 495–498.

Rubinsztein, J. S., Fletcher, P. C., Rogers, R. D., Ho, L. W., Aigbirhio, F. I., Paykel, E. S., Robbins, T. W., & Sahakian, B. J. (2001). Decision-making in mania: A PET study. *Brain, 124,* 2550–2563.

Sassi, R. B., Brambilla, P., Hatch, J. P., Nicoletti, M. A., Mallinger, A. G., Frank, E., Kupfer, D. J., Keshavan, M. S., & Soares, J. C. (2004). Reduced left anterior cingulate volumes in untreated bipolar patients. *Biological Psychiatry, 56,* 467–475.

Sax, K. W., Strakowski, S. M., Zimmerman, M. E., DelBello, M. P., Keck, P. E., Jr., & Hawkins, J. M. (1999). Frontosubcortical neuroanatomy and the continuous performance test in mania. *American Journal of Psychiatry, 156,* 139–141.

Sharma, V., Menon, R., Carr, T. J., Densmore, M., Mazmanian, D., & Williamson, P. C. (2003). An MRI study of subgenual prefrontal cortex in patients with familial and non-familial bipolar I disorder. *Journal of Affective Disorders, 77,* 167–171.

Silfverskiold, P., & Risberg, J. (1989). Regional cerebral blood flow in depression and mania. *Archives of General Psychiatry, 46,* 253–259.

Sprengelmeyer, R., Rausch, M., Eysel, U. T., & Przuntek, H. (1998). Neural structures associated with recognition of facial expressions of basic emotions. *Procceedings of the Royal Society of London. Series B, 265,* 1927–1931.

Strakowski, S. M., Adler, C. M., & DelBello, M. P. (2002). Volumetric MRI studies of mood disorders: do they distinguish unipolar and bipolar disorder? *Bipolar Disorders, 4,* 80–88.

Strakowski, S. M., Adler, C. M., Holland, S. K., Mills, N., & DelBello, M. P. (2004). A preliminary FMRI study of sustained attention in euthymic, unmedicated bipolar disorder. *Neuropsychopharmacology, 29,* 1734–1740.

Strakowski, S. M., DelBello, M. P., Sax, K. W., Zimmerman, M. E., Shear, P. K., Hawkins, J. M., & Larson, E. R. (1999). Brain magnetic resonance imaging of structural abnormalities in bipolar disorder. *Archives of General Psychiatry, 56,* 254–260.

Surguladze, S. A., Brammer, M. J., Young, A. W., Andrew, C., Travis, M. J., Williams, S. C., & Phillips, M. L. (2003). A preferential increase in the extrastriate response to signals of danger. *Neuroimage, 19,* 1317–1328.

Thompson, P.J. (1991). Antidepressants and Memory. *Annual Review of Psychopharmacology, 6,* 79–90.

Tohen, M., Hennen, J., Zarate, C. M., Jr., Baldessarini, R. J., Strakowski, S. M., Stoll, A. L., Faedda, G. L., Suppes, T., Gebre-Medhin, P., & Cohen, B. M. (2000). Two-year syndromal and functional recovery in 219 cases of first-episode major affective disorder with psychotic features. *American Journal of Psychiatry, 157,* 220–228.

Venn, H. R., Gray, J. M., Montagne, B., Murray, L. K., Michael, Burt D., Frigerio, E., Perrett, D. I., & Young, A. H. (2004). Perception of facial expressions of emotion in bipolar disorder. *Bipolar Disorder, 6,* 186–293.

Videbech, P., & Ravnkilde, B. (2004). Hippocampal volume and depression: a meta-analysis of MRI studies. *American Journal of Psychiatry, 161,* 1957–1966.

Williams, L. M., Das, P., Harris, A. W., Liddell, B. B., Brammer, M. J., Olivieri, G., Skerrett, D., Phillips, M. L., David, A. S., Peduto, A., & Gordon, E. (2004). Dysregulation of arousal and amygdala-prefrontal systems in paranoid schizophrenia. *American Journal of Psychiatry, 161,* 480–489.

Yurgelun-Todd, D. A., Gruber, S. A., Kanayama, G., Killgore, W. D., Baird, A. A., & Young, A. D. (2000). fMRI during affect discrimination in bipolar affective disorder. *Bipolar Disorders, 2,* 237–248.

Zubieta, J. K., Huguelet, P., O'Neil, R. L., & Giordani, B. J. (2001). Cognitive function in euthymic bipolar I disorder. *Psychiatry Research, 102,* 9–20.

COGNITIVE NEUROPSYCHIATRY
2006, 11 (3), 250–271

Emotional processing in schizophrenia

Christian G. Kohler and Elizabeth A. Martin

University of Pennsylvania, Philadelphia, PA, USA

Introduction. Persons with schizophrenia have impaired emotional processing, involving experience, expression, and recognition of emotions.

Methods. This article reviews the historical descriptions and more recent work on emotion processing in schizophrenia.

Results. Although abilities of emotional processing relate directly to interpersonal communication and psychosocial functioning, methodological issues exist in the current body of studies and resultant knowledge, which limit translation to novel treatment options.

Conclusions. Further improvement in emotion processing in persons with stable schizophrenia are unlikely to result from conventional pharmacotherapy of psychosis. New treatment modalities and behavioural interventions offer possible improvements in quality of life and psychosocial functioning.

Schizophrenia (SZP) has traditionally been viewed as a psychiatric illness with prominent clinical features of psychosis or positive symptoms, negative symptoms, and cognitive dysfunction. Deficits in cognition, considered a stable hallmark of SZP, have long been described and in the early part of this century were used to differentiate SZP from affective illnesses. Investigations have shown quite marked neuropsychological functioning deficits in SZP, of a magnitude similar to performance of patients with brain injury (for a review, see Heaton & Crowley, 1981), and these impairments are present in patients treated with medications (Braff et al., 1991), as well as in neuroleptic naive patients with first-episode SZP (Censits, Ragland, Gur, & Gur, 1997; Saykin et al., 1994).

Emotional processing can be parsed along dimensions of emotion experience, expression, and recognition. Early descriptions of the phenomenology of SZP included disturbances in emotional processing, such as abnormal expression and abnormal experience as symptoms inherent, but not always characteristic to the illness. Kraepelin's (1896) Binary Model proposed an exclusivity of SZP and

Correspondence should be addressed to Dr Christian G. Kohler, Neuropsychiatry Section, 10 Gates Building, Hospital of the University of Pennsylvania, 3400 Spruce St., Philadelphia, PA 19104, USA.

http://www.psypress.com/cogneuropsychiatry   DOI:10.1080/13546800500188575

affective phenomena and delineated a clear distinction between dementia praecox and manic-depressive illness. However, by 1919, Kraepelin (1919/1971) reported affective disturbances that were present at the onset of dementia praecox "... usually anxious, despondent, they weep and lament, would like to die...". and became less prominent during later stages of the illness with more prominent somatic preoccupation and self-neglect. Eugen Bleuler (1911), whose views have been influential on our understanding of SZP, divided the phenomenology of SZP into primary and secondary symptoms. Primary symptoms—disturbances in affect, association, ambivalence and, autism—were seen as partial, but necessary for the diagnosis. Secondary symptoms, which included not only delusions and hallucinations but also depressed mood, could be absent or could change without any alteration in the underlying process.

Similarly, impaired interpersonal skills have been described as hallmarks of the illness, and both expression and recognition of facial emotions are viewed as major components of interpersonal communication. With respect to expression, although affective flattening is an established symptom of SZP, little is known about its characteristics and course and, except for clinical ratings, limited quantitative data are available. An increasing body of literature has examined emotion recognition deficits in SZP. Once acute psychotic symptoms are stabilised, the ability to express and recognise emotions substantially relates to interpersonal and social functioning.

Over the past 30 years, these dimensions of emotional processing and their respective dysfunctions have been subjected to increasing clinical attention and research. As noted above, SZP presents as a heterogeneous illness with wide-ranging symptoms encompassing positive and negative symptoms, dysfunction in cognition and emotion processing, and psychosocial impairment. Approaches to treatment have moved beyond treatment of acute psychosis and, in people who are in the chronic or residual phases of the illness, have increasingly focused on improvement in negative symptoms, cognition, emotional processing, and psychosocial remediation. This article describes the recent literature on experience, recognition, and expression in SZP, and delineates possible future directions to investigate and remediate these areas of dysfunction, which in turn may ameliorate psychosocial functioning and quality of life in persons with SZP.

NEUROBIOLOGY OF EMOTIONAL PROCESSING

Different concepts exist regarding the constituents of emotions, and most theories include the combination of a physical and cognitive, or attributional, component. The Jamesian Model (James, 1884/1922) postulates that physical changes as the result of an external experience are sufficient to qualify for an emotional experience. Cannon (1927/1987) argued that the central component of emotional experience is not the physical sensation, but a brain-based feeling, which he claimed to be located in the thalamus. Schachter and Singer (1962) expanded the Jamesian Model in that emotional experience is based on the cognitive attribution to bodily changes or arousal.

According to Tomkins (1962), emotions are motor and glandular responses originating in the face and other bodily regions, which are triggered by sub-cortical affect programmes and provide sensory feedback to cortical brain regions. It is unclear whether this model proposes the brain-based experience to represent the trigger or the consequence of the emotion. However, important for further research on emotions, it emphasises the face as a principal constituent in the processing of emotions. Similarly, Damasio (1994) postulated that the content of emotional experience consists of bodily changes, juxtaposed to the precipitant or cause of the emotional experience and the associated change in one's mode of thinking.

Processing of emotions is supported by distributed neural systems, and as lesion studies show, preferentially of the right hemisphere. There are two main theories regarding the hemispheric specialisation in processing emotions (Borod et al., 1998). The hemispheric hypothesis posits that the right hemisphere is specialised to process all emotions, whereas the valence hypothesis regards the right hemisphere as superior for processing negative and the left hemisphere superior for positive emotions. Common negative emotions are sadness, fear, and anger, common positive emotions are happiness and, possibly, surprise. In human and primate studies, the amygdala, which receives input from sensory cortical areas and via subcortical input from the visual pathways of the midbrain and thalamus, is thought to be preferentially involved in the processing of fear and other emotions. A recent model based on animal and human studies (Phillips, Drevets, Rauch, & Lane, 2003) proposes that emotion perceptions may be dependent on two neural systems. The ventral limbic system, including amygdala, insula, ventral striatum, and ventral regions of the anterior cingulate gyrus and prefrontal cortex, is vital for identification of the emotional sig-nificance of a stimulus and the subsequent production of the affective state. The dorsal system includes the hippocampus and dorsal regions of the anterior cingulated gyrus and prefrontal cortex, and is important in executive functioning required for the regulation of affective states. In schizophrenia, which affects most functions of the limbic system, all dimensions of emotional processing, including experience, expression, and recognition are commonly affected. Impairment in these areas may be most relevant in persons who have achieved remission of stability with respect to acute psychosis.

There is limited information concerning brain regions and their dysfunction associated with euphoric and manic mood states. In idiopathic and secondary mania, functional imaging studies have revealed asymmetric temporal lobe activity (Gyulai et al., 1997; Migliorelli et al., 1993; Starkstein et al., 1990), which may remit with stabilisation of mood (Gyulai et al., 1997). Functional imaging studies in idiopathic depression (Baxter et al., 1985; Dolan & Friston,

1989; Drevets, 1999; Mayberg, Lewis, Regenold, & Wagner, 1994) and depression associated with schizophrenia (Kohler, Swanson, Gur, Harper Mozley, & Gur, 1998), stroke (Robinson, Kubos, Starr, Rao, & Price, 1984), epilepsy (Bromfield et al., 1992), and neurodegenerative disorders (Mayberg et al., 1990; Mayberg, Starkstein, Peyser, Brandt, & Dannals, 1992) have implicated left inferior frontal and cingulate brain dysfunction.

EMOTION EXPERIENCE

Emotional Intensity

In a healthy individual, issues of emotional experience and intensity remain poorly understood. Difficulties lie in measuring one's emotional experience, gauging its quality, and quantifying its intensity. Measurements of emotional experience via emotion induction have included presentation of emotional faces and pictures, exposure to emotive music, and the recall of one's own emotional experiences.

Historically, SZP was thought to involve decreased range of emotional experience. According to Sass and Parnas (2003), SZP is defined as an ipseity disturbance and anhedonia, defined as diminished ability to experience pleasure, represents both a crucial element of such a lack of self-experience and a characteristic, common negative symptom of SZP. Lack of emotional experience is typically inferred from a deficiency to identify one's own emotional experience and/or impairment in facial expression of emotions, also referred to as flattening of affect.

It has been described that persons with SZP may be unreliable reporters of their own emotional experience (Jaeger, Bitter, Czobor, & Volavka, 1990). However, others have described that SZP subjects report similar emotional experience in comparison with depression (Berenbaum, 1992; Sison, Alpert, Fudge, & Stern, 1996) and healthy controls (Kring & Neale, 1996). Kring and Neale (1996) found that in response to emotionally stimulating film clips, patients with SZP are less facially expressive than healthy controls but report similar emotional experiences and greater autonomic responses.

Employing an emotional startle paradigm, Volz, Hamm, Kirsch, and Rey (2003) reported that in response to unpleasant pictures, people with SZP exhibited lessened affective modulation upon early but not late tone presentations. This suggests delayed responses to affective stimuli in schizophrenia. Lastly, blunted facial expression of emotions in SZP may not correlate with emotional experience (Earnst et al., 1996; Kring, Kerr, Smith, & Neale, 1993; Myin-Germeys, Delespaul, & de Vries, 2000; Sison et al., 1996), which in some of these studies has been described as similar to emotional experience in healthy controls.

Applying a mood induction procedure with happy and sad faces to 40 SZP individuals and gender-matched healthy controls, Schneider, Gur, Gur, and

Shtasel (1995) found that patients exhibited impaired ability to respond to mood induction, particularly for happiness irrespective of medication status and gender. Performance on mood induction was positively correlated with hallucinations, and negatively correlated with the negative symptom complex of anhedonia. Taylor, Liberzon, Decker, and Koeppe (2002) examined emotional experience and processing in SZP and healthy subjects using positron emission tomography and found that while patients reported similar subjective experience to aversive stimuli, the groups differed in brain activation consistent with impaired processing of emotional stimuli in SZP.

Future directions and investigations into emotional experience in SZP may include presentation of emotional stimuli in conjunction with self-rating measures during neuroimaging procedures, which will elucidate the neural substrate of feelings and the putative alteration of its function in SZP.

Depression

Relationship to treatment. Following the introduction of antipsychotic medications in treating SZP, clinical reports appeared that described a dramatic increase in the incidence of depression and suicide (Beisser, 1961; Hussar, 1962). Experience with the antihypertensive agent reserpine, also used to treat SZP and known to cause depression in some patients, created the concern that depression might result from pharmacotherapy in SZP. This led to the introduction of the term "pharmacogenic depression" (Galdi, 1983; Helmchen & Hippius, 1967). A further suggestion was that treatment with typical antipsychotics may cause depressive symptoms due to extrapyramidal motor disturbances or "akinetic depression" (Craig, Richardson, Pass, & Bregman, 1985; Johnson, 1981; Rifkin, Quitkin, & Klein, 1975; Van Putten & May, 1978). Subsequent studies refuted the association between antipsychotics and depression in general and describe that depression occurs most commonly during the onset of psychosis (Bowers & Astrachan, 1967; House, Bostock, & Cooper, 1987; Johnson, 1981; Knights & Hirsch, 1981; Koreen et al., 1993; Mayer-Gross, Slater, & Roth, 1955; McGlashan & Carpenter, 1976; Roth, 1970; Steinberg, Green, & Durell, 1967; Stern, Pillsbury, & Sonnenberg, 1972). Reduction of acute symptoms and clinical stabilisation are associated with decline of depressive symptoms (House et al., 1987; Knights & Hirsch, 1981; Shanfield, Tucker, Marrow, & Detre, 1970), that may re-emerge during each relapse (Shanfield et al., 1970; Johnson, 1981; Koreen et al., 1993). Depression appears less common with increasing chronicity of illness, perhaps because its symptoms are gradually replaced by negative symptoms (House et al., 1987).

Relationship to onset of illness. Koreen et al. (1993) followed 70 men and women with first-episode SZP for up to 5 years. Before initiation of treatment, three fourths of the subjects experienced significant symptoms of depression, as measured by the Hamilton Rating Scale for Depression, and approximately one third experienced syndromatic criteria of major depression. Symptoms of depression remitted with stabilisation of psychosis and without specific anti-depressant treatment. In an attempt to examine the differentiation between SZP and major depression, Wassink, Flaum, Nopoulos, and Andreasen (1999) reported on 75 persons with recent-onset SZP who were followed for 5 years and about one third met the algorithmic criteria for a major depressive episode, while no symptoms were present in about one tenth of persons. The findings highlight that depressive symptoms are common early in the course of SZP with potential implications for diagnostic and treatment practices. In addition, these studies offer support of depression in schizophrenia being associated with positive symptoms.

Suicidality.   An increased risk of suicide attempts by people with SZP has been identified (Harkavy-Friedman, Nelson, Venarde, & Mann, 2004). Between 8% and 13% of people with SZP commit suicide (Meltzer & Okayli, 1995; Miles, 1977; Nyman & Jonsson, 1986), and suicide presents as a common cause of premature death in SZP (Palmer, Pankratz, & Bostwick, 2005). The majority of suicide completers were depressed in the few months directly preceding their deaths (Cohen, Leonard, Farberow, & Shneidman, 1964; Planansky & Johnston, 1971) underscoring the need for treatment of depression in SZP.

Another and less dramatic, but pernicious consequence, is the pervasive negative effect of depression on enjoyment of life and psychosocial functioning (Hofer et al., 2004), which is already quite impaired in persons with SZP who do not experience depression.

Relationship to negative and positive symptoms.   A major difficulty in evaluating depression in SZP stems from the potential overlap of negative symptoms with depression. While several studies found little or no association between depressive and negative features (Goldman, Tandon, Liberzon, & Greden, 1992; Kibel, Laffont, & Liddle, 1993; Kuck, Zisook, Moranville, Heaton, & Braff, 1992), other studies (Craig et al., 1985; Kulhara et al., 1989; Prosser et al., 1987) found an association between negative and vegetative features of depression. Vegetative symptoms of depression consist of somatic and nonspecific behavioural disturbances, such as anergia, anhedonia, insomnia, and lack of appetite, and can be found in many psychiatric disorders. Kitamura and Suga (1991) reported an association between depressive ratings and nega-tive ratings, specifically for avolition-apathy and anhedonia-asociality, and Ring et al. (1991) noted a correlation between negative and depressive symptoms but only in male patients. No study found a link between negative symptoms and depressive cognitions, which are more specific to depression and consist of sadness, anxiety, guilt, tension, and somatic concern.

In an effort to separate the effects of depression from symptoms primarily attributable to SZP, such as negative and positive symptoms, we compared a group of SZP subjects with depression to a group without depression (Kohler, Gur, Swanson, Petty, & Gur, 1998). There were 63 patients (35 men, 28 women) in the high (HD) and 81 patients (52 men, 29 women) in the low depression (LD) group. The groups were compared on demographic, clinical, and eight neuropsychological domains. They differed in age at onset of illness (later in HD group), delusional thinking (more severe in HD group), and performance in a single neuropsychological domain, attention (more impaired in HD group). The presence of specific attentional impairment associated with depressive symptoms in SZP is consistent with the hypothesis of frontal lobe dysfunction in depression, as these regions have been implicated in maintaining a euthymic mood state and in attentional processes. In people from this group who underwent magnetic resonance imaging (MRI) and PET, we found larger temporal lobes and relatively decreased left anterior cingulate metabolism in HD. Although the former finding was not expected, it may indicate that intact temporal lobes are necessary for emotional experience. The finding on decreased left medial frontal metabolism is consistent with other studies in idiopathic depression and depression in brain-related disorders as outlined above.

Studies on the treatment of depression in SZP have suffered methodological limitations concerning criteria and scales for assessing depression. Most studies have centred on the treatment of depressive symptoms in chronic institutionalised patients and only a few have examined the role of antidepressant treatment in patients suffering from an acute episode. Studies, which evaluated the presence of depressed mood in patients with acute psychosis, reported improvement in both psychotic and depressive symptoms in patients with SZP who were treated with mostly typical (Johnson, 1981; Knights & Hirsch, 1981; Koreen et al., 1993; McGlashan & Carpenter, 1976) and atypical antipsychotics (Arvaniitis & Miller, 1997; Keck et al., 1998; Meltzer, Lee, & Ranjan, 1994; Tollefson, Sanger, Lu, & Thieme, 1998).

Two comprehensive reviews (Plasky, 1991; Siris, 1991) of the literature on depressive symptoms in SZP preceding the widespread use of atypical antipsychotics evaluated over 30 publications and found only three papers that clearly support the benefit of antidepressant treatment. Many studies were difficult to interpret due to flawed designs, such as inadequate assessment of depression and small number of patients.

According to a more recent review of studies on the treatment of depression in SZP by Levinson, Umapathy, and Musthaq (1999), the beneficial effect of antidepressants is limited to patients who were treated as outpatients or exhibited more stable psychotic symptoms. Antidepressants show no benefit in patients without clear depressive symptoms, with florid psychotic symptoms, and of questionable or limited benefit in chronic inpatients and patients with unstable psychotic symptoms. Coinciding with the advent of atypical anti-psychotics, there is a lack of treatment studies on depression in SZP using newer generation selective serotonin and noradrenalin-serotonin reuptake inhibitor medications.

Over the last 10 years atypical neuroleptics, which affect serotonergic pathways, have found widespread usage in the treatment of SZP. Of this group of medications, clozapine and olanzapine have been investigated for specific antidepressant effect in SZP and mood disorders (Meltzer et al., 1994; Weisler, Ahearn, Davidson, & Wallace, 1997; Zarate, Tohen, & Baldessarini, 1995). In a large cohort of patients with acute exacerbation of chronic SZP, average dosed olanzapine treatment was found to improve anxious-depressed symptoms, when compared to placebo and haloperidol. This effect was found to be independent of improvement in positive, negative and extrapyramidal symptoms (Tollefson et al., 1998; Tran et al., 1997). To a lesser extent, there is similar evidence for improvement of mood symptoms in SZP as the result of treatment with quetiapine (Arvanitis & Miller, 1997) and ziprasidone (Keck et al., 1998) and no clear evidence for risperidone (Ceskova & Svestka, 1993; Müller et al., 1998; Tran et al., 1997). In addition, atypical antipsychotics in general (Barak, Mirecki, Knobler, Natan, & Aizenberg, 2004), and clozapine in particular (Meltzer & Okayli, 1995), have been found to reduce suicidality and completed suicide.

While depression is a well-described comorbidity of SZP, future goals remain in improved treatment of depression and prevention of suicidality. Depression has been associated with worse quality of life in SZP (Hofer et al., 2004), and its improvement will lead to better psychosocial functioning. Apart from medication treatment for depression, there has been increased interest in applying psychotherapy beyond supportive measures, most recently employing cognitive-behavioural therapy (CBT). This therapy is based on the premise that thoughts exert influence on a person's emotions and behaviour. Identifying and correcting cognitive distortions can lead to improvement in a person's emotional state and behaviour. Unlike supportive therapy, which is not time-limited, CBT represents a structured and time-limited approach, typically consisting of 20 sessions over 6–9 months. Patients learn to view delusions and hallucinations as symptoms, that are part of their psychiatric disorder, rather than as frightening and believable entities. Over the past 10 years a number of studies (Beck & Rector, 2000; Drury, Birchwood, Cochrane, & Macmillan, 1996; Kingdon & Tuckington, 1991; Kuipers et al., 1997; Lewis et al., 2002; Pinto, La Pia, Mennella, Giorgio, & DeSimone, 1999; Sensky et al., 2000; Tarrier et al., 2000) on the benefit of cognitive therapy in schizophrenia. Although most studies focused on positive and negative symptom improvement, a single study (Sensky et al., 2000) showed significant and lasting reduction of depressive symptoms over a period of nine months.

Mania

Unlike depression in SZP, mania has been much less commonly described. Bleuler (1911) postulated that any affective symptoms may occur in the setting of SZP, provided that criteria for certain fundamental schizophrenic symptoms were met: splitting of cognition from emotion and behaviour, formal thought disorder, flat or blunted affect, autism, and ambivalence.

Manic symptoms in the setting of SZP may represent a short-lived schizomanic state or warrant the diagnosis of schizoaffective disorder. Patients with SZP sometimes display manic symptoms (Tsuang & Loyd, 1988) and become agitated, irritable, impulsive, and insomniac as part of an acute psychotic exacerbation or in response to hallucinations and delusions. Usually, these symptoms are temporary and the behavioural picture lacks more typical manic symptoms (e.g., pressured speech, grandiosity, and elated mood). Kasanin (1933/1994) coined the term "schizoaffective psychosis" to describe a group of patients with sudden onset in youth of prominent affective and schizophrenic symptoms, who experienced an external stressor and had good premorbid adjustment. The initial description did not specify the relationship of schizoaffective disorder to affective disorders or SZP.

The primary difficulty in diagnosing schizoaffective disorder is the differentiation from SZP with an atypical affective disorder or from a mood disorder with incongruent psychotic features. Thus, the existence of schizoaffective disorder as a separate clinical entity has repeatedly been questioned. In addition, bipolar disorder (BPD) and SZP may share genetic factors as evidenced by epidemiologic characteristics, family studies, and overlap in confirmed linkages of BPD and/or SZP (Craddock, O'Donovan, & Owen, 2005; Murray et al., 2004). Treatment of manic symptoms in SZP beyond antipsychotics includes mood stabilisers, such as valproate, which are frequently used as secondary medications in SZP (Casey et al., 2003). However, their utility remains controversial (Basan, Kissling, & Leucht, 2004).

FACIAL EXPRESSION OF EMOTIONS

Healthy individuals

The ability to produce and recognise facial expressions of emotion represents an important component of interpersonal communication in humans and primates (Darwin, 1872). Six basic emotions—happiness, sadness, anger, fear, disgust, and surprise—and their corresponding facial expressions are recognised across different cultures (Eibl-Eibesfeldt, 1970; Ekman, Friesen, & Ellsworth, 1972; Huber, 1931; Izard, 1994). Although universal emotions are recognised across different cultural and ethnic groups, social emotions, such as guilt, shame, arrogance, admiration, and flirtatiousness, are particular to culture specific interactions.

Schizophrenia

Diminished affect, the facial expression of emotion, has been described since Bleuler (1911) as a core symptom in SZP. Impairment commonly consists of flat or inappropriate affect, may precede the onset of psychosis by many years (Walker, Grimes, Davis, & Smith, 1993) and can be worsened by administration of neuroleptics with strong nigrostriatal dopaminergic blockade (Krakowski, Czobor, & Volavka, 1997; Rifkin et al., 1975; Van Putten & May, 1978).

Measurement

The main difficulty in studying flat affect is the lack of reliable, objective, and efficient methods for quantifying facial expressions. Whereas there are widely used and validated instruments that measure and parse aspects of cognitive dysfunction and its neurobiology, overall assessment of negative symptoms have been limited to observer-based rating scales, such as the Scale for the Assessment of Negative Symptoms (SANS; Andreasen, 1984) and the Positive and Negative Symptom Scale (PANSS; Kay, Fiszbein, & Opler, 1987). Initial studies on facial affect in SZP beyond measurement with rating scales found both intact posed (Gottheil, Thornton, & Exline, 1976) and decreased spontaneous expressions (Gottheil, Paredes, Exline, & Winkelmayer, 1970).

The Facial Active Coding System (FACS), created by Ekman and Friesen (1978), remains the "gold standard" for qualitative analysis of facial emotional expressions. Unfortunately, FACS presents as a subjective rating measure that requires extensive training and still falls short of yielding measures thata are sensitive to subtle effects. The FACS has been simplified and adapted for clinical research, yielding EMFACS (Friesen, 1986) and FACES (Kring et al., 1993). While EMFACS identifies the presence or absence of muscle movements associated with the predicted expression of the particular emotion, FACES rates overall dynamic facial changes, according to number of positive and negative expressions, their intensity, and duration. Limitations of these methods include that EMFACS catalogues only those facial movements which Ekman and Friesen determined as part of posed facial expressions, while FACES does not rate individual muscle movements or action units. Using EMFACS (Berenbaum, 1992; Berenbaum & Oltmanns, 1992), persons with depression, but not SZP, exhibited fewer happy expressions during happy induction and more anger expressions during disgust induction. However, this difference may not be disorder-specific, as SZP compared to controls, but not psychosomatic probands (Steimer-Krause, Krause, & Wagner, 1990), displayed decreased variability of spontaneous expressions. While viewing brief emotion-inducing film clips, SZP probands exhibited less expressivity, as measured by FACES, but similar experience (Kring et al., 1993). Two recent studies examined posed (Trémeau et al., 2005) and spontaneous (Gaebel & Wölwer, 2004; Trémeau et al., 2005) expressions of emotions in persons with SZP during acute and post-acute stages of illness, and depression. Both patient groups exhibited less spontaneous expressions, irrespective of typical or atypical antipsychotic medication effect (Gaebel & Wölwer, 2004; Trémeau et al., 2005) and did not differ according to illness acuity in SZP. Studies that measured facial EMG in response to emotional films (Earnst et al., 1996; Mattes, Schneider, Heimann, & Birbaumer, 1995) and pictures (Kring, Kerr, & Earnst, 1999) reported similar (Earnst et al., 1996; Mattes et al., 1995) and maybe inappropriate expressions (Kring et al., 1999) in SZP. Limitations in these studies consisted of placing foreign objects (i.e. electrodes), over only two selected facial muscles and possibly over-identifying expressions, including micro-expressions which cannot be discerned in real-life settings. The potential influence of extrapyramidal side-effects on emotion expression remains unclear. While antipsychotics, in particular typicals, have been associated with akinesia, recent studies (Earnst et al. 1996; Kring et al., 1999) examined patients both on and off antipsychotics and revealed no clear effect on expressivity and emotional experience.

These studies provide evidence for the presence of affective flattening in SZP and its independence from emotion experience and medication effects. However, they fail to elucidate and more thoroughly characterise facial expression of emotions in SZP, which in the clinical realm presents as an inherent and stable symptom of SZP, associated with poor prognosis (Edwards, McGorry, Waddell, & Harrigan, 1999; Ho, Nopoulos, Flaum, Arndt, & Andreasen, 1998; Shatsel, Gur, Gallacher, Heimberg, & Gur, 1992). None of above-described studies employed classic or traditional FACS ratings, which may account for the lack of findings specific to SZP. Conversely to FACES or EMFACS, which provide holistic assessments and take into consideration previous predictions on facial expressions, FACS allows for ratings of individual muscle movements across all regions of the face.

Future studies that examine emotion expression in SZP, and possible improvement, will need to employ better quantification of emotion expression. Our group has developed a set of algorithms for highly automated analysis of facial expressions (Verma et al., 2005), which can quantify differences in expression. We anticipate that reliable quantification of affective flattening and emotion expression in persons with stable SZP in conjunction with novel medications or remediation treatment, may provide improvement in theses characteristic and debilitating symptoms of SZP.

FACIAL EMOTION RECOGNITION

Over the last 15 years, a large body of literature has examined emotion recognition, as measured by the ability to identify the emotional quality of facial expression, in brain-related disorders and healthy people and documented impairment in right brain-injured people (Adolphs, Damasio, Tranel, & Damasio, 1996; Borod, Martin, Alpert, Brozgold, & Welkowitz, 1993), SZP (for reviews, see Kohler et al., 2003; Mandal, Pandey, & Prasad, 1998; Morrison, Bellack, & Mueser, 1988) depression (Feinberg, Rifkin, Schaffer, & Walker, 1986; Gur et al., 1992; Mikhailova, Vladimirova, Iznack, Tsusulkovskaya, & Sushko, 1996), bipolar disorder (Addington & Addington, 1998; Lembke & Ketter, 2002), Alzheimer disease (for a review, see Kohler et al., 2005), and Huntington's chorea (Jacobs, Shuren, & Heilman, 1995).

Few studies have examined brain functioning in schizophrenia during emotion recognition. An earlier study in which persons judged the emotional intensity of faces showed increased amygdala activation in patients as the possible result of impaired sensory gating and impaired inhibition of amygdalar response (Kosaka et al., 2002). Two subsequent studies (Gur et al., 2002; Hempel, Hempel, Schonknecht, Stippich, & Schroder, 2003) found decreased activation during emotion recognition, in concordance with previous findings of amygdala activation deficits in schizophrenia (Phillips et al., 1999; Schneider et al., 1998).

Methodological limitations

Whereas cognitive deficits are well characterised in SZP, the findings of emotion recognition impairment in SZP are limited by the use of differing emotional stimuli and different stages of illness. More recent emotion recognition studies in SZP have employed standardised face stimuli and better characterised samples and have reported on associations of emotion processing in SZP, duration of illness (Mueser et al., 1996; Silver, Shlomo, Turner, & Gur, 2002), and symptomatology (Bryson, Bell, & Lysaker, 1997; Kohler et al., 2003; Mandal et al., 1998; Penn et al., 2000; Schneider et al., 1995). For example, in institutionalised patients, duration and severity of illness, and social competence (Mueser et al., 1997; Silver et al., 2002) were found to correlate with emotion recognition. In addition, research using standardised face stimuli to examine cognition found a relationship between cognitive abilities and affect perception in SZP in general (Bozikas, Kosmidis, Anexoulaki, Giannakou, & Karavatos, 2004), and more specifically, a link between deficits in emotional recognition and cognitive abilities (Kohler, Bilker, Hagendoorn, Gur, & Gur, 2000; Sachs, Steger-Wuchse, Kryspin-Exner, Gur, & Katschnig, 2004).

Another issue raised is whether a differential deficit (Chapman & Chapman, 1978) can be demonstrated against the more general impairment in facial processing (Archer, Hay, & Young, 1994; Edwards, Pattison, Jackson, & Wales, 2001; Johnston, Katsikitis, & Carr, 2001; Kerr & Neale, 1993; Kohler et al., 2000; Novic, Luchins, & Perline, 1984; Penn et al., 2000; Salem, Kring, & Kerr, 1996). Some of the initial studies reported a differential deficit, but the majority of recent investigations (Kerr & Neale, 1993; Penn et al., 2000; Salem et al.,

1996) failed to support that notion. Regardless of whether differential or part of general impairment, emotion recognition abilities will exert effects on psychosocial functioning independent of the presence and severity of positive and negative symptoms and cognitive difficulties. Impaired emotion recognition may also be related to the tendency of persons with SZP to visually scan features of the face that are not important in the expression of a particular emotion, as has been shown with computerised scanpath procedures (Loughland, Williams, & Gordon, 2002).

Comparison with affective disorders

Findings of emotion recognition impairment in SZP are limited by the relative lack of comparison with other patient groups with psychosis, such as major depression or bipolar disorder. Studies on SZP using emotion recognition tasks found that patients performed more poorly than depressed patient groups and controls (Feinberg et al., 1986; Gessler, Cutting, Frith, & Weinman, 1989; Schneider, Koch, Mattes, & Heimann, 1992; Walker, McGuire, & Bettes, 1984; Zuroff & Colussy, 1986). Improvement of emotion recognition has been reported in persons with major depression (Mikhailova et al., 1996) and BPD (Addington & Addington, 1998) after treatment response, however, the deficit may be more stable in SZP (Gaebel & Wölwer, 1992). More recently, first-episode patients with SZP were found to perform worse than affective psychosis patients and controls, particularly in recognition of fear and sadness. Similarly, a single study (Addington & Addington, 1998) that compared emotion recognition in young persons with stable SZP and BPD found impaired affect identification and discrimination in SZP outpatients.

Treatment

Recently, there has been increased emphasis on identifying targets of treatment beyond positive symptoms and improvement in psychosocial functioning. The MATRICS programme (Green & Nuechterlein, 2004; Marder, Fenton, & Youens, 2004) has underscored that cognitive dysfunction, including social cognition as one of seven domains, accounts for considerable residual psychosocial impairment in outpatient SZP populations. Social cognition—including recognition of emotional behaviour and its context—has been described as independent of clinical symptoms in persons with acute SZP (Penn et al., 2002), and its improvement is related to social abilities to a greater extent than nonsocial cognition or neurocognition (Penn, Corrigan, Bentall, Racenstein, & Newman, 1997). In a recent large scale effort on cognitive remediation in persons with stable schizophrenia (Hogarty et al., 2004), cognitive enhancement therapy but not supportive therapy produced improvement in social cognition over a period of 2 years. While emotion recognition impairments have implications for persons with mental illness regardless of stage of illness, the ability to recognise nonverbal communication, specifically facial expressions of emotions, may be most problematic once psychotic symptoms have stabilised and treatment goals have been focused on improving psychosocial functioning (i.e., interpersonal relationships, work, and education). In support of possible malleability of emotion recognition abilities and underscoring the potential link to psychosocial functioning in SZP, recent attempts have shown an effect with even brief remediation (Penn et al., 2000; Silver, Goodman, Knoll, & Isakov, 2004) and for prolonged cognitive remediation on emotion perception (van der Gaag, Kern, van den Bosch, & Liberman, 2002; Frommann, Streit, & Wölwer, 2003), but not neurocognition (van der Gaag et al., 2002). While these attempts aimed at mostly chronic and institutionalised patients, a 12-week training programme (Frommann et al., 2003) showed emotion recognition improvement in the majority of 16 post-acute SZP patients. Persons with SZP who are hospitalised or have been ill for many years may benefit from improved emotion recognition, yet young persons who are clinically stable will derive the greatest benefit from improved emotional processing and the effect on psychosocial functioning. Such rehabilitation measures may take into account recent findings showing an selective effect of eye regions on brain-based processing of emotions (Whalen et al., 2004), in particular fear, and successful remediation of fear recognition impairment by training a person with amygdala damage to focus on the eyes (Adolphs, Tranel, & Buchanan, 2005) Remediation may also be guided by training people to focus on facial features that are emotionally salient, using behavioural techniques or scanpath methods.

CONCLUSIONS AND FUTURE DIRECTIONS

We have outlined the dimensions of emotion processing—experience, expression and recognition—with respect to historical perspectives and the recent increase in efforts to understand their dysfunction in SZP. In all three areas there are methodological issues, which limit our understanding of their respective impact and our ability to pursue novel potential modalities of treatment. However, and as recent studies show, further improvement in emotion processing in persons with stable SZP are unlikely to result from conventional pharmacotherapy of psychosis. In the illness of schizophrenia, which includes heterogeneous symptoms of psychosis, negative symptoms, dysfunction in cognition and emotional processing, and resultant marked psychosocial impairment, it is imperative to pursue novel treatment modalities to alleviate symptoms of this multifaceted and vexing illness. Such treatment modalities may include medications that exert differential effects on the dopaminergic system, similar to aripiprazole, or selectively affect nicotinic receptors, which may improve abilities of emotion expression and recognition. Similarly, more novel and selective behavioural interventions that target areas of emotional processing offer possible improvements in quality of life and psychosocial functioning.

REFERENCES

Addington, J., & Addington, D. (1998). Facial affect recognition and information processing in schizophrenia and bipolar disorder. *Schizophrenia Research*, *32*, 171–181.

Adolphs, R., Damasio, H., Tranel, D., & Damasio, A. R. (1996). Cortical systems for the recognition of emotion in facial expressions. *Journal of Neuroscience*, *16*, 7678–7687.

Adolphs, R., Tranel, D., & Buchanan, T.W. (2005). Amygdala damage impairs emotional memory for gist but not details of complex stimuli. *Nature Neuroscience*, *8*, 512–518.

Andreasen, N. C. (1984). *The scale for the Assessment of Negative Symptoms (SANS)*. Iowa City: University of Iowa.

Archer, J., Hay, D. C., & Young, A. W. (1994). Movement, face processing, and schizophrenia: Evidence of a differential deficit in expression analysis. *British Journal of Clinical Psychology*, *33*, 517–528.

Arvanitis, L. A., & Miller, B. G. (1997). Multiple fixed doses of "Seroquel" (quetiapine) in patients with acute exacerbation of schizophrenia: A comparison with haloperidol and placebo. The Seroquel Trial 13 Study Group. *Biological Psychiatry*, *42*, 233–246.

Barak, Y., Mirecki, I., Knobler, H. Y., Natan, Z., & Aizenberg, D. (2004). Suicidality and second generation antipsychotics in schizophrenia patients: A case-controlled retrospective study during a 5-year period. *Psychopharmacology (Berl)*, *175*, 215–219.

Basan, A., Kissling, W., & Leucht, S. (2004). Valproate as an adjunct to antipsychotics for schizophrenia: A systematic review of randomized trials. *Schizophrenia Research*, *70*, 33–37.

Baxter, L. R., Phelps, M. E., Mazziotta, J. C., Schwartz, J. M., Gerner, R. H., Selin, C. E., et al. (1985). Cerebral metabolic rates for glucose in mood disorders. *Archives of General Psychiatry*, *42*, 441–447.

Beisser, A. R. (1961). Study of suicide in mental hospitals. *Diseases of the Nervous System*, *22*, 365–369.

Beck, A. T., & Rector, N. A. (2000). Cognitive therapy of schizophrenia: A new therapy for the new millennium. *American Journal of Psychotherapy*, *54*, 291–300.

Berenbaum, H. (1992). Posed facial expressions of emotion in schizophrenia and depression. *Psychological Medicine*, *22*, 929–937.

Berenbaum, H., & Oltmanns, T. F. (1992). Emotional experience and expression in schizophrenia and depression. *Journal of Abnormal Psychology*, *101*, 37–44.

Bleuler, E. (1911). *Dementia Praeox oder die Gruppe der Schizophrenien*. Aschaffensburg Handbuch. Leipzig, Germany: Deutike.

Borod, J. C., Cicero, B. A., Obler, L. K., Welkowitz, J., Erhan, H. M., Santschi, C., et al. (1998). Right hemisphere emotional perception: Evidence across multiple channels. *Neuropsychology*, *12*, 446–458.

Borod, J. C., Martin, C. C., Alpert, M., Brozgold, A., & Welkowitz, J. (1993). Perception of facial emotion in schizophrenic and right-brain damaged patients. *Journal of Nervous and Mental Disease*, *181*, 494–502.

Bowers, M. B., & Astrachan, B. M. (1967). Depression in acute schizophrenic psychosis. *American Journal of Psychiatry*, *123*, 976–979.

Bozikas, V. P., Kosmidis, M. H., Anexoulaki, D., Giannakou, M., & Karavatos, A. (2004). Relationship of affect recognition with psychopathology and cognitive performance in schizophrenia. *Journal of International Neuropsychological Society*, *10*, 549–558.

Braff, D. L., Heaton, R., Kuck, J., Cullum, M., Moranville, J., Grant, I., et al. (1991). The generalized pattern of neuropsychological deficits in outpatients with chronic schizophrenia with heterogeneous Wisconsin card sorting test results. *Archives of General Psychiatry, 48*, 891–898.

Bromfield, E. B., Altshuler, L., Leiderman, D. B., Balish, M., Ketter, T. A., Devinsky O., et al. (1992). Cerebral metabolism and depression in patients with complex partial seizures. *Archives of Neurology, 49*, 617–623.

Bryson, G., Bell, M., & Lysaker, P. (1997). Affect impairment in schizophrenia: A function of global impairment or a specific cognitive deficit. *Psychiatry Research, 71*, 105–113.

Cannon, W. B. (1987). The James-Lange theory of emotions: A critical examination and an alternative theory. By Walter B. Cannon, 1927. *American Journal of Psychology, 100*, 567–586.

Casey, D. E., Daniel, D. G., Wassef, A. A., Tracy, K. A., Wozniak, P., & Sommerville, K. W. (2003). Effect of divalproex combined with olanzapine or risperidone in patients with an acute exacerbation of schizophrenia. *Neuropsychopharmacology, 28*, 182–192.

Censits, D. M., Ragland, J. D., Gur, R. C., & Gur, R. E. (1997). Neuropsychological evidence supporting a neurodevelopmental model of schizophrenia: A longitudinal study. *Schizophrenia Research, 24*, 289–298.

Ceskova , E., & Svestka, J. (1993). Double-blind comparison of risperidone and haloperidol in schizophrenic and schizoaffective psychoses. *Pharmacopsychiatry, 26*, 121–124.

Chapman, L. J., & Chapman, J. P. (1978). The measurement of differential deficit. *Journal of Psychiatry Research, 14*, 303–311.

Cohen, S., Leonard, C. V., Farberow, N. L., & Shneidman, E. (1964). Tranquilizers and suicide in the schizophrenic patient. *Archives of General Psychiatry, 11*, 312–321.

Craddock, N., O'Donovan, M. C., & Owen, M. J. (2005). The genetics of schizophrenia and bipolar disorder: Dissecting psychosis. *Journal of Medical Genetics, 42*, 193–204.

Craig, T. J., Richardson, M. A., Pass, R., & Bregman, Z. (1985). Measurement of mood and affect in schizophrenic inpatients. *American Journal of Psychiatry, 142*, 1272–1277.

Damasio, A. R. (1994). *Descartes' error*. London: MacMillan.

Darwin, C. (1892). *The expression of emotions in man and animals*. New York: Philosophical Library.

Dolan, R. J., & Friston, K. J. (1989). Positron emission tomography in psychiatric and neuropsychiatric disorders. *Seminars in Neurology, 9*, 330–337.

Drevets, W. C. (1999). Prefrontal cortical-amygdalar metabolism in major depression. *Annals of the New York Academy of Science, 877*, 614–637.

Drury, V., Birchwood, M., Cochrane, R., & Macmillan, F. (1996). Cognitive therapy and recovery from acute psychosis: A controlled trial: I. Impact on psychotic symptoms. *British Journal of Psychiatry, 169*, 593–601.

Earnst, K. S., Kring, A. M., Kadar, M. A., Salem, J. E., Shepard, D. A., & Loosen, P. T. (1996). Facial expression in schizophrenia. *Biological Psychiatry, 40*, 556–558.

Edwards, J., McGorry, P. D., Waddell, F. M., & Harrigan, S. M. (1999). Enduring negative symptoms in first-episode psychosis: Comparison of six methods using follow-up data. *Schizophrenia Research, 40*, 147–158.

Edwards, J., Pattison, P. E., Jackson, H. J., & Wales, R. J. (2001). Facial affect and affective prosody recognition in first-episode schizophrenia. *Schizophrenia Research, 48*, 235–253.

Eibl-Eibesfeldt, I. (1970). *Ethology: The biology of behavior*. New York: Holt, Rinehart & Winston.

Ekman P., Friesen W.V., & Ellsworth, P. (1972). *Emotion in the human face: Guidelines for research and an integration of findings*. New York: Pergamon.

Ekman, P., & Friesen, W. V. (1978). *Manual of the Facial Action Coding System (FACS)*. Palo Alto, CA: Consulting Psychologists Press.

Feinberg, T. E., Rifkin, A., Schaffer, C., & Walker, E. (1986). Facial discrimination and emotional recognition in schizophrenia and affective disorders. *Archives of General Psychiatry, 43*, 276–279.

Friesen, W. (1986). Recent developments in FACS-EMFACS. *Face value: Facial Measurement Newsletter, 1*, 1–2.

Frommann, N., Streit, M., & Wölwer, W. (2003). Remediation of facial affect recognition impairments in patients with schizophrenia: A new training program. *Psychiatry Research, 117*, 281–284.

Gaebel, W., & Wölwer, W. (1992). Facial expression and emotional face recognition in schizophrenia and depression. *European Archives of Psychiatry and Clinical Neuroscience, 242*, 46–52.

Gaebel, W., & Wölwer, W. (2004). Facial expressivity in the course of schizophrenia and depression. *European Archives of Psychiatry and Clinical Neuroscience, 254*, 335–342.

Galdi, J. (1983). The causality of depression in schizophrenia. *British Journal of Psychiatry, 142*, 621–625.

Gessler, S., Cutting, J., Frith, C. D., & Weinman J. (1989). Schizophrenic inability to judge facial emotion: A controlled study. *British Journal of Clinical Psychology, 28*, 19–29.

Goldman, R. S., Tandon, R., Liberzon, I., & Greden, J. F. (1992). Measurement of depression and negative symptoms in schizophrenia. *Psychopathology, 25*, 49–56.

Gottheil, E., Paredes, A., Exline, R. V., & Winkelmayer, R. (1970). Communication of affect in schizophrenia. *Archives of General Psychiatry, 22*, 439–444.

Gottheil, E., Thornton, C. C., & Exline, R. V. (1976). Appropriate and background affect in facial displays of emotion. *Archives of General Psychiatry, 33*, 565–568.

Green, M. F., & Nuechterlein, K. H. (2004). The MATRICS initiative: Developing a consensus cognitive battery for clinical trials. *Schizophrenia Research, 72*, 1–3.

Gur, R. C., Erwin, R. J., Gur, R. E., Zwil, A. S., Heimberg, C., & Kraemer, H. C. (1992). Facial emotion discrimination: II. Behavioral findings in depression. *Psychiatry Research, 42*, 241–251.

Gur, R. E., McGrath, C., Chan, R. M., Schroeder, L., Turner, T., Turetsky B. I., et al. (2002). An fMRI study of facial emotion processing in patients with schizophrenia. *American Journal of Psychiatry, 159*, 1992–1999.

Gyulai, L., Alavi, A., Broich, K., Reilley, J., Ball, W. B., & Whybrow, P. C. (1997). I-123 iofetamine single-photon computed emission tomography in rapid cycling bipolar disorder: A clinical study. *Biological Psychiatry, 41*, 152–161.

Harkavy-Friedman, J. M., Nelson, E. A, Venarde, D. F., & Mann, J. J. (2004). Suicidal behavior in schizophrenia and schizoaffective disorder: Examining the role of depression. *Suicide & Life-Threatening Behavior, 34*, 66–76.

Heaton, R. K., & Crowley, T. J. (1981). Effects of psychiatric disorders and their somatic treatments on neuropsychological test results. In S. B. Filskov & T. J. Boll (Eds.), *Handbook of clinical neuropsychology* (pp. 481–525). New York: Wiley-Interscience.

Helmchen, H., & Hippius, H. (1967). Depressive Syndrome im Verlauf neuroleptischer Therapie. *Nervenarzt, 38*, 445.

Hempel, A., Hempel, E., Schonknecht, P., Stippich, C., & Schroder, J. (2003). Impairment in basal limbic function in schizophrenia during affect recognition. *Psychiatry Research, 122*, 115–124.

Ho, B. C., Nopoulos, P., Flaum, M., Arndt, S., & Andreasen, N. C. (1998). Two-year outcome in first-episode schizophrenia: Predictive value of symptoms for quality of life. *American Journal of Psychiatry, 155*, 1196–1201.

Hofer, A., Kemmler, G., Eder, U., Edlinger, M., Hummer, M., & Fleischhacker, W. W. (2004). Quality of life in schizophrenia: The impact of psychopathology, attitude toward medication, and side effects. *Journal of Clinical Psychiatry, 65*, 932–9.

Hogarty, G. E., Flesher, S., Ulrich, R., Carter, M., Greenwald, D., Pogue-Geile, M., et al. (2004). Cognitive enhancement therapy for schizophrenia: Effects of a 2-year randomized trial on cognition and behavior. *Archives of General Psychiatry, 61*, 866–876.

House, A., Bostock, J., & Cooper, J. (1987). Depressive syndromes in the year following onset of a first schizophrenic illness. *British Journal of Psychiatry, 151*, 773–779.

Huber E. (1931). *Evolution of facial musculature and facial expression*. Baltimore, MD: Johns Hopkins Press.

Hussar, A. E. (1962). Effect of tranquilizers on medical mortality and morbidity in mental hospitals. *Journal of the American Medical Association, 179*, 682–686.

Izard, C. E. (1994). Innate and universal facial expressions: Evidence from developmental and cross-cultural research. *Psychological Bulletin, 115*, 288–299.

Jaeger, J., Bitter, I., Czobor, P., & Volavka, J. (1990). The measurement of subjective experience in schizophrenia: The Subjective Deficit Syndrome Scale. *Comprehensive Psychiatry, 31*, 216–226.

Jacobs, D. H., Shuren, J., & Heilman, K. H. (1995). Impaired perception of facial identity and facial affect in Huntington's disease. *Neurology, 45*, 1217–1218.

James, W. (1922). What is an emotion? In K. Dunlap (Ed.), *The emotions* (pp. 11–30). Baltimore, MD: Williams & Wilkins. (Original work published 1884)

Johnson, D. A. W. (1981). Studies of depressive symptoms in schizophrenia: I. The prevalence of depression and possible causes: II. A two-year longitudinal study of symptoms: III. A double-blind trial of placebo against orphenadrine: IV. A double-blind trial of nortriptyline for depression in chronic schizophrenia. *British Journal of Psychiatry, 139*, 89–101.

Johnston, P. J., Katsikitis, M., & Carr, V. J. (2001). A generalised deficit can account for problems in facial emotion in schizophrenia. *Biological Psychology, 58*, 203–227.

Kasanin, J. (1994). The acute schizoaffective psychoses. *American Journal of Psychiatry, 151*(Suppl. 6), 144–154. (Original work published 1933)

Kay, S. R., Fiszbein, A., & Opler, L. A. (1987). The Positive and Negative Syndrome Scale (PANSS) for schizophrenia. *Schizophrenia Bulletin, 13*, 261–276.

Keck, Jr., P., Buffenstein, A., Ferguson, J., Feighner, J., Jaffe, W., Harrigan, E. P., et al. (1998). Ziprasidone 40 and 120 mg/day in the acute exacerbation of schizophrenia and schizoaffective disorder: A 4-week placebo-controlled trial. *Psychopharmacology (Berl), 140*, 173–184.

Kerr, S. L., & Neale, J. M. (1993). Emotion perception in schizophrenia: Specific deficit or further evidence of generalized poor performance? *Journal of Abnormal Psychology, 102*, 312–318.

Kibel, D. A., Laffont, I., & Liddle, P. F. (1993). The composition of the negative features of chronic schizophrenia. *British Journal of Psychiatry, 162*, 744–750.

Kingdon, D., & Turkington, D. (1991). The use of cognitive behavior therapy with a normalizing rationale in schizophrenia. *Journal of Nervous and Mental Disease, 179*, 207–211.

Kitamura, T., & Suga, R. (1991). Depressive and negative symptoms in major psychiatric disorders. *Comprehensive Psychiatry, 32*, 88–94.

Knights, A., & Hirsch, S. R. (1981). "Revealed" depression and drug treatment for schizophrenia. *Archives of General Psychiatry, 38*, 806–811.

Kohler, C. G., Anselmo-Gallagher, G., Bilker, W. B., Karlawish, J., Gur, R. E. & Clark, C. (2005). Emotion discrimination deficits in mild Alzheimer disease. *American Journal of Geriatric Psychiatry, 13*, 926–933.

Kohler, C. G., Bilker, W., Hagendoorn, M., Gur, R. E., & Gur, R. C. (2000). Emotion recognition deficit in schizophrenia: Association with symptomatology and cognition. *Biological Psychiatry, 48*, 127–36.

Kohler, C. G., Gur, R. C., Swanson, C. S., Petty, R., & Gur, R. E. (1998). Depression in schizophrenia: I. Association with neuropsychological deficits. *Biological Psychiatry, 43*, 165–172.

Kohler, C. G., Swanson, C. S., Gur, R. C., Harper Mozley, L., & Gur, R. E. (1998). Depression in schizophrenia: II. MRI and PET findings. *Biological Psychiatry, 43*, 173–180.

Kohler, C. G., Turner, T. T., Bilker, W. B., Brensinger, C., Siegel, S. J., Kanes, S. J., et al. (2003). Facial emotion recognition in schizophrenia: Intensity effects and error pattern. *American Journal of Psychiatry, 160*, 1168–1174.

Koreen, A. R., Siris, S. G., Chakos, M., Alvir, J., Mayerhoff, D., & Lieberman, J. (1993). Depression in first-episode schizophrenia. *American Journal of Psychiatry, 150*, 1643–1648.

Kosaka, H., Omori, M., Murata, T., Iidaka, T., Yamada, H., Okada, T., et al. (2002). Differential amygdala response during facial recognition in patients with schizophrenia: An fMRI study. *Schizophrenia Research*, *57*, 87–95.

Kraepelin, E. (1896). *Psychiatrie: Ein Lehrbuch für Studirende und Aerzte 5*. Vollständig Umgearb. Leipzig, Germany: Johann Ambrosius Barth.

Kraepelin, E. (1971). *Dementia praecox and paraphrenia* (R. M. Barcley & G. M. Robertson, Trans.). Edinburgh: E.&S. Livingstone. (Original work published 1919)

Krakowski, M., Czobor, P., & Volavka, J. (1997). Effect of neuroleptic treatment on depressive symptoms in acute schizophrenic episodes. *Psychiatry Research*, *71*, 19–26.

Kring, A. M., Kerr, S. L., & Earnst, K. S. (1999). Schizophrenic patients show facial reactions to emotional facial expressions. *Psychophysiology*, *36*, 186–192.

Kring, A. M., Kerr, S. L., Smith, D. A., & Neale, J. M. (1993). Flat affect in schizophrenia does not reflect diminished subjective experience of emotion. *Journal of Abnormal Psychology*, *102*, 77–106.

Kring, A. M., & Neale, J. M. (1996). Do schizophrenic patients show a disjunctive relationship among expressive, experiential, and psychophysiological components of emotion? *Journal of Abnormal Psychology*, *105*, 249–257.

Kuck, J., Zisook, S., Moranville, J. T., Heaton, R. K., & Braff, D.L. (1992). Negative symptomatology in schizophrenic outpatients. *Journal of Nervous and Mental Disease*, *180*, 510–515.

Kuipers, E., Garety, P., Fowler, D., Dunn, G., Bebbington, P., Freeman, D., et al. (1997). London–East Anglia randomised controlled trial of cognitive–behavioral therapy for psychosis: I. Effects of the treatment phase. *British Journal of Psychiatry*, *171*, 319–327.

Kulhara, P., Avasthi, A., Chadda, R., Chandiramani, K., Mattoo, S. K., Kota, S. K., et al. (1989). Negative and depressive symptoms in schizophrenia. *British Journal of Psychiatry*, *154*, 207–211.

Lembke, A., & Ketter, T. A. (2002). Impaired recognition of facial emotion in mania. *American Journal of Psychiatry*, *159*, 302–304.

Levinson, D. F., Umapathy, C., & Musthaq, M. (1999). Treatment of schizoaffective disorder and schizophrenia with mood symptoms. *American Journal of Psychiatry*, *156*, 1138–1148.

Lewis, S., Tarrier, N., Haddock, G., Bentall, R., Kinderman, P., Kingdon, D., et al. (2002). Randomised controlled trial of cognitive-behavioral therapy in early schizophrenia: Acute-phase outcomes. *British Journal of Psychiatry Supplementum*, *43*, 91–97.

Loughland, C. M., Williams, L. M., & Gordon, E. (2002). Visual scanpaths to positive and negative facial emotions in an outpatient schizophrenia sample. *Schizophrenia Research*, *55*, 159–170.

Mandal, M. K., Pandey, R., & Prasad, A. B. (1998). Facial expressions of emotions and schizophrenia: Review. *Schizophrenia Bulletin*, *24*, 399–341.

Marder, S. R., Fenton, W., & Youens, K. (2004). Schizophrenia: IX. Cognition in schizophrenia—The MATRICS initiative. *American Journal of Psychiatry*, *161*, 25.

Mattes, R. M., Schneider, F., Heimann, H., & Birbaumer, N. (1995). Reduced emotional response of schizophrenic patients in remission during social interaction. *Schizophrenia Research*, *17*, 249–255.

Mayberg, H. S., Lewis, P. J., Regenold, W., & Wagner, Jr., H. N. (1994). Paralimbic hypoperfusion in unipolar depression. *Journal of Nuclear Medicine*, *35*, 929–934.

Mayberg, H. S., Starkstein, S. E., Peyser, C. E., Brandt, J., & Dannals, R. F. (1992). Paralimbic frontal lobe hypometabolism in depression associated with Huntington's disease. *Neurology*, *42*, 1791–1797.

Mayberg, H. S., Starkstein, S. E., Sadzot, B., Preziosi, T., Andrezejewski, P. L., Dannals, R. F., et al. (1990). Selective hypometabolism in the inferior frontal lobe in depressed patients with Parkinson's disease. *Annals of Neurology*, *28*, 57–64.

Mayer-Gross, W., Slater, E., & Roth, M. (1955). *Clinical psychiatry*. Baltimore, MD: Williams & Wilkins.

McGlashan, T., & Carpenter, W. T. (1976). An investigation of the postpsychotic depressive syndrome. *American Journal of Psychiatry, 133*, 4–19.

Meltzer, H. Y., Lee, M. A., & Ranjan, R. (1994). Recent advances in the pharmacotherapy of schizophrenia. *Acta Psychiatrica Scandinavica. Supplementum, 384*, 95–101.

Meltzer, H. Y., & Okayli, G. (1995). Reduction of suicidality during clozapine treatment of neuroleptic-resistant schizophrenia: Impact on risk-benefit assessment. *American Journal of Psychiatry, 152*, 183–190.

Migliorelli, R., Starkstein, S. E., Teson, A., de Quiros, G., Vazquez, S., Leiguarda, R., et al. (1993). SPECT findings in patients with primary mania. *Journal of Neuropsychiatry and Clinical Neurosciences, 5*, 379–383.

Mikhailova, E. S., Vladimirova, T. V., Iznack, A. F., Tsusulkovskaya, E. J., & Sushko, N. V. (1996). Abnormal recognition of facial expression of emotions in depressed patients with major depression disorder and schizotypal personality disorder. *Biological Psychiatry, 40*, 697–705.

Miles, C. (1977). Conditions predisposing to suicide: A review. *Journal of Nervous and Mental Disease, 164*, 231–246.

Morrison, R. L., Bellack, A. S., & Mueser, K. T. (1988). Deficits in facial-affect recognition and schizophrenia. *Schizophrenia Bulletin, 14*, 67–83.

Mueser, K. T., Doonan, R., Penn, D. L., Blanchard, J. J., Bellack, A. S., & Nishith, P. (1996). Emotion recognition and social competence in chronic schizophrenia. *Journal of Abnormal Psychology, 105*, 271–275.

Müller-Seicheneder, F., Müller, M. J., Hillert, A., Szegedi, A., Wetzel, H., & Benkert, O. (1998). Risperidone versus haloperidol and amitriptyline in the treatment of patients with a combined psychotic and depressive syndrome. *Journal of Clinical Psychopharmacology, 18*, 111–120.

Murray, R. M., Sham, P., Van Os, J., Zanelli, J., Cannon, M., & McDonald C. (2004). A developmental model for similarities and dissimilarities between schizophrenia and bipolar disorder. *Schizophrenia Research, 71*, 405–416.

Myin-Germeys, I., Delespaul, P. A., & de Vries, M. W. (2000). Schizophrenia patients are more emotionally active than is assumed based on their behavior. *Schizophrenia Bulletin, 26*, 847–854.

Novic, J., Luchins, D. J., & Perline, R. (1984). Facial affect recognition in schizophrenia. Is there a differential deficit? *British Journal of Psychiatry, 144*, 533–537.

Nyman, A. K., & Jonsson H. (1986). Patterns of self-destructive behaviour in schizophrenia. *Acta Psychiatrica Scandinavica, 73*, 252–262.

Palmer, B. A., Pankratz, V. S., & Bostwick, J. M. (2005). The lifetime risk of suicide in schizophrenia: A reexamination. *Archives of General Psychiatry, 62*, 247–253.

Penn, D. L., Combs, D. R., Ritchie, M., Francis, J., Cassisi, J., Morris, S., et al. (2000). Emotion recognition in schizophrenia: Further investigation of generalized versus specific deficit models. *Journal of Abnormal Psychology, 109*, 512–516.

Penn, D. L., Corrigan, P. W., Bentall, R. P., Racenstein, J. M., & Newman, L. (1997). Social cognition in schizophrenia. *Psychological Bulletin, 121*, 114–132.

Penn, D. L., Ritchie, M., Francis, J., Combs, D., & Martin, J. (2002). Social perception in schizophrenia: The role of context. *Psychiatry Research, 109*, 149–159.

Phillips, M. L., Drevets, W. C., Rauch, S. L., & Lane, R. (2003). Neurobiology of emotion perception. I: The neural basis of normal emotion perception. *Society of Biological Psychiatry, 54*, 504–514.

Phillips, M. L., Williams, L., Senior, C., Bullmore, E. T., Brammer, M. J., & Andrew, C. (1998). A differential neural response to threatening and non-threatening negative facial expressions in paranoid and non-paranoid schizophrenics. *Psychiatry Research, 92*, 11–31.

Pinto, A., La Pia, S., Mennella, R., Giorgio, D., & DeSimone, L. (1999). Cognitive-behavioral therapy and clozapine for clients with treatment-refractory schizophrenia. *Psychiatric Services, 50*, 901–904.

Planansky, K., & Johnston, R. (1971). The occurrence and characteristics of suicidal preoccupation and acts in schizophrenia. *Acta Psychiatrica Scandinavica, 47,* 473–483.

Plasky, P. (1991). Antidepressant usage in schizophrenia. *Schizophrenia Bulletin, 17,* 649–657.

Prosser, E. S., Csernansky, J. G., Kaplan, J., Thiemann, S., Becker, T. J., & Hollister, L. E. (1987). Depression, parkinsonian symptoms and negative symptoms in schizophrenics treated with neuroleptics. *The Journal of Nervous and Mental Disease, 175,* 100–105.

Rifkin, A., Quitkin, F., & Klein, D. F. (1975). Akinesia. *Archives of General Psychiatry, 332,* 672–674.

Ring, N., Tantam, D., Montague, L., Newby, D., Black, D., & Morris, J. (1991). Gender differences in the incidence of definite schizophrenia and atypical psychosis- Focus on negative symptoms of schizophrenia. *Acta Psychiatrica Scandinavica, 84,* 489–496.

Robinson, R. G., Kubos, K. L., Starr, L. B., Rao, K., & Price, T. G. (1984). Mood disorders in stroke patients. *Brain, 107,* 81–93.

Roth, S. (1970). The seemingly ubiquitous depression following acute schizophrenic episodes, a neglected area of clinical discussion. *American Journal of Psychiatry, 127,* 51–58.

Sachs, G., Steger-Wuchse, D., Kryspin-Exner, I., Gur, R. C., & Katschnig, H. (2004). Facial recognition deficits and cognition in schizophrenia. *Schizophrenia Research, 68,* 27–35.

Salem, J. E., Kring, A. M., & Kerr, S. L. (1996). More evidence for generalized poor performance in facial emotion perception in schizophrenia. *Journal of Abnormal Psychology, 105,* 480–483.

Sass, L. A., & Parnas, J. (2003). Schizophrenia, consciousness, and the self. *Schizophrenia Bulletin, 29,* 427–444.

Saykin, A. J., Shtasel, D. L., Gur, R. E., Kester, D. B., Mozley, L. H., Stafiniak, P., et al. (1994). Neuropsychological deficits in neuroleptic naive patients with first-episode schizophrenia. *Archives of General Psychiatry, 51,* 124–131.

Schachter, S., & Singer, J. E. (1962). Cognitive, social, and physiological determinants of emotional state. *Psychological Review, 69,* 379–399.

Schneider, F., Gur, R. C., Gur, R. E., & Shtasel, D. L. (1995). Emotional processing in schizophrenia: Neurobehavioral probes in relation to psychopathology. *Schizophrenia Research, 17,* 67–75.

Schneider, F., Koch, J. D., Mattes, R., & Heimann, H. (1992). The recognition of emotions from the facial expression in divided visual half field presentations in schizophrenic and depressive patients. *Nervenarzt, 63,* 545–550.

Schneider, F., Weiss, U., Kessler, C., Salloum, J. B., Posse, S., Grodd, W., et al. (1998). Differential amygdala activation in schizophrenia during sadness. *Schizophrenia Research, 34,* 133–142.

Sensky, T., Turkington, D., Kingdon, D., Scott, J. L., Scott, J., Siddle, R., et al. (2000). A randomized controlled trial of cognitive-behavioral therapy for persistent symptoms in schizophrenia resistant to medication. *Archives of General Psychiatry, 57,* 165–172.

Shanfield, S., Tucker, G. J., Marrow, M., & Detre, T. (1970). The schizophrenic patient and depressive symptomatology. *Journal of Nervous Mental Diseases, 151,* 203–210.

Shatsel, D. L., Gur, R. E., Gallacher, F. V., Heimberg, C., & Gur, R. C. (1992). Gender differences in the clinical expression of schizophrenia. *Schizophrenia Research, 7,* 225–232.

Silver, H., Goodman, C., Knoll, G., & Isakov, V. (2004). Brief emotion training improves recognition of facial emotions in chronic schizophrenia. A pilot study. *Psychiatry Research, 128,* 147–154.

Silver, H., Shlomo, N., Turner, T., & Gur, R. C. (2002). Perception of happy and sad facial expressions in chronic schizophrenia: Evidence for two evaluative systems. *Schizophrenia Research, 55,* 171–177.

Siris, S. G. (1991). Diagnosis of secondary depression in schizophrenia. *Schizophrenia Bulletin, 17,* 75–97.

Sison, C. E., Alpert, M., Fudge, R., & Stern, R. M. (1996). Constricted expressiveness and psychophysiological reactivity in schizophrenia. *Journal of Nervous and Mental Disease, 184,* 589–597.

Starkstein, S. E., Mayberg, H. S., Berthier, M. L., Fedoroff, P., Price, T. R., Dannals, R. F., et al. (1990). Mania after brain injury: Neuroradiological and metabolic findings. *Annals of Neurology, 27*, 652–659.

Stern, M. J., Pillsbury, J. A., & Sonnenberg, S. M. (1972). Postpsychotic depression in schizophrenics. *Comprehensive Psychiatry, 123*, 976–979.

Steimer-Krause, E., Krause, R., & Wagner, G. (1990). Interaction regulations used by schizophrenic and psychosomatic patients: Studies on facial behavior in dyadic interactions. *Psychiatry, 53*, 209–228.

Steinberg, H. R., Green, R., & Durell, J. (1967). Depression occurring during the course of recovery from acute schizophrenic symptoms. *American Journal of Psychiatry, 124*, 699–702.

Tarrier, N., Kinney, C., McCarthy, E., Humphreys, L., Wittkowski, A., & Morris, J. (2000). Two-year follow-up of cognitive-behavioral therapy and supportive counseling in the treatment of persistent symptoms in chronic schizophrenia. *Journal of Consulting and Clinical Psychology, 68*, 917–922.

Taylor, S. F., Liberzon, I., Decker, L. R., & Koeppe, R. A. (2002). A functional anatomic study of emotion in schizophrenia. *Schizophrenia Research, 58*, 159–172.

Tollefson, G. D., Sanger, T. M., Lu, Y., & Thieme, M. E. (1998). Depressive signs and symptoms in schizophrenia. *Archives of General Psychiatry, 55*, 250–258.

Tomkins, S. S. (1962). *Affect, imagery, and consciousness: Vol. 1. The positive affects.* New York: Springer.

Tran, P. V., Hamilton, S. H., Kuntz, A. J., Potvin, J. H., Andersen, S. W., Beasley, C., et al. (1997). Double-blind comparison of olanzapine versus risperidone in the treatment of schizophrenia and other psychotic disorders. *Journal of Clinical Psychopharmacology, 17*, 407–418.

Trémeau, F., Malaspina, D., Duval, F., Corrêa, H., Hagar-Budny, M., Coin-Bariou, L., et al. (2005). Facial expressiveness in patients with schizophrenia compared to depressed patients and non-patients comparison subjects. *American Journal of Psychiatry, 162*, 92–101.

Tsuang M. T., & Loyd, D. W. (1988). Other psychotic disorders. In R. Michels (Ed.), *Psychiatry.* Philadelphia: Lippincott.

van der Gaag, M., Kern, R. S., van den Bosch, R. J., & Liberman, R. P. (2002). A controlled trial of cognitive remediation in schizophrenia. *Schizophrenia Bulletin, 28*, 167–176.

Van Putten, T., & May, P. R. (1978). Akinetic depression in schizophrenia. *Archives of General Psychiatry, 35*, 1101–1107.

Verma, R., Davatzikos, C., Loughead, J., Indersmitten, T., Hu, R., Kohler, C., et al. (2005). Quantification of facial expressions using high dimensional shape transformations. *Journal of Neuroscience Methods, 141*, 61–73.

Volz, M., Hamm, A. O., Kirsch, P., & Rey, E. R. (2003). Temporal course of emotional startle modulation in schizophrenia patients. *International Journal of Psychophysiology, 49*, 123–137.

Walker, E. F., Grimes, K. E., Davis, D. M., & Smith, A. J. (1993). Childhood precursors of schizophrenia: Facial expressions of emotion. *American Journal of Psychiatry, 150*, 1654–1660.

Walker, E., McGuire, M., & Bettes, B. (1984). Recognition and identification of facial stimuli by schizophrenics and patients with affective disorders. *British Journal of Clinical Psychology, 23*, 37–44.

Wassink, T. H., Flaum, M., Nopoulos, P., & Andreasen, N. C. (1999). Prevalence of depressive symptoms early in the course of schizophrenia. *American Journal of Psychiatry, 156*, 315–316.

Weisler, R. H., Ahearn, E. P., Davidson, J. R., & Wallace, C. D. (1997). Adjunctive use of olanzapine in mood disorders: Five case reports. *Annals of Clinical Psychiatry, 9*, 259–262.

Whalen, P. J., Kagan, J., Cook, R. G., Davis, F. C., Kim, H., Polis, S., et al. (2004). Human amygdala responsivity to masked fearful eye whites. *Science, 306*, 2061.

Zarate, C. A., Tohen, M., & Baldessarini, R. J. (1995). Clozapine in severe mood disorders. *Journal of Clinical Psychiatry, 56*, 411–417.

Zuroff, D. C., & Colussy, S. A. (1986). Emotion recognition in schizophrenic and depressed patients. *Journal of Clinical Psychology, 42*, 411–417.

COGNITIVE NEUROPSYCHIATRY
2006, 11 (3), 272–284

Object-location memory in schizophrenia: Interference of symbolic threatening content

Mascha van't Wout

*Helmholtz Institute, Utrecht University and
University Medical Center, The Netherlands*

André Aleman

BCN Neuroimaging Center, University of Groningen, The Netherlands

Roy P. C. Kessels

*Helmholtz Institute, Utrecht University and
University Medical Center, The Netherlands*

René S. Kahn

University Medical Center, The Netherlands

Introduction. Monitoring environmental stimuli for their emotional relevance is inherently associated with spatial processing. In schizophrenia, deficits in spatial working memory on one hand, and abnormal emotion processing on the other, have been documented, but these have not been related to each other. In the present study, we investigated whether a specific aspect of spatial memory (i.e., object-location memory), is impaired in patients with schizophrenia. Moreover, we hypothesised that symbolic threatening content of objects would interfere with spatial processing in patients with schizophrenia but not in healthy controls.
Methods. Spatial memory for symbolic pictorial stimuli was assessed in 40 patients with schizophrenia compared to 41 healthy matched control participants using an object-relocation task.
Results. Patients with schizophrenia performed worse in relocating objects, independent of overall intellectual ability. More specifically, patients were particularly worse in the relocation of objects with a symbolic threatening content.

Correspondence should be addressed to Mascha van't Wout, Helmholtz Institute, Department of Psychonomics, Utrecht University, Heidelberglaan 2, NL-3584 CS Utrecht, The Netherlands; e-mail: M.vantWout@fss.uu.nl

We would like to thank E. Caspers and W. Cahn for their help in recruitment of the patients. M. v.'t Wout and A. Aleman were supported by a Vernieuwingslmpuls grant (No. 016.026.027) and R. Kessels was supported by a VENI grant (No. 451.02.037) both from the Netherlands Organisation for Scientific Research (NWO).

    DOI:10.1080/13546800500214041

Conclusions. These results suggest that a threatening semantic emotional content of schematic stimuli can interfere with spatial processing in schizophrenia. We hypothesise that a disproportional influence of the amygdala on other brain areas, such as the hippocampus, might underlie this specific emotional interference.

In schizophrenia, profound deficits in cognitive functioning have been consistently documented (Aleman, Hijman, de Haan, & Kahn, 1999; Heinrichs & Zakzanis, 1998), which cannot be explained by medication effects (Aleman & de Haan, 2000). Additionally, impairments in spatial working memory have also been reported in schizophrenia (Cameron et al., 2003; Carter et al., 1996; Fleming et al., 1997; Keefe, LeesRoitman, & Dupre, 1997; McGrath, Chapple, & Wright, 2001; Park & Holzman, 1992). Park and Holzman (1992) demonstrated that patients with schizophrenia show deficits on an oculomotor and haptic spatial delayed-response task independent of nonspatial working memory and sensory control tasks. This suggests that patients with schizophrenia are less able to maintain visuospatial representations. Consistent with this finding, Fleming et al. (1997) also reported marked deficits in spatial working memory in schizophrenia in the presence of intact perceptual abilities.

A specific aspect of spatial memory concerns object location. Object-location memory concerns knowledge of the exact position of objects and their relative relationship with each other (Kessels, de Haan, Kappelle, & Postma, 2001). Although spatial working memory has been investigated in schizophrenia, object-location memory has not. The investigation of location-memory is of value as it enables identification, classification, and location of items used in everyday life (cf. Milner, Johnsrude, & Crane, 1997). Importantly, deficits in location-memory may contribute to the difficulties with activities of daily living observed in schizophrenia.

With regard to the neural basis of spatial memory and object-location memory, the temporal lobes have been shown to play a crucial role. More specifically, the hippocampal region is important for memory, in particular, the encoding of information, and receives input from the parahippocampal region. Intact functioning of the parahippocampal region is crucial for spatial memory (Bohbot et al., 1998; Kessels et al., 2001). Interestingly, a reduction in volume in the (para)hippocampal region has been reported in schizophrenia (Seidman et al., 2003; Wright et al., 2000), which might account for the deficits in spatial memory observed in schizophrenia.

In addition to cognitive dysfunction, emotional dysfunction is increasingly recognised as a core feature of schizophrenia (Lane, 2003). This emotional dysfunction includes disturbances in the expression of emotions and perception of affective information and may contribute to social isolation, hamper independent living, and negatively affect professional and community functioning (Hooker & Park, 2002; Kee, Green, Mintz, & Brekke, 2003; Poole, Tobias, & Vinogradov, 2000). More specifically, behavioural research has shown deficits in facial affect recognition (Addington & Addington, 1998; Habel et al., 2000; Kohler et al., 2000; Mueser et al., 1996; Penn et al., 2000; Schneider, Gur, Gur, & Shtasel, 1995; Wolwer, Streit, Polzer, & Gaebel, 1996), particularly in the processing of threat-related faces and potentially threatening social scenes (Green, Williams, & Davidson, 2003; Phillips, Senior, & David, 2000). It is important to note that affective disturbance in schizophrenia does not only pertain to reduced levels of emotional expression, but may also concern increased levels of emotional arousal (e.g., raised anxiety levels) (Delespaul, deVries, & van Os, 2002; Kring & Neale, 1996).

In recent years, neural models of schizophrenia have been advanced that hypothesise an imbalance between the amygdala and other brain areas (Grace, 2000; Grossberg, 2000). Specifically, Grace (2000) hypothesised an increased influence of the amygdala on cortical areas resulting from a disruption of cortical regulation of subcortical systems in schizophrenia. As the emotional relevance of information is processed through the amygdala (Morris et al., 1996), such overactivation of the amygdala could lead to the signalling of actual threat where there is none. According to the model proposed by Grace (2000), in these circumstances the amygdala overrides hippocampal circuits, thus inhibiting the processing of historical and contextual information, and giving priority to emotional processing. A behavioural prediction might be that presentation of threat-related information might disrupt performance on a spatial task, relative to neutral information. Because the monitoring of environmental stimuli for their emotional relevance is inherently associated with spatial processing, the study of spatial memory for emotional stimuli in patients with schizophrenia might indirectly test this hypothesis.

To the best of our knowledge, object-location memory and, more specifically, the influence of affective information on object-location memory in schizophrenia have not yet been investigated. The aim of the present study was twofold. First, we tested the hypothesis that patients with schizophrenia show a specific deficit in their memory for locations of objects after controlling for overall intellectual ability. Second, we tested the hypothesis that patients with schizophrenia show threat-related interference in object-location memory. We hypothesised that there would be no threat-related interference in healthy comparison participants as the stimuli are highly symbolic and nonarousing and will therefore not serve as a distractor in healthy participants.

Object-location memory was measured with the emotional object-relocation task, an adapted version of Object Relocation (Kessels, Postma, & de Haan, 1999). Participants had to remember the location of schematic images of everyday objects (icons) presented on a computer screen. The stimuli concerned threatening, neutral, positive, and obsessive-compulsive disorder-related symbolic information (the last three were considered to be nonthreatening). Subsequently, participants were asked to relocate these icons in an empty frame as accurately as possible.

METHODS

Participants

A total of 40 patients with a diagnosis of schizophrenia were recruited from the University Medical Centre, Utrecht. All patients fulfilled DSM-IV criteria for schizophrenia as confirmed with the Comprehensive Assessment of Symptoms and History (CASH; Andreasen, Flaum, & Arndt, 1992). Patients were clinically stable and 37 received medication at the time of the study. Of patients, 24 received only atypical antipsychotics (clozapine, risperidone, olanzapine, and quetiapine) and 13 patients also received other medication (besides antipsychotic medication), such as classic antipsychotics, antidepressants, mood stabilisers, and benzodiazepines. Symptoms were rated with the Positive and Negative Syndrome Scale (PANSS; Kay, Opler, & Fiszbein, 1987). The clinical characteristics of the patient sample are listed in Table 1.

A total of 41 nonpsychiatric healthy control participants were drawn from the general population using advertisements in local newspapers and through an institute for volunteers. Inclusion criteria for both patients and healthy control participants were age between 18 and 65 years and being physically healthy. Exclusion criteria for all participants were neurological conditions or history of head injury with loss of consciousness, recent history of alcohol and substance abuse, and mental retardation. None of the control participants had a history of psychiatric illness confirmed with the Mini-International Neuropsychiatric Interview (MINI; Sheehan et al., 1998). Control participants were recruited to match the patient sample with respect to age, gender, handedness, and educational level. The demographic characteristics of the patients with schizophrenia and the healthy control participants are listed in Table 2. The study was approved by the local ethics committee and all participants provided written

TABLE 1
Clinical characteristics of 40 patients with schizophrenia

Clinical characteristic	Mean (SD)
Duration of illness (years)	8.14 (6.67)
Age of onset (years)	23.09 (6.22)
Medication (no. of patients)	
Antipsychotics	clozapine (17); risperidone (5); olanzapine (10); quetiapine (2); sulpiride (1); bromperidol (1); pimozide (1)
Antidepressants	paroxetine (2); fluoxetine (2); citalopram (3)
Mood stabilisers	lithium (1); valproate (1)
Benzodiazepines	oxazepam (3); temazepam (1); alprazolam (1)
Positive scale PANSS	11.48 (3.58)
Negative scale PANSS	12.58 (3.71)
General psychopathology PANSS	25.0 (5.29)

TABLE 2
Demographic characteristics of 40 patients with schizophrenia and 41 healthy control participants

	Schizophrenia patients	Healthy control participants	
	Mean (SD)	Mean (SD)	p
Age (years)	31.53 (7.71)	31.41 (9.17)	.95
Male/Female	26/14	26/15	.88
Education (years)	15.0 (2.81)	14.73 (2.58)	.68
Handedness (right/left/ambidexter)	37/2/1	37/3/1	.77

informed consent after the procedure had been fully explained and prior to testing.

Measures

Intellectual ability. Two tests were used to index intellectual function. The first was the Dutch translation of the National Adult Reading Test (NART; Nelson, 1982; Schmand, Bakker, Saan, & Louman, 1991). The NART provides an estimate of verbal IQ based on the high correlation between reading ability, specifically of irregular words, with intelligence in the normal population. The test comprises a list of 50 irregular words (i.e., pronunciation does not follow the normal phonetic rules) printed in order of increasing difficulty. Participants are required to read these words aloud and, on the basis of the number of errors made in pronunciation, a reliable estimate of WAIS-R IQ can be calculated (Willshire, Kinsella, & Prior, 1991).

In addition, we used the Raven Advanced Progressive Matrices to obtain a reliable measurement of nonverbal reasoning (Lezak, 1995). This test consists of 12 pictures of matrices (i.e., related patterns), each of which is a figural design with a part removed. Participants must choose the correct missing part from eight options. On the basis of the number of errors made by participants an estimate of IQ can be calculated.

Object-relocation. The emotional memory task is an adapted version from Kessels et al. (1999) and is a measure of spatial memory for affective objects. The test consisted of three trials and in each trial, 8 different icons of everyday objects were presented. The icons were categorised into four affective types: neutral (e.g., tree, house); threatening (e.g., skull, danger signal); obsessive-compulsive disorder-related (e.g., toilet, towels); and positive (e.g., smiling face). For the main analysis, threatening icons were contrasted with the nonthreatening icons. The obsessive-compulsive disorder-related icons were chosen to serve as control stimuli as they have a threatening emotional meaning for a different psychiatric disorder—obsessive-compulsive disorder (OCD; Wilhelm, McNally, Baer, & Florin, 1996). However, these icons are not considered to be threatening to patients with schizophrenia. The icons for the emotional memory task were selected on the basis of valence ratings of 20 persons with formal psychological training and two ratings from experienced clinicians. Only icons with unanimous ratings were included as stimuli.

In each trial the icons were displayed for 12s in different locations within a 180 cm × 180 cm frame on a computer screen. Participants were placed in front of the computer at a distance of approximately 90 cm. After 12 s encoding, the frame would reappear with the eight icons in a horizontal line above the empty frame (see Figure 1). Participants then had to try to relocate the icons to their original position using the touch-sensitive computer screen. There was no time limit during relocation of the icons and participants were allowed to make corrections. Following relocation of the icons, the next trial was presented.

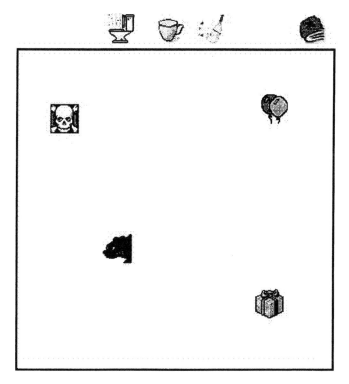

Figure 1.   Example of an image display in object-relocation (actual size 18 cm × 18 cm).

Participants were told to try to relocate the icons to their original position as accurately as possible. The absolute deviation in millimetres between the original and relocated position was computed for each of the stimulus types and time of relocating the icons in seconds was measured. The procedure for this is described in more detail by Kessels et al. (1999).

RESULTS

Intellectual ability.   Using the Dutch translation of the NART, patients and control participants had a mean estimated IQ of 105.08 (*SD* 8.89) and 107.39 (*SD* 9.51), respectively. The calculated IQ, using the Raven test was 98.63 (*SD* 17.22) for patients and 107.60 (*SD* 12.85) for control participants. *t*-tests of these measures revealed a significant difference between the groups on the estimated IQ using the Raven test ($t = 2.60, p = .01$), but no significant group difference on the estimated IQ by the NART ($t = -1.11, p = .27$).

Object-relocation.   A 2 × 4 within-subjects ANOVA with diagnosis (patient or control participant) as grouping variable and the different affective object types (neutral, positive, threatening, and OCD-related) as within-subjects variables, demonstrated that, overall, patients with schizophrenia were less accurate in relocating the icons than control participants, $F(1, 79) = 15.61, MSE = 3882.99, p < .0001$. Additionally, patients and control participants differed significantly on intellectual ability as measured with the Raven test, where patients with schizophrenia made more errors. However, the difference in object-location memory remained significant when performance on the Raven test was entered as a covariate, $F(1, 75) = 9.78, MSE = 3781.09, p = .003$.

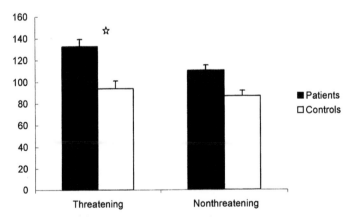

Figure 2.   Mean deviations (mm) of relocated objects in the object-relocation task on threatening and nonthreatening icons for patients with schizophrenia and healthy control participants, *$p = .05$.

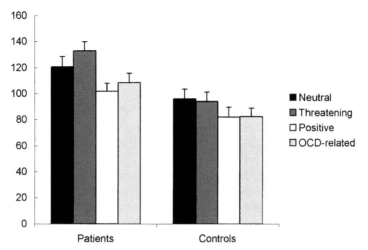

Figure 3.   Mean deviations (mm) for relocated objects compared with their original position of the different affective icons for patients with schizophrenia and healthy control participants.

With regard to the affective content, the main analysis concerned threatening vs. nonthreatening icons, which included neutral, positive, and OCD-related icons. A 2 × 2 within-subjects ANOVA with Group (patient versus control participant) and Threat (accuracy of threatening versus non-threatening objects) showed that patients performed significantly worse on the relocation of threatening objects compared to non-threatening objects, $F(1, 79) = 3.88$, $MSE = 600.09, p = .05$) (see Figure 2). A 2 × 2 within-subjects ANOVA of the individual affective stimuli categories demonstrated no differences between the two groups in accuracy of relocation of neutral objects vs. objects: threatening, $F(1, 79) = 2.63$, $MSE = 743.48, p = .11$; OCD-related, $F(1, 79) = 0.10$, $MSE = 1410.21, p = .92$; positive, $F(1, 79) = 0.19$, $MSE = 1999.92, p = .66$) (see Figure 3).

DISCUSSION

The aim of the present study was to investigate object-location memory in schizophrenia. We also investigated whether a symbolic threatening content would interfere with object-location memory in schizophrenia. As hypothesised, patients with schizophrenia performed worse in relocating everyday objects into space, independent of overall intellectual ability. This is in agreement with research that demonstrated spatial working memory deficits in schizophrenia (Burglen et al., 2004; Fleming et al., 1997; Keefe et al., 1995; Leiderman & Strejilevich, 2004; Park & Holzman, 1992).

With regard to the neural basis of spatial memory, involvement of a network comprising the hippocampus, dorsolateral prefrontal, and parietal cortex has been demonstrated (Belger et al., 1998; Carlson et al., 1998; Geffen et al., 1997;

McCarthy et al., 1994, 1996; Moulden, Picton, & Stuss, 1997; Rolls, 2000). In addition, the importance of the hippocampus in object-location memory has been established (Kessels et al., 2001; Rolls, 2000). In schizophrenia, research has reported that deficits in spatial learning were associated with impairments in the function of the frontal lobes and medial temporal regions, including the hippocampus (Gruzelier, Seymour, Wilson, Jolley, & Hirsch, 1988). Hypothetically, the present result of a specific deficit in object-location memory in schizophrenia might be consistent with the large body of evidence indicating structural and functional abnormalities of the prefrontal cortex and hippocampus in schizophrenia (Crespo-Facorro et al., 2001; Lawrie & Abukmeil, 1998; Shenton, Dickey, Frumin, & McCarley, 2001; Wright et al., 2000).

To investigate whether there was more interference in spatial memory due to negative rather than positive or neutral content in schizophrenia, we compared relocation accuracy of threatening objects with nonthreatening objects. Our results showed that patients with schizophrenia were disproportionally worse at relocating threatening objects, in contrast to the healthy control group. These results suggest that schizophrenia can be associated with an increased interference in spatial short-term memory for highly symbolic threatening stimuli, as used in the object relocation task. A related issue that deserves attention is the perceived intensity of threat, as schizophrenia patients might have experienced these objects as more threatening. Although we do not have these ratings of patients or control participants, implicit processes of relocating threatening objects as used here are not necessarily accompanied by an increase in overt threat perception. For instance, in anxiety disorder, individuals are usually unaware that they process threatening stimuli highly automatically, making it difficult to control the anxiety (Beck & Clark, 1997).

The increased interference of threatening stimuli in spatial cognition in schizophrenia could be explained by Grace (2000), who hypothesised that a disruption of cortical regulation of subcortical systems may eventually lead to an exaggerated influence of the amygdala on the other brain areas, such as prefrontal cortex and hippocampus. More specifically, the neural model proposed by Grace (2000) assumes that under normal conditions, people perform tasks based on past experiences or current context, which is mediated through the hippocampus. However, when a threatening object appears, the brain has to signal whether this potentially threatening object requires action. In such circumstances, the amygdala has an overriding influence over the hippocampus in order to trigger flight behaviour. In schizophrenia, the amygdala might become hyperactive due to an imbalance in dopamine systems. Eventually, the processing of the affective connotation of a stimulus (amygdala) may acquire excessive priority, at the cost of contextual or historical information (hippocampus) or a motor plan (prefrontal cortex) (Grace, 2000, 2003). Indeed, schizophrenia has been associated with abnormalities in prefrontal-temporal circuits (Egan & Weinberger, 1997; Shenton et al., 2001; Torrey, 2002), which includes brain areas that are crucial for cognition and emotion. Therefore, the influence of emotion on cognition might be disturbed in schizophrenia.

A limitation of the present study is that our design does not differentiate between problems in either the encoding or retrieval of threat-related information. Object identification at encoding has been shown to affect significantly object-location memory (Kohler, Moscovitch, & Melo, 2001) and spatial processing deficits in schizophrenia have also been suggested to arise during encoding (Leiderman & Strejilevich, 2004). To investigate whether encoding or retrieval is specifically disturbed in schizophrenia, a memory task using both free recall and recognition should be administered. In case of deficits in encoding, patients will demonstrate problems both during recall and recognition. Deficits in retrieval on the other hand, will only result in problems during recall with intact recognition of the objects. Although the aim of the present study was to investigate the influence of symbolic threat, future research could investigate object-location memory with the use of affective faces (Putman, van Honk, Kessels, Mulder, & Koppeschaar, 2004; Van Honk et al., 2003). This may provide insight of the presence of a threat-related bias in object-relocation memory when it concerns biologically more relevant stimuli. Additionally, the use of neuroimaging techniques can also further elucidate the neural basis of dysfunctional spatial memory for emotional information in schizophrenia.

To summarise, patients with schizophrenia revealed deficits in object-location memory, independent of overall intellectual ability. This finding corroborates and extends research that demonstrated spatial working memory deficits in schizophrenia (Fleming et al., 1997; Gruzelier et al., 1988; Park & Holzman, 1992) and implicates dysfunctions of prefrontal-hippocampal circuits in schizophrenia. With regard to the interaction between emotion and cognition, schizophrenia can be associated with an increased influence of threatening content on spatial cognition (e.g., object-location memory). We hypothesise that this result might be due to a dysregulation of prefrontal-amygdala circuits in schizophrenia.

REFERENCES

Addington, J., & Addington, D. (1998). Facial affect recognition and information processing in schizophrenia and bipolar disorder. *Schizophrenia Research, 32*, 171–181.

Aleman, A., & de Haan, E. H. F. (2000). Antipsychotics and working memory in schizophrenia. *Science, 289*, 56–57.

Aleman, A., Hijman, R., de Haan, E. H. F., & Kahn, R. S. (1999). Memory impairment in schizophrenia: A meta-analysis. *American Journal of Psychiatry, 156*, 1358–1366.

Andreasen, N. C., Flaum, M., & Arndt, S. (1992). The Comprehensive Assessment of Symptoms and History (CASH)—an instrument for assessing diagnosis and psychopathology. *Archives of General Psychiatry, 49*, 615–623.

Beck, A. T., & Clark, D. A. (1997). An information processing model of anxiety: Automatic and strategic processes. *Behaviour Research and Therapy, 35*, 49–58.

Belger, A., Puce, A., Krystal, J. H., Gore, J. C., Goldman-Rakic, P., & McCarthy, G. (1998). Dissociation of mnemonic and perceptual processes during spatial and nonspatial working memory using fMRI. *Human Brain Mapping, 6,* 14–32.

Bohbot, V. D., Kalina, M., Stepankova, K., Spackova, N., Petrides, M., & Nadel, L. (1998). Spatial memory deficits in patients with lesions to the right hippocampus and to the right para-hippocampal cortex. *Neuropsychologia, 36,* 1217–1238.

Burglen, F., Marczewski, P., Mitchell, K. J., van der Linden, M., Johnson, M. K., Danion, J.-M., et al. (2004). Impaired performance in a working memory binding task in patients with schizophrenia. *Psychiatry Research, 125,* 247–255.

Cameron, A. M., Geffen, G. M., Kavanagh, D. J., Wright, M. J., McGrath, J. J., & Geffen, L. B. (2003). Event-related potential correlates of impaired visuospatial working memory in schizophrenia. *Psychophysiology, 40,* 702–715.

Carlson, S., Martinkauppi, S., Rama, P., Salli, E., Korvenoja, A., & Aronen, H. J. (1998). Distribution of cortical activation during visuospatial n-back tasks as revealed by functional magnetic resonance imaging. *Cerebral Cortex, 8,* 743–752.

Carter, C., Robertson, L., Nordahl, T., Chaderjian, M., Kraft, L., & OshoraCelaya, L. (1996). Spatial working memory deficits and their relationship to negative symptoms in unmedicated schizophrenia patients. *Biological Psychiatry, 40,* 930–932.

Crespo-Facorro, B., Wiser, A. K., Andreasen, N. C., O'Leary, D. S., Watkins, G. L., Ponto, L. L. R., et al. (2001). Neural basis of novel and well-learned recognition memory in schizophrenia: A positron emission tomography study. *Human Brain Mapping, 12,* 219–231.

Delespaul, P., deVries, M., & van Os, J. (2002). Determinants of occurrence and recovery from hallucinations in daily life. *Social Psychiatry and Psychiatric Epidemiology, 37,* 97–104.

Egan, M. F., & Weinberger, D. R. (1997). Neurobiology of schizophrenia. *Current Opinion in Neurobiology, 7,* 701–707.

Fleming, K., Goldberg, T. E., Binks, S., Randolph, C., Gold, J. M., & Weinberger, D. R. (1997). Visuospatial working memory in patients with schizophrenia. *Biological Psychiatry, 41,* 43–49.

Geffen, G. M., Wright, M. J., Green, H. J., Gillespie, N. A., Smyth, D. C., Evans, D. M., et al. (1997). Effects of memory load and distraction on performance and event-related slow potentials in a visuospatial working memory task. *Journal of Cognitive Neuroscience, 9,* 743–757.

Grace, A. A. (2000). Gating of information flow within the limbic system and the pathophysiology of schizophrenia. *Brain Research Reviews, 31,* 330–341.

Grace, A. A. (2003). Gating within limbic-cortical circuits and its alteration in a developmental disruption model of schizophrenia. *Clinical Neuroscience Research, 3,* 333–338.

Green, M. J., Williams, L. M., & Davidson, D. (2003). Visual scanpaths to threat-related faces in deluded schizophrenia. *Psychiatry Research, 119,* 271–285.

Grossberg, S. (2000). The imbalanced brain: From normal behavior to schizophrenia. *Biological Psychiatry, 48,* 81–98.

Gruzelier, J., Seymour, K., Wilson, L., Jolley, A., & Hirsch, S. (1988). Impairments on neuro-psychologic tests of temporohippocampal and frontohippocampal functions and word fluency in remitting schizophrenia and affective disorders. *Archives of General Psychiatry, 45,* 623–629.

Habel, U., Gur, R. C., Mandal, M. K., Salloum, J. B., Gur, R. E., & Schneider, F. (2000). Emotional processing in schizophrenia across cultures: Standardized measures of discrimination and experience. *Schizophrenia Research, 42,* 57–66.

Heinrichs, R. W., & Zakzanis, K. K. (1998). Neurocognitive deficit in schizophrenia: A quantitative review of the evidence. *Neuropsychology, 12,* 426–445.

Hooker, C., & Park, S. (2002). Emotion processing and its relationship to social functioning in schizophrenia patients. *Psychiatry Research, 112,* 41–50.

Kay, S. R., Opler, L. A., & Fiszbein, A. (1987). The positive and negative syndrome rating scale (PANSS) for schizophrenia. *Schizophrenia Bulletin, 13,* 261–276.

Kee, K. S., Green, M. F., Mintz, J., & Brekke, J. S. (2003). Is emotion processing a predictor of functional outcome in schizophrenia? *Schizophrenia Bulletin, 29,* 487–497.

Keefe, R. S. E., LeesRoitman, S. E., & Dupre, R. L. (1997). Performance of patients with schizophrenia on a pen and paper visuospatial working memory task with short delay. *Schizophrenia Research, 26,* 9–14.

Keefe, R. S. E., Lees Roitman, S. E., Harvey, P. D., Blum, C. S., DuPre, R. L., Prieto, D. M., et al. (1995). A pen-and-paper human analogue of a monkey prefrontal cortex activation task: Spatial working memory in patients with schizophrenia. *Schizophrenia Research, 17,* 25–33.

Kessels, R. P. C., de Haan, E. H. F., Kappelle, L. J., & Postma, A. (2001). Varieties of human spatial memory: A meta-analysis on the effects of hippocampal lesions. *Brain Research Reviews, 35,* 295–303.

Kessels, R. P. C., Postma, A., & de Haan, E. H. F. (1999). Object Relocation: A program for setting up, running, and analyzing experiments on memory for object locations. *Behavior Research Methods Instruments and Computers, 31,* 423–428.

Kohler, C. G., Bilker, W., Hagendoorn, M., Gur, R. E., & Gur, R. C. (2000). Emotion recognition deficit in schizophrenia: Association with symptomatology and cognition. *Biological Psychiatry, 48,* 127–136.

Kohler, S., Moscovitch, M., & Melo, B. (2001). Episodic memory for object location versus episodic memory for object identity: Do they rely on distinct encoding processes? *Memory and Cognition, 29,* 948–959.

Kring, A. M., & Neale, J. M. (1996). Do schizophrenic patients show a disjunctive relationship among expressive, experiential, and psychophysiological components of emotion? *Journal of Abnormal Psychology, 105,* 249–257.

Lane, R. D. (2003). The neural substrates of affect impairment in schizophrenia. *American Journal of Psychiatry, 160,* 1723–1725.

Lawrie, S. M., & Abukmeil, S. S. (1998). Brain abnormality in schizophrenia: A systematic and quantitative review of volumetric magnetic resonance imaging studies. *British Journal of Psychiatry, 172,* 110–120.

Leiderman, E. A., & Strejilevich, S. A. (2004). Visuospatial deficits in schizophrenia: Central executive and memory subsystems impairments. *Schizophrenia Research, 68,* 217–223.

Lezak, M. D. (1995). *Neuropsychological assessment* (3rd ed.). New York: Oxford University Press.

McCarthy, G., Blamire, A. M., Puce, A., Nobre, A. C., Bloch, G., Hyder, F., et al. (1994). Functional magnetic-resonance-imaging of human prefrontal cortex activation during a spatial working-memory task. *Proceedings of the National Academy of Sciences USA, 91,* 8690–8694.

McCarthy, G., Puce, A., Constable, R. T., Krystal, J. H., Gore, J. C., & GoldmanRakic, P. (1996). Activation of human prefrontal cortex during spatial and nonspatial working memory tasks measured by functional MRI. *Cerebral Cortex, 6,* 600–611.

McGrath, J., Chapple, B., & Wright, M. (2001). Working memory in schizophrenia and mania: Correlation with symptoms during the acute and subacute phases. *Acta Psychiatrica Scandinavica, 103,* 181–188.

Milner, B., Johnsrude, I., & Crane, J. (1997). Right medial temporal-lobe contribution to object-location memory. *Philosophical Transactions of the Royal Society of London Series B: Biological Sciences, 352,* 1469–1474.

Morris, J. S., Frith, C. D., Perrett, D. I., Rowland, D., Young, A. W., Calder, A. J., et al. (1996). A differential neural response in the human amygdala to fearful and happy facial expressions. *Nature, 383,* 812–815.

Moulden, D. J. A., Picton, T. W., & Stuss, D. T. (1997). Event-related potential evidence of right prefrontal activity during a visuospatial working memory task. *Brain and Cognition, 35,* 392–395.

Mueser, K. T., Doonan, R., Penn, D. L., Blanchard, J. J., Bellack, A. S., Nishith, P., et al. (1996). Emotion recognition and social competence in chronic schizophrenia. *Journal of Abnormal Psychology*, *105*, 271–275.

Nelson, H. E. (1982). *National adult reading test (NART): Test manual.* Windsor, UK: NFER.

Park, S., & Holzman, P. S. (1992). Schizophrenics show spatial working memory deficits. *Archives of General Psychiatry*, *49*, 975–982.

Penn, D. L., Combs, D. R., Ritchie, M., Francis, J., Cassisi, J., & Morris, S. (2000). Emotion recognition in schizophrenia: Further investigation of generalized versus specific deficit models. *Journal of Abnormal Psychology*, *109*, 512–516.

Phillips, M. L., Senior, C., & David, A. S. (2000). Perception of threat in schizophrenics with persecutory delusions: An investigation using visual scan paths. *Psychological Medicine*, *30*, 157–167.

Poole, J. H., Tobias, F. C., & Vinogradov, S. (2000). The functional relevance of affect recognition errors in schizophrenia. *Journal of the International Neuropsychological Society*, *6*, 649–658.

Putman, P., van Honk, J., Kessels, R. P. C., Mulder, M., & Koppeschaar, H. P. F. (2004). Salivary cortisol and short and long-term memory for emotional faces in healthy young women. *Psychoneuroendocrinology*, *29*, 953–960.

Rolls, E. T. (2000). Memory systems in the brain. *Annual Review of Psychology*, *51*, 599–630.

Schmand, B., Bakker, D., Saan, R., & Louman, J. (1991). De Nederlandse Leestest voor Volwassenen: een maat voor het premorbide intelligentieniveau [The Dutch Reading test for Adults: a measure of premorbide intelligence]. *Tijdschrift voor Gerontologie en Geriatrie*, *22*, 15–19.

Schneider, F., Gur, R. C., Gur, R. E., & Shtasel, D. L. (1995). Emotional processing in schizophrenia—neurobehavioral probes in relation to psychopathology. *Schizophrenia Research*, *17*, 67–75.

Seidman, L. J., Pantelis, C., Keshavan, M. S., Faraone, S. V., Goldstein, J. M., Horton, N. J., et al. (2003). A review and new report of medial temporal lobe dysfunction as a vulnerability indicator for schizophrenia: A magnetic resonance imaging morphometric family study of the parahippocampal gyrus. *Schizophrenia Bulletin*, *29*, 803–830.

Sheehan, D. V., Lecrubier, Y., Sheehan, K. H., Amorim, P., Janavs, J., Weiller, E., et al. (1998). The Mini-International Neuropsychiatric Interview (MINI): The development and validation of a structured diagnostic psychiatric interview for DSM-IV and ICD-10. *Journal of Clinical Psychiatry*, *59*, 22–33.

Shenton, M. E., Dickey, C. C., Frumin, M., & McCarley, R. W. (2001). A review of MRI findings in schizophrenia. *Schizophrenia Research*, *49*, 1–52.

Torrey, E. F. (2002). Studies of individuals with schizophrenia never treated with antipsychotic medications: a review. *Schizophrenia Research*, *58*, 101–115.

Van Honk, J., Kessels, R. P. C., Putman, P., Jager, G., Koppeschaar, H. P. F., & Postma, A. (2003). Attentionally modulated effects of cortisol and mood on memory for emotional faces in healthy young males. *Psychoneuroendocrinology*, *28*, 941–948.

Wilhelm, S., McNally, R. J., Baer, L., & Florin, I. (1996). Directed forgetting in obsessive-compulsive disorder. *Behaviour Research and Therapy*, *34*, 633–641.

Willshire, D., Kinsella, G., & Prior, M. (1991). Estimating WAIS-R IQ from the National Adult Reading Test—a cross-validation. *Journal of Clinical and Experimental Neuropsychology*, *13*, 204–216.

Wolwer, W., Streit, M., Polzer, U., & Gaebel, W. (1996). Facial affect recognition in the course of schizophrenia. *European Archives of Psychiatry and Clinical Neuroscience*, *246*, 165–170.

Wright, I. C., Rabe-Hesketh, S., Woodruff, P. W. R., David, A. S., Murray, R. M., & Bullmore, E. T. (2000). Meta-analysis of regional brain volumes in schizophrenia. *American Journal of Psychiatry*, *157*, 16–25.

COGNITIVE NEUROPSYCHIATRY
2006, 11 (3), 285–306

Unmasking feigned sanity: A neurobiological model of emotion processing in primary psychopathy

Jack van Honk and Dennis J. L. G. Schutter

Utrecht University, The Netherlands

Introduction. The neurobiological basis of primary psychopathy, an emotional disorder characterised by a lack of fear and empathy, on the one hand, and extremely violent, antisocial tendencies, on the other, is relatively unknown. Nevertheless, theoretical models that emphasise the role of fearlessness, imbalanced motivation, defective somatic markers, and dysfunctional violence inhibition mechanisms have complementary proposals regarding motivations and brain mechanisms involved.
Methods. Presently, incorporating the heuristic value of these models and further theorising on the basis of recent data from neuropsychology, neuroendocrinology, neuroimaging, and repetitive transcranial magnetic stimulation (rTMS), an attempt is made to construct a neurobiological framework of emotion processing in primary psychopathy with clinical applicability.
Results. According to this framework, defective emotional processing in primary psychopathy results from bottom-up hormone-mediated imbalances at: (1) the subcortical level; (2) in subcortico-cortical "cross-talk"; that end up in an instrumental stance at the cortical level (3). An endocrine dual-system approach for the fine-tuned restoration of these hormone-mediated imbalances is proposed as a possible clinical application.
Discussion. This application may be capable of laying a neurobiological foundation for more successful sociotherapeutic interventions in primary psychopathy.

In his now classic work *The Mask of Sanity* (1941), Cleckley defines psychopathy in such an elaborate and elegant manner that most of his observations have survived until today. When reading *The Mask* one becomes absorbed by the vivid descriptions of the emotional poverty, shamelessness, manipulativeness, superficial charm, fearlessness, and remorselessness displayed by the world's

Correspondence should be addressed to Jack van Honk, Helmholtz Research Institute, Affective Neuroscience Section, Utrecht University, Heidelberglaan 2, 3584 CS Utrecht, The Netherlands; e-mail: J.vanHonk@fss.uu.nl

This work was sponsored by an Innovational Research Grant (No. 016-005-060) from the Netherlands Organisation for Scientific Research (NWO). We thank an anonymous referee for excellent comments that have in our opinion substantially improved the manuscript.

http://www.psypress.com/cogneuropsychiatry   DOI:10.1080/13546800500233728

most cruel intraspecies predator. The psychopath is suggested to be a morally insane and untreatable misfit whose violent, antisocial behaviour needs little or no stimulation; it is instrumentally driven. The motivational basis for unrestrained social aggression is provided by *lack* of fear and empathy, and access to prey is secured by an impenetrable mask of sanity. Cleckley's (1941) extensive clinical descriptions of the personality characteristics of the psychopath have been widely accepted, and his definition was included in the second edition of the *Diagnostic and Statistical Manual of Mental Disorders* (DSM-II). Gradually, from the DSM-III onwards, however, more behaviourally based descriptions were used, because these are more reliable measurable (Salekin, 2002). These behavioural classifications then again proved to be too narrow to distinguish psychopathy from antisocial personality disorder (ASPD). This is rather problematic because ASPD is a nonspecific classification that virtually overlaps with criminality. Up to 75% of convicted criminals in the United States can be diagnosed with ASPD on the basis of key DSM characteristics, such as the tendency to disregard the rights of others and the rules of society. These ASPD characteristics of course also apply to the psychopath; according to the DSM-IV descriptions of ASPD most psychopaths factually suffer from ASPD. The opposite can of course not said to be true, since ASPD is found in 4% of the general population whereas the prevalence of psychopathy in less than 1% (Pitchford, 2001).

A diagnostic gap was bridged with the development of the Psychopathy Checklist (PCL; Hare, 1980) and especially its revised version (PCL-R; Hare, 1991). The PCL-R is a large step forward in the definition, classification, and diagnostisation of psychopathy. The list consists of 20 items from which two main factors can be derived: Factor 1 refers to defective socioaffective characteristics and involves items, such as superficial charm, pathological lying, lack of empathy, and shallow affect, wheras Factor 2 assesses the chronic antisocial lifestyle of the psychopath with items, such as parasitic lifestyle, proneness to boredom, and impulsivity. The two factors are of course not fully independent because a chronic antisocial lifestyle logically supervenes on a defective emotional system. However, the PCL-R's real weakness relates to the interaction between psychopathic severity and expected treatment outcome, which roots in its relationship with anxiety.

PCL-R AND ANXIETY

Although the PCL-R has proven to be a great improvement in the diagnostisation of psychopathy, it is a pity that it does not clearly incorporate factors of fear and anxiety (Newman & Lorenz, 2003). As a result, anxious individuals can be diagnosed with psychopathy, which is "a contradiction in terms" for the influential low fear models of psychopathy (Lykken, 1995; Patrick, 1994). To deal with this problem, researchers in the field of psychopathy have adopted the strategy to add an anxiety scale to the PCL-R to distinguish the secondary (high anxious) from the primary (low anxious) psychopath (e.g., Newman, Patterson, Howland, & Nichols, 1990). Several studies demonstrated that the anxiety index of passive avoidance is dysfunctional in the primary psychopath exclusively (see Arnett, 1997). This begs the question whether the secondary psychopath does not better fit in a subcategory of ASPD. Moreover, the above diagnostic problems extend to questions regarding the neurobiology underlying psychopathy, because the presence or absence of fear and anxiety clearly involves different physiological substrates on both the endocrinological and the neuroanatomical level (Rosen & Schulkin, 1998).

In sum, the PCL-R was initially intended to diagnose Cleckley's psychopath, but it falls short. Since socioemotional learning is largely driven by punishments, the relative neglect of fear paradigms, such as punishment sensitivity in the assessment of psychopathy, obscures insights in therapeutic treatment outcome. Furthermore, the PCL-R's underassessment of fear and anxiety necessarily results in overdiagnostisation. When lack of fear hallmarks psychopathy, individuals diagnosed with psychopathy should lack fear. When not, the overlap with ASPD becomes substantial and psychopathy and ASPD become fuzzy categories.

In the present review we will address hypothetical considerations about defective brain circuits and dysfunctional emotional processing in *primary* psychopathy.

Psychopathy and emotional processing

Various models on emotional dysfunction in psychopathy have been proposed since Phillippe Pinel, almost two centuries ago, coined the term *insanity without a delirium*. The term refers to emotional dysfunction in absence of emotional distress, which typifies psychopathy. For centuries, labelling emotional behaviour as disordered has been based on the rather vulnerable observation-description method. Dysfunctions in emotional processing can, however, additionally be assessed by, for instance, the selective attentional or physiological response to threat. Hypervigilant cognitive and psychophysiological affective responses are often observed in both highly and clinically anxious subjects (Williams, Mathews, & MacLeod, 1996), while hypovigilance marks ASDP and in particular the primary psychopath (Arnett, 1997). Both the former preoccupation with environmental threat and the latter neglect of threat arguably plays an important role in the aetiology and maintenance of emotional disorders such as melancholic depression, social phobia, and psychopathy (Schulkin, 2003a; Van Honk & de Haan, 2001; Williams et al., 1996). Thus the psychopath displays an inattentiveness to threat, a risky behavioural strategy that leaves more room for attending to the rewarding aspects of the environment. In social phobia and melancholic depression, sensitivity for the punishing consequences of (threatening) social encounters should result in socially avoidant behaviour, while in the psychopath punishment insensitivity defensibly leads to unrestrained and socially aggressive forms of behavioural approach (Arnett, 1997; Raine, 1996). In sum, hypophobia in psychopathy seems to predispose for violence and social aggression through defective inhibition in antisocial behaviour. This theoretical notion has its roots in the groundbreaking findings of Lykken (1957) that have recently been further elaborated by Patrick (1994). In the next section of this review the four most influential theoretical models of psychopathy are discussed.

THEORETICAL MODELS OF PSYCHOPATHY

Low fear model of psychopathy

The low fear model of psychopathy states that the psychopathic disturbance is rooted in and nourished by the absence of fear. Fearlessness secures for an inability to respond to and learn from the punishing consequences of antisocial and violent behaviour. Almost half a century ago David Lykken (1957) started to explore this low fear model using the concept of passive avoidance. In aversive-conditioning paradigms it was repeatedly demonstrated that psychopaths have a lesser tendency to avoid behaviour that had previously been associated with punishment in the form of mild electric shocks. Many theorists regarded fearlessness as one of the main characteristics of psychopathy (Cleckley, 1982; Fowles, 1980; Lykken, 1957). The findings of Lykken are exemplary according to Fowles (2000), because the observation of poor aversive conditioning in psychopaths later on proved to be one of the most reliable phenomena in psychopathology-related psychophysiological research. Lykken's (1957) findings have also been supported with the use of the startle reflex as an index for fearfulness. Reduced startle reflexes to threatening visual stimuli (Patrick, Bradley, & Lang, 1993) and to imagined fearful situations (Patrick, Cuthbert, & Lang, 1994) have been demonstrated in psychopaths.

All this has led to the notion that psychopaths have problems with passive avoidance or punishment-induced behavioural inhibition. Societal control over individuals' violent and antisocial behaviour is liable to fail in absence of punishment sensitivity, because attempts for social correction have no effect. However, explanations for poor passive avoidance in the psychopath often refer to punishment insensitivity or low levels of fear, which is somewhat weak since the notion that the preservation of behaviour that has been punished is due to insensitivity for punishment may have descriptive value but surely no explanatory value. One could perhaps better state that psychopaths do poorly on anxiety-mediated avoidance learning, and seek for an explanation on the brain-system level, where the anxiety-related physiological responses are generated and interpreted. In particular the quest for identifying neurobiological mechanisms underlying defective passive avoidance in psychopathy would be of interest (Arnett, 1997).

Thus, the low fear hypothesis for psychopathy has found strong support during decades of research, which makes it all the more problematic that the clinical selection criterion applied, the PCL-R, does not directly assess anxiety (Newman & Lorenz, 2003). When the absence of anxiety is a pivotal feature in primary psychopathy, additional measures to index anxiety seem necessary. Moreover, the low anxious or true psychopath (Fowles, 2000) is of prime interest for scientific enquiry because the expectancy for successful psycho- or sociotherapeutic interventions in these subjects is extremely low (Salekin, 2002). Another crucial issue which relates to the psychopaths' punishment insensitivity tends to escape attention; punishment is particularly ineffective in psychopaths when it conflicts with reward. Short-term reward is favoured even with the knowledge that this will be followed by extreme future punishment. Moreover, the motivational systems of behavioural inhibition (BIS) and behavioural activation (BAS) are mutually inhibitory (Fowles, 1980), hence the insensitivity for punishment logically allows a fuller expression of BAS, as can be seen in a hypersensitivity for reward in the psychopath. Important studies that relate to this issue have been performed by Arnett, Howland, Smith, & Newman (1993) and Arnett (1997) who showed that heart rate increases to monetary incentives (i.e., approach cues) were observed in psychopaths, but only in those who were low anxious (i.e., behaviourally inhibited). These findings fit best with Fowles' (1980) explanation of psychopathy in terms of the balancing properties of BIS and BAS. In sum, evidence from behavioural and psychophysiological studies suggest a weak inhibition and a strong activation system in psychopathy; the motivational imbalance model of psychopathy (Arnett, 1997).

Motivational imbalance model of psychopathy

In his comprehensive review of automatic responsivity in psychopathy, Arnett (1997) heavily builds on the personality model of Gray (1987) and Fowles (1980) for the construction of an elegant framework of imbalanced motivation in psychopathy. Arnett convincingly argues for the mutually inhibitory properties of the key motivational systems and suggests that a weak BIS when connected with a strong BAS has high explanatory value in the etiology and maintenance of psychopathy. It should however be noted that this reciprocal inhibition between the BIS and BAS systems was already an important feature in Fowles' (1980) model. Arnett (1997), however, evaluates a large amount of data and specifically defends the notion of motivational imbalance in the "primary" form of psychopathy. It is in this conception of motivational imbalance that defective inhibition resulting from weak BIS allows fuller expression of the BAS, behaviourally expressed in disinhibition accompanied by reward-seeking tendencies (Arnett, 1997; Lovelace & Gannon, 1999). In secondary psychopathy, the strength of BIS (anxiety) should be less weakened and perhaps of a more fluctuating nature, opening the possibility for successful sociotherapeutic intervention (cf. Salekin, 2002). Simply stated, when categorised in the above fashion, the secondary psychopath is unpredictably bad, but the primary psychopath is bad to the bone.

However, although there is considerable evidence of weak BIS in psychopathy, the evidence for strong BAS is far less convincing. This is most likely due to the fact that research in the latter area is much scarcer (Arnett, 1997). Some evidence is nevertheless available in the larger heart rate responses or increases to reward in count–up paradigms (e.g., Arnett, Smith, & Newman, 1997; Hare, Frazelle, & Cox, 1978) a true manifestation of enhanced sensitivity for the rewarding aspects of the environment in psychopathy. Nevertheless, evidence suggests a kind of imbalance in the psychopaths' BIS and BAS. The mutually inhibitory nature of these systems is responsible for the fact that the insensitivity for punishment observed in psychopathy is in particular evident when reward is pending (Arnett, 1997).

In the Arnett (1997) review, this concept of mutual inhibition between the BIS and the BAS is elaborated on, and the imbalanced strength of systems found in psychopathy is argued to find its reflection in depression, where strong BIS in conjunction with an already weakened BAS results in pathological withdrawal (Van Honk, Hermans, Putnam, Montagne, & Schutter, 2002b). This should particularly be true in a psychopathological state frequently observed; anxious depression (Rosen & Schulkin, 1998). In agreement, recent studies that investigated the connectional nature of the mutually exclusive BIS-BAS on basis of questionnaires have found evidence for strong BIS and weak BAS in depression, and crucially in the present respect strong BAS and weak BIS were observed in psychopathy (Kasch, Rottenberg, Arnow, & Gotlib, 2002; Lovelace & Gannon, 1999). It seems that a continuum of prototypical psychopathology can be constructed on the basis of the relative imbalanced involvement of approach- and withdrawal-related emotion. Anxious depressed subjects can be characterised by extreme forms of social withdrawal, whereas the psychopath shows uninhibited approach tending towards a violent, antisocial level.

Arnett's mutually inhibitory system can easily be fitted within an influential theoretical framework of the neurobiology of emotion that largely builds on data from patients with lesions to the orbitofrontal and medial regions of the prefrontal cortex (OMPFC); the somatic marker hypothesis (SMH).

Somatic marker hypothesis of psychopathy

According to Damasio's (1994) SMH, emotional learning is established by somatic or bodily feelings that consciously or unconsciously mark behaviours that have negative or positive outcome for the individual (Tranel, Bechara, & Damasio, 2000; but see Maia & McClelland (2004) for a critical note). Hence, adaptive emotional learning depends on the balanced induction of punishment-related inhibition and reward-related enhancement of specific behavioural choices. Decision making is thus dependent on bioregulatory markers that signal incentives for approach or avoidance in an attempt to maintain homeostasis and ensure survival. Emotions occupy the top level of this bioregulatory response system and neurological evidence indicates that damage to the OMPFC or the amygdala precludes the ability to guide decisions advantageously because somatic (emotional) signals can not be read or are simply absent (Bechara, Damasio, Damasio, & Lee, 1999).

With respect to psychopathy, the SMH seems to provide a neurobiological foundation for Arnett's (1997) model of motivational imbalance, by framing the neural substrates of adaptive and balanced motivational tendencies that guide emotional decision making (Damasio, 1994). In the proposed neural circuitry of these motivated choices, the key roles are again played by the amygdala and the OMPFC (Bechara et al., 1999). Evidence largely stems from experiments with the Iowa gambling task. In this task subjects are instructed to try to earn as much money as possible while drawing cards from four different decks (Bechara, Damasio, Damasio, & Lee, 1994). In the task, decisions to choose from decks of cards should become motivated by preprogrammed punishment and reward schedules. Insensitivity for punishment together with a strong reward dependency results in impaired performance. The fact that impaired gambling performance has been demonstrated in both clinical (Blair, Colledge, & Mitchell, 2001a; Mitchell, Colledge, Leonard, & Blair, 2002) and subclinical psychopaths (Van Honk, Hermans, Putman, Montagne, & Schutter, 2002b) links the SMH to psychopathy. Although the SMH initially emphasises the role of the OMPFC in emotional learning, the amygdala is also crucial. Patients with damage to either the OMPFC or the amygdala show defective decision making on the Iowa gambling task (Bechara et al., 1999). While amygdala patients are unable to grasp the situation's affective value because markers are simply absent, OMPFC cannot interpret affective value for guiding their decisions advantageously. Important in this respect, preliminary data from neuroimaging studies point at defective OMPFC-amygdaloid networks in psychopathy (Veit et al., 2002). Another important theorist in the field of psychopathy is James Blair, and his theoretical framework in particular distinguishes primary from secondary psychopathy.

Defective violence inhibition mechanisms in primary psychopathy

According to Blair (2003b) the SMH builds on evidence coming from patients with so-called "acquired sociopathy" whose aggression is impulsive and reactive in nature (i.e., frustration/threat-induced) rather than instrumental and goal-directed. According to Blair, both instrumental and reactive forms of aggression can be observed in primary psychopaths, but secondary psychopaths demonstrate almost exclusively reactive aggression. In this model, the orbitofrontal cortex is more strongly involved in reactive aggression, while the amygdala is particularly involved in instrumental aggression.

Blair (2003b) furthermore proposes a violence inhibition mechanism (VIM) that relates in particular to the primary psychopath. The VIM theory argues that a particular neurocognitive deficit plays a major role in the etiology of psychopathy. Putting relatively more weight on lack of empathy and building on ethological work in social animals by Lorenz (1966) and Eibl-Eibesfeldt (1970), evolved signalling mechanisms for the control of social aggression are suggested. The rule is that when a conspecific aggressor encounters submissive cues, such as the display of fear, attack will be terminated by the VIM. The VIM secures obedience to the rule in a fully automatic fashion. Activation of VIM by cues of fear and distress starts up the "empathic" response that goes accompanied by decreases in autonomic activity and attention to the victim. Although Blair is not very explicit on this, it is with respect to primary psychopathy very important to distinguish between cognitive and affective forms of empathy. The primary psychopath should of course possess "mind reading skills" to predict the behaviour of a victim to be, but lacks the affective forms of empathy that work by feeling and understanding other people's pleasures and pains (Decety & Jackson, 2004). It should furthermore be noted that Blair sees primary psychopathy as a developmental disorder carrying a breakdown in social moralisation. The neurological locus of this "neurocognitive" impairment in psychopathy is the amygdala, and when seen in the light of the ability to recognise the submissive cue of fear this view also finds support. One of the most replicated findings in neuropsychological research is the relationship between the amygdala and the processing of fearful faces (Calder, Lawrence, & Young, 2002). Moreover, it has been demonstrated repeatedly that subjects with psychopathic characteristics are impaired in the recognition of fearful facial expressions (Blair, 2003a, 2003b; Montagne et al., 2005). Moreover, Blair's theory not only pays attention to lack of empathy but also to lack of fear (Blair, 2003b), and there is evidence for poor passive avoidance (e.g., Lykken, 1957) and an attenuated fear-potentiated startle in psychopathy (Herpertz et al., 2001). In conclusion, according to Blair, amygdala dysfunction is revealed in primary psychopathy in the face of danger or when affective empathy is requested. Although the model of Blair is rather different from the other models discussed above there are commonalities.

Theoretical integration

It is most interesting to observe that the above theoretical proposals are not contradictory in any strong manner, surely not when evaluated in terms of fundamental issues of the sensitivity to punishment and reward. The low fear model of Lykken findings (1957) was especially focused on the aspects of fear and punishment sensitivity. In recent years, however, theorists have directed more attention to the involvement of rewarding properties of the environment as elucidators of punishment insensitivity in psychopathy (for a review, see Arnett, 1997). Thus, the low fear model preceded and partly founded the motivational imbalance model of psychopathy (Arnett, 1997; Fowles, 1980). Next, Damasio's SMH discusses a neurobiological principle of balanced and imbalanced motivational stances by proposing involvement of a neural network encompassing the OMPFC and the amygdala. Punishment- and reward-learning seems to depend on OMPFC's accessibility to amygdala-generated bodily signals. Finally, Blair (2003a, 2003b) discusses a specific subcortically driven neurobiological mechanism (VIM) seemingly defective in psychopathy. Nevertheless, in its manifestations this defect can be seen as a specific imbalance in the sensitivity for punishment and reward. Extreme reward sensitivity predisposes for social aggression, but the final execution of aggression needs disinhibition which is provided by low fear and empathy (cf. Keltner, Moffitt, & Stouthamer-Loeber, 1996). In the remainder of this review we will attempt to integrate the above models of dysfunctional emotional processing in primary psychopathy into a neurobiological triple balance model of emotion that serves as a research heuristic with possible clinical applications. According to this model, three neurobiological balances in processing punishments and rewards and control homeostasis in socioemotional functioning: a subcortical balance (1); a sub-cortico-cortical communication balance (2); and a cortical balance (3). It is furthermore proposed that the end-products of the hypothalamic-pituitary-adrenal (HPA) and hypothalamic-pituitary-gonadal (HPG) axes, testosterone and cortisol play crucial roles in setting these emotional balances. The details of how this translates to the processing of punishment and reward, and primary psychopathy are discussed below.

TRIPLE BALANCE HYPOTHESIS OF EMOTION

1. Subcortical balance

A fine-tuned balance in reaction to punishment and reward is crucial for survival and signifies psychobiological homeostasis (Ressler, 2004). Extremities in the processing of punishment and rewards lead to emotional disorders (Van Honk et al., 2004). From an evolutionary point of view, approach- or withdrawal-related response to reward or punishment are illustrated by the fight-flight cascade that is initiated in subcortical affective circuits and controlled by endocrine-autonomic nervous system interactions (Decatanzaro, 1999). A crucial hypothesis in the triple balance model of emotion is that the end-products of the HPA and (HPG) axes, the steroid hormones cortisol and testosterone are pivotally involved in homeostatic emotion regulation through their antagonistic actions on the biological and psychological level. This antagonism begins with the mutually inhibitory functional interaction between the HPA and HPG axis (Viau, 2002), which concurs with mutually inhibitory connection between the BIS and the BAS (Arnett, 1997). Cortisol suppresses the activity of the HPG axis at all its levels, diminishes the production of testosterone and inhibits the action of testosterone at the target tissues (Johnson, Kamilaris, Chrousos, & Gold, 1992). Testosterone in its turn inhibits the stress-induced activation of the HPA axis at the level of the hypothalamus (Viau, 2002). The steroids cortisol and testosterone are suggested to act on the brain by binding to amygdaloid-centred steroid-responsive neuronal networks (Wood, 1996) where they regulate and facilitate the neuropeptide gene expression that changes the probability of approach (testosterone) or withdrawal (cortisol) when confronted with environmental threat (Schulkin, 2003). Thus, the steroids cortisol and testosterone are capable of inducing neurochemical changes advancing from the subcortical level that influence the way in which organisms act in the presence of threat.

Cortisol

The glucocorticoid cortisol is a crucial neuroendocrine mediator of the emotion fear. Elevated levels of cortisol act on the amygdala to facilitate corticotropin-releasing hormone (CRH) gene expression that potentiates the state of fear (Rosen & Schulkin, 1998). In agreement, evidence indicates a role for cortisol in the disorders of fear and anxiety and in the anxious manifestations of depression. High levels of cortisol have been observed in anxious depressed patients (Schulkin, 2003) and also in nonclinical anxious (Brown et al., 1996) and depressed subjects (Van Honk et al., 2003a). In contrast, and in support of the low fear model of psychopathy (Lykken, 1957), low levels of cortisol have been observed in subjects with aggressive antisocial tendencies (McBurnett et al., 1991; Vanyukov et al., 1993; Virkkunen, 1985). Inconsistent findings have however also been reported (Schulz, Halperin, Newcorn, Sharma, & Gabriel, 1997), but can be explained in terms of secondary forms of psychopathy (McBurnett, Lahey, Rathouz, & Loeber, 2000) and put emphasis on differential emotion processing in primary and secondary psychopathy (Arnett, 1997). In sum, the association between low levels of cortisol and low fear vs. high social aggression suggests a possible role for cortisol in the primary form of psychopathy. Such a role would nicely fit Arnett's motivational imbalance model (Arnett, 1997) that emphasises the role of punishment insensitivity (fearlessness) and reward dependency (anger proneness) in primary psychopathy. Moreover, as noted earlier, the insensitivity for punishment together with a strong reward dependency results in impaired performance on the Iowa gambling task. Indeed, such impaired decision-making performance was recently observed in subjects with low levels of cortisol (Van Honk, Schutter, Hermans, & Putman, 2003b).

Testosterone

Opposed to the amplifying effects of cortisol on fear, testosterone has not only rewarding properties, but also leads to reductions in fear (Boissy & Boussiou, 1994). Elevated levels of testosterone should in theory lead to a more disadvantageous pattern of decision making on the Iowa gambling task. This hypothesis was recently confirmed when the effects of a single administration of testosterone on decision making in the gambling task were investigated. Testosterone was hypothesised to induce a shift in motivational balance towards decreased punishment sensitivity and enhanced reward sensitivity. As expected, after testosterone administration subjects made overall more disadvantageous decisions on the task (Van Honk et al., 2004). Animal research has already shown that testosterone treatment reduces the sensitivity for punishment (Boissy & Bouissou, 1994) while enhancing the sensitivity for reward (Carr, Fibirger, & Phillips, 1989). These changes would precisely induce the imbalance in the core motivational tendencies that predisposes for primary psychopathy (Arnett, 1997; Fowles, 1980). In concordance, elevated testosterone levels have been related to psychopathy as measured on the Karolinska Scales of Personality (KSP; Stalenheim, Eriksson, Von Knorrig, & Wide, 1998). Furthermore, testosterone has been associated with antisocial tendencies, such as aggressive dominance and criminal violence, in both males (Dabbs, Carr, Frady, & Riad, 1995; Dabbs & Morris, 1990) and females (Dabbs & Haregrove, 1997; Dabbs, Ruback, Frady, Hopper, & Sgoutas, 1988). Importantly in this respect, testosterone is argued to be involved in instrumental forms of aggression (Van Honk et al., 2004), which are rather selectively observed in the primary psychopath (Blair, 2001, 2003a). Note, however, that a role of testosterone in primary *but not* secondary psychopathy is far from evident. Interestingly, low serotonergic central neurotransmission strongly relates to the reactive forms of aggression observed in secondary psychopathy, and reactive aggression manifests itself often in highly comorbid forms involving anxiety and depression (e.g., borderline disorder). Given the evidence for fear-reducing and antidepressant properties of testosterone (Van Honk, Peper, & Schutter, 2005), it might be argued that in primary psychopathy heightened levels of testosterone go accompanied by relatively normal serotonin activity while in secondary psychopathy low serotonin and high testosterone levels in the central nervous system predispose for more impulsive forms of aggression (cf. Birger et al., 2003). Given the evidence for testosterone and serotonin inhibiting each other's actions (McEwen & Seeman, 2003) the neurobiological interactions seem to fit best in secondary psychopathy.

In the neurobiological mechanisms underlying the effects of cortisol and testosterone on the sensitivity for punishment and reward construct, a crucial role seems reserved for the amygdala. As noted, steroid hormones act by binding to amygdala-centred steroid-responsive neuronal networks in the brain (Meisel

& Sachs, 1994; Wood, 1996). Moreover, animal data indicate that cortisol acts on the amygdala to facilitate CRH gene expression which increases the sensitivity for punishment (Schulkin, 2003a) whereas testosterone facilitates vasopressin gene expression at the amygdala which increases the sensitivity for reward (DeVries, DeVries, Taymans, & Carter, 1995).

2. Subcortico-cortical balance

Appropriate communication between the subcortical and cortical regions of the emotional brain is argued to be crucial for healthy socioemotional functioning (Mayberg et al., 1999). Concerning amygdala-OMPFC communication, for instance, the amygdala attributes affective value to a stimulus, while the OMPFC provides for the more complex affective evaluation that plays a role in the decision for proper action. In agreement, patients with amygdala lesions have problems in assigning affective value to a stimulus and OMPFC patients have difficulties in making appropriate reactions to emotional situations (Bechara et al., 1999). Thus these brain structures highly depend on each other, with the workings of the amygdala finding their appreciation on the OMPFC level, and the OMPFC depending on correct amygdala input to guide emotional behaviour appropriately. Not unexpectedly, neuroimaging data from psychopaths (Kiehl et al., 2001; Veit et al., 2002) and from ASPD patients (Raine, Lencz, Bihrle, Lacasse, & Colletti, 2000) can easily be interpreted in terms of communication deficits between the amygdala and OMPFC.

In the latter study, Raine et al. (2000) found reductions in PFC grey matter in ASPD diagnosed inmates, accompanied by reductions in skin conductance, which is an index for fear (Fowles, 2000). It must be noted that both primary and secondary psychopaths were likely present in the ASDP population of Raine et al. (2000). Nevertheless, theoretical considerations of Damasio (2000) pinpointed the abnormalities observed by Raine to the orbitofrontal cortex (OFC). To provide more definitive answers concerning a role of the OFC in skin conductance, Van Honk et al. (2001a) transiently reduced OFC grey matter excitability of eight normal subjects by applying inhibitory repetitive transcranial magnetic stimulation (rTMS). Significant reductions in skin conductance were shown, consistent with the findings of Raine et al. (2000) and the theoretical considerations of Damasio (2000). These rTMS data might have implications for treatment protocols in psychopathy since it indicates that rTMS is able to modulate punishment sensitivity at the psychophysiological level by changing neuronal excitability of the OFC. Note that fast rTMS over the fronto-polar cortex should enhance OFC activity and upgrade the inhibitory functions of the OFC (Sack & Linden, 2003) and may thus upgrade weakened punishment learning.

Recent findings suggest that subcortico-cortical communication is particularly sensitive to steroid hormone manipulation. This evidence builds on an evolutionary theory wherein the phylogenetically different brain systems relate to the subcortically generated slow wave and cortically generated fast wave oscillations as indexed with electroencephalography (EEG) (Knyazav & Slobodskaya, 2003; Schutter & Van Honk, 2004). Relative increases or decreases in subcortico-cortical "cross-talk" are computed by correlating the change in power between the low and high frequency bands, and it has been repeatedly demonstrated that increased subcortico-cortical cross-talk as indexed by EEG is accompanied by elevated punishment sensitivity (Knyazev & Slobodskaya, 2003; Knyazev, Savostyanov & Levin, 2004). On the endocrine level, increased levels of cortisol have been associated with enhanced punishment relative to reward sensitivity and are accompanied by increased subcortico-cortical cross-talk (Schutter & Van Honk, 2005). This might not only explain the relationships between cortisol and prefrontal asymmetry discussed, but also the absence of a relation between both testosterone and left-sided frontal asymmetry since in an opposite fashion, reductions in subcortico-cortical communication have been observed after administration of testosterone (Schutter & Van Honk, 2004). The cortical cognitive-emotional system in the end depends fully on the primordial subcortical emotional systems to get fuelled with emotion (Panksepp & Panksepp, 2000). Since testosterone, at least to an extent, decouples the cortical and the subcortical regions (Schutter & Van Honk, 2005), the cortical processing mode becomes more purely cognitive; thus cold and instrumental.

3. Cortical balance

Although in very simple animals, the subcortical affective circuits in the brain are fully responsible for the reflexive responses to punishment and reward (Panksepp & Panksepp, 2000) in the course of evolution the neocortex expanded and the left and the right prefrontal cortices became involved in more sophisticated forms of approach and withdrawal (Davidson, 1992). Multiple hypotheses have been postulated regarding the asymmetrical involvement of the cerebral cortex in emotional processing. The right hemisphere hypothesis, the prevalent view for more than a century (Jackson, 1887), argues that most of our emotional processing is biased to the right hemisphere (Borod, 1993). However, evidence for this notion is largely based on lesion studies with human patients and animals that not only have methodological weaknesses in terms of plasticity problems but are also hampered by the fact that lesions can go accompanied by defective inter- and intrahemispheric cross-talk (Leuchter et al., 1997).

Moreover, the right hemisphere hypothesis has recently lost even more ground. The work of Davidson and colleagues who recorded electrical brain activity and repeatedly found evidence for the lateralisation of approach and withdrawal related emotion led to the valence hypothesis. This hypothesis states that the left prefrontal cortex (PFC) is involved in approach-related positive affect and the right PFC in withdrawal-related negative affect (Davidson, 1992). Although the link between approach- and withdrawal-related affect and anterior asymmetry proved highly reliable over the years, the positive-negative distinction became difficult to defend in recent years especially with respect to the "negative" emotion anger (Harmon-Jones, 2003). Anger is an energising emotion driven by motives of reward with tendencies for aggression (Harmon-Jones, 2004), the prototypical emotion of approach (Van Honk & Schutter, 2005).

Findings and theoretical elaborations of Harmon-Jones (2003) provide for a revision of common notions in approach- and reward-related psychopathological processing. On basis of an extensive line of evidence demonstrating links between the left PFC, anger, and aggression, Harmon-Jones (2003, 2004) proposed a model of motivational direction that drops the "positive-negative" valence dimension and simply suggests that approach-related emotion is linked to the left PFC and the withdrawal-related emotion to the right PFC.

Support for this new wave in anterior asymmetry and emotion was provided by data from rTMS. Using the proper frequency parameter settings, rTMS enables transient changes in asymmetrical brain activation (Van Honk & Schutter, 2004). For instance, a deactivation of the right prefrontal cortex induces reductions in contralateral inhibition between the hemispheres ending up in left prefrontal activation (Schutter, Van Honk, d'Alfonso, Postma, & De Haan, 2001). In accordance with the dimensional model of approach and withdrawal of Harmon-Jones (2003) the induction of relatively more left prefrontal activity results in reductions in attention to fearful facial expressions and enhanced attention to angry facial expressions (Van Honk & Schutter, 2004; Van Honk et al., 2002a; Van Honk, Schutter, d'Alfonso, Kessels, & De Haan, 2002c; d'Alfonso, Van Honk, Hermans, Postma, & De Haan, 2000). Finally, concurring with our data on cortisol and testosterone, recent evidence was found for anterior asymmetry being predictive for the balance between the sensitivity for punishment and reward as assessed by the Iowa gambling task (Schutter, De Haan, & Van Honk, 2004). This instigates the idea that balanced homeostasis between emotional approach and withdrawal (Arnett, 1997; Van Honk & Schutter, 2005) can work by way of the antagonistic features of the emotions fear and anger (Keltner et al., 1995). Note that the core negative emotions are, in such a view, no longer stigmatized but their pivotal role in cognitive and motivational aspects of attention, learning, and decision making is recognised, as well as their indispensable counter-regulatory socioemotional functions and crucial life-saving properties (Dimberg & Öhman, 1996; Van Honk et al., 2001b). Moreover, on the notion that evolution provided organisms with a rich set of mechanisms to maintain homeostasis (Schulkin, 2003b), the idea that left-dominant asymmetrical processing in the PFC would be associated with psychobiological well-being seems counterintuitive (but see Davidson, 2004). Reasoned from the evolutionary perspective the homeostatic state (or psychobiological well-being) is more likely symmetrical in nature and defensibly an emergent property of the balance between emotional approach and withdrawal (Van Honk & Schutter, 2005).

Several reports link fearfulness and high levels of cortisol to right-sided dominance in frontal asymmetry (Buss et al., 2003; Kalin, Larson, Shelton, & Davidson, 1998; Tops et al., 2004) but there is no evidence for such inter-relationships between testosterone, aggression, and left-sided dominant frontal asymmetry. This could be explained by the fact that testosterone induces hypocoupling whereas cortisol induces hypercoupling between the subcortical and cortical structures (Schutter & Van Honk, 2004, 2005). The cortisol-mediated anxious-depressive stance is clearly reflected on the cortical level as a result of subcortico-cortical hypercommunication, but the psychopathic stance remains "masked in sanity" because testosterone decouples the upper and the lower brain structures.

Triple balance model of emotion applied to primary psychopathy

In the preceding section, the triple balance model of emotion was intro-duced. It was stated that hormonal imbalances induce motivational imbal-ances on and between the different levels of the brain. In the primary psychopath, this hormonal imbalance should be observed ratiowise as low-ered activity of the HPA vs. heightened activity of the HPG axis. This ends up in relative low levels of cortisol vs. high levels of testosterone, the hormo-nal imbalance that provides for a motivational stance of low punishment vs. high reward sensitivity, on (1) the subcortical level (DeVries et al., 1995; Schulkin, 2003a; Van Honk et al., 2004). This imbalance also reduces (2) subcortico-cortical communication (Schutter & Van Honk, 2004, 2005), depriving the cortical balance (3) from necessary emotion input for guiding social behaviour appropriately (Blair, 2003b). This triple balance model of emotion might have potential for the diagnosis and treatment of primary psy-chopathy. The standard method of diagnosis by observation and interview could be supplemented with and compared to a fine-grained neurobiological measurement of the activity of the HPA and HPG axes (Balance 1). Further-more, EEG recordings might be applied to provide information on the sub-cortico-cortical cross-talk (Balance 2), and frontal asymmetry of emotion (Balance 3). If imbalances (Figure 1) are observed they could be restored in a bottom-up manner by endocrinological manipulations targeting the activity of the HPA and HPG axis or the levels of their end-products (Viau, 2002). Research in clinical populations is however necessary to find under what tonic levels of activation of the endocrine axes the ratio imbalances reveal themselves in particular. Nevertheless, although we must take a provisional stance on the issue, an endocrinological dual systems approach that aims to restore the imbalances within and between the HPA and HPG axes may have the potential for laying a neurobiological foundation for more success-ful psycho- and sociotherapeutic interventions in primary psychopathy.

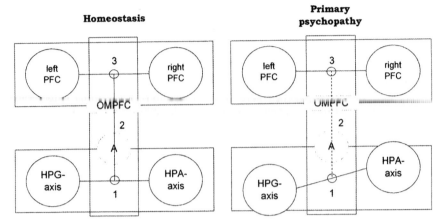

Figure 1. (1) Subcortical (horizontal) balance; (2) subcortico-cortical coupling (vertical balance); (3) cortical (horizontal) balance. Schema represents vector-based model [i.e., direction of possible imbalance for horizontal balances (1) + (2), and strength of processing (thickness of line) for vertical balance (3)]. PFC, prefrontal cortex; OMPFC, orbito-medial prefrontal cortex; HPA axis, hypothalamic-pituitary-adrenal axis; HPG axis, hypothalamic-pituitary-gonadal axis; A, amygdala. *Primary psychopathy.* HPG over HPA dominance, subcortico-cortical hypocoupling, and the emotionless-cortical balance that provides for the mask of sanity. Socioaggressive tendencies find no cortical inhibition and, conversely, the cortical system has low emotion input resulting in lack of conscience and empathy; an aggression-disinhibition-cold cognition syndrome resulting in instrumental acts. *Prototypical affective homeostasis.* Overall balanced processing; Psychobiological well-being.

Figure 1 delineates the main features of the triple balance model of emotion and shows how it relates to primary psychopathy.

DISCUSSION

In this review, concurring theoretical proposals have been outlined regarding the relative involvement of the core motives punishment and reward sensitivity in primary psychopathy. Fitting with these notions, experimental evidence from several lines of neurobiological research suggest specific neuroanatomical and neurohormonal substrates to be defective in psychopathy. The primary psychopath shows an extreme motivational imbalance in terms of low sensitivity for punishment and high sensitivity for reward, which is argued to depend importantly on imbalances in the activity in and between the HPA and HPG axes, measured in terms of the ratio of cortisol and testosterone levels. An imbalanced ratio will be reflected in: (1) a reward-driven motivational imbalance at the subcortical level; (2) defective subcortico-cortical communication; and (3) an emotionally flattened cortical stance. An endocrine dual-systems approach was proposed for restoring the motivational imbalances observed in psychopathy working by way of fine-tuned cortisol and testosterone manipulations to sensitise the psychopath's emotional system for traditional therapeutic approaches. This method might have efficacy in the treatment of primary psychopathy, a still untreatable emotional disorder that distinguishes itself particularly by bringing greater misery to victims and society than to the patients themselves.

REFERENCES

Aikey, J. L., Nyby, J. G., Anmuth, D. M., & James, P. J. (2002). Testosterone rapidly reduces anxiety in male house mice (*Mus musculus*). *Hormones and Behavior, 42*, 448–460.

Arnett, P. A. (1997). Autonomic responsivity in psychopaths: A critical review and theoretical proposal. *Clinical Psychology Review, 17*, 903–936.

Arnett, P. A., Howland, E. W., Smith, S. S., & Newman, J. P. (1993). Autonomic responsivity during passive avoidance in incarcerated psychopaths. *Personality and Individual Differences, 14*, 173–184.

Arnett, P. A., Smith, S. S., & Newman, J. P. (1997). Approach and avoidance motivation in incarcerated psychopaths during passive avoidance. *Journal of Personality and Social Psychology, 72*, 1413–1428.

Bechara, A., Damasio, A. R., Damasio, H., & Anderson, S. W. (1994). Insensitivity to future consequences following damage to the human prefrontal cortex. *Cognition, 50*, 7–15.

Bechara, A., Damasio, H., Damasio, A. R., & Lee, G. P. (1999). Different contributions of the human amygdala and ventromedial prefrontal cortex to decision-making. *Journal of Neuroscience, 19*, 5473–5481.

Birger, M., Swartz, M., Cohen, D., Alesh, Y., Grishpan, C., & Kotelr, M (2003). Aggression: The testosterone-serotonin link. *Israel Medical Association Journal, 5*, 653–658.

Blair, R. J. (2001). Neurocognitive models of aggression, antisocial personality disorder, and psychopathy. *Journal of Neurology Neurosurgery and Psychiatry, 71*, 727–731.

Blair, R. J. R. (2003a). Neurobiological basis of psychopathy. *British Journal of Psychiatry, 182*, 5–7.

Blair, R. J. R. (2003b). Facial expressions, their communicatory functions and neuro-cognitive substrates. *Philosophical Transactions of the Royal Society of London B, 358*, 561–572.

Blair, R. J. R., Colledge, E., & Mitchell, D. G. V. (2001a). Somatic markers and response reversal: Is there orbitofrontal cortex dysfunction in boys with psychopathic tendencies? *Journal of Abnormal Child Psychology, 29*, 499–511.

Blair, R. J. R., Colledge, E., Murray, L., & Mitchell, D. G. V. (2001b). A selective impairment in the processing of sad and fearful expressions in children with psychopathic tendencies. *Journal of Abnormal Child Psychology, 29*, 491–498.

Blair, R. J. R., Morris, J. S., Frith, C. D., Perett, D. I., & Dolan, R. J. (1999). Dissociable neural responses to facial expressions of sadness and anger. *Brain, 122*, 883–893.

Boissy, A., & Bouissou, M. F. (1994). Effects of androgen treatment on behavioral and physiological responses of heifers to fear-eliciting situations. *Hormones and Behavior, 28*, 66–83.

Borod, J. C. (1993). Cerebral mechanism underlying facial, prosodic, and lexical emotional expression: A review of neuropsychological studies and methodological issues. *Neuropsychology, 7*, 445–463.

Brown, L. L., Tomarken, A. J., Orth, P. N., Losen, P. T., Kalin, N. H., & Davidson, R. J. (1996). *Journal of Personal Social Psychology, 70*, 362–371.

Buss, K. A., Schumacher, J. R., Dolski, I., Kalin, N. H., Goldsmith, H. H., & Davidson, R. J. (2003). Right frontal brain activity, cortisol, and withdrawal behavior in 6-month-old infants. *Behavioral Neuroscience, 117*, 11–20.

Calder, A. J., Lawrence, A. D., & Young, A. W. (2001). Neuropsychology of fear and loathing. *Nature Reviews Neuroscience, 2*, 352–363.

Carr, G. D., Fibiger, H. C., & Phillips, A. G. (1989). Conditioned place preference as a measure of drug reward. In J. M. Leibman & S. J. Cooper (Eds.), *Oxford reviews in psychopharmacology: Vol.1. Neuropharmacological basis of reward* (pp. 265–319). New York: Oxford University Press.

Cleckley, H. (1957). *The mask of sanity*. St Louis, MO: Mosby.

Dabbs, J. M., Jr., Carr, T. S., Frady, R. L., & Riad, J. K. (1995). Testosterone, crime, and misbehavior among 692 male prison inmates. *Personality and Individual Differences, 9*, 269–275.

Dabbs, J. M. Jr., & Hargrove, M. F. (1997). Age, testosterone, and behavior among female prison inmates. *Psychosomatic Medicine, 59*, 477–480.

Dabbs, J. M. Jr., & Morris, R. (1990). Testosterone, social class, and antisocial behavior in a sample of 4,462 men. *Psychological Science, 1*, 209–211.

Dabbs, J. M., Jr., Ruback, R. B., Frady, R. L., Hopper, C. H., & Sgoutas, D. S. (1988). Saliva testosterone and criminal violence among women. *Personality and Individual Differences, 9*, 269–275.

d'Alfonso, A., Van Honk, J., Hermans, E. J., Postma, A., & De Haan, E. (2000). Laterality effects in selective attention to threat after repetitive transcranial stimulations at the prefrontal cortex in female subjects. *Neuroscience Letters, 280*, 195–198.

Damasio, A. R. (1994). *Descartes' error: Emotion, reason, and the human brain*. New York: Grosset/Putnam.

Damasio, A. R. (2000). The neural basis of sociopathy. *Archives of General Psychiatry, 57*, 128–129.

Davidson, R. J. (1992). Anterior brain asymmetry and the nature of emotion. *Brain and Cognition, 20*, 125–151.

Davidson, R. J. (2004). What does the prefrontal cortex "do" in affect: Perspectives on frontal EEG. *Biological Psychology, 67*, 219–233.

Decantazaro, D. A (1999). *Motivation and emotion: Evolutionary, physiological and social perspectives*. New Jersey: Prentice Hall.

Decety, J., & Jackson, P. L. (2004). The functional architecture of human empathy. *Behavioral and Cognitive Neuroscience Reviews, 3*, 71–100.

DeVries, A. C., DeVries, M. B., Taymans, S., & Carer, C. S. (1995). Modulation of pair binding in female voles by corticosterone. *Proceedings of the National Academy of Sciences USA, 92*, 7744–7748.

Dimberg, U., & Öhman, A. (1996). Behold the wrath: Psychophysiological responses to facial stimuli. *Motivation and Emotion, 20*, 149–182.

Eibl-Eibesfeldt, I. (1970). *Ethology: The biology of behaviour*. New York: Holt, Rinehart & Winston.

Fowles, D. C. (1980). The three arousal model: Implications of Gray's two-factor learning theory for heart rate, electrodermal activity, and psychopathy. *Psychophysiology, 17*, 87–104.

Fowles, D. C. (2000). Electrodermal hyporeactivity and antisocial behavior: Does anxiety mediate the relationship? *Journal of Affective Disorders, 61*, 177–189.

Gray, J. A. (1987). *The psychology of fear and stress*. New York: Cambridge University Press.

Hare, R. D. (1980). A research scale for the assessment of psychopathy in criminal populations. *Personality and Individual Differences, 1*, 111–120.

Hare, R. D. (1991). *The Hare psychopathy checklist–revised*. Toronto: Multi-Health Systems.

Hare, R.D. (1993). *Without conscience: The disturbing world of the psychopaths among us*. New York: Pocket Books.

Hare, R. D., Frazelle, J., & Cox, D. N. (1978). Psychopathy and physiological responses to threat of an aversive stimulus. *Psychophysiology, 15*, 165–172.

Harmon-Jones, E. (2003). Clarifying the emotive functions of asymmetrical frontal cortical activity. *Psychophysiology, 40*, 838–848.

Harmon-Jones, E. (2004). Contributions from research on anger and cognitive dissonance to understanding the motivational functions of asymmetrical frontal brain activity. *Biological Psychology, 67*, 51–76.

Harmon-Jones, E., & Allen, J. J. B. (1998). Anger and frontal brain activity: EEG asymmetry consistent with approach motivation despite negative affective valence. *Journal of Personality and Social Psychology, 74*, 1310–1316.

Harmon-Jones, E., & Sigelman, J. (2001). State anger and prefrontal brain activity: Evidence that insult-related relative left-prefrontal activation is associated with experienced anger and aggression. *Journal of Personality and Social Psychology, 80*, 797–803.

Hermans, E. J., Van Honk, J., Putman, P., Tuiten, A., De Haan, E., & Van Doornen, L. (1999). Anxiety, vagal tone, and selective attention to mask fearful faces. *Psychophysiology, 36*, S45.

Herpertz, S. C., Werth, U., Luka, G., Qunaibi, M., Schuerkens, A., Kunert, H., Freese, R., Flesch, M., Mueller, R., Osterheider, M., & Sass, H. (2001). Emotion in criminal offenders with psychopathy and borderline personality disorder. *Archives of General Psychiatry, 58*, 737–745.

Jackson, J. H. (1887). The evolution and the dissolution of the nervous system. *Journal of Mental Science, 33*, 25–48.

Johnson, E. O., Kamilaris, T. C., Chrousos, G. P., & Gold, P. W. (1992). Mechanisms of stress: A dynamic overview of hormonal and behavioral homeostasis. *Neuroscience and Biobehavioral Reviews, 16*, 115–130.

Kalin, N. H., Larson, C., Shelton, S. E., & Davidson, R. J. (1998). Asymmetric frontal brain activity, cortisol, and behavior associated with fearful temperament in rhesus monkeys. *Behavioral Neuroscience, 112*, 286–292.

Kasch, K. L., Rottenberg, J., Arnow, B. A., & Gotlib, I. H. (2002). Behavioral activation and inhibition systems and the severity and course of depression. *Journal of Abnormal Psychology, 111*, 589–597.

Keltner, D., Moffitt, T. E., & Stouthamer-Loeber, M. (1995). Facial expressions of emotion and psychopathology in adolescent boys. *Journal of Abnormal Psychology, 104*, 644–652.

Kiehl, K. A., Smith, A. M., Hare, R. D., Mendrek, A., Forster, B. B., Brink, J., & Liddle, P. F. (2001). Limbic abnormalities in affective processing by criminal psychopaths as revealed by functional magnetic resonance imaging. *Biological Psychiatry, 50*, 677–684.

Knyazev, G. G., & Slobodskaya, H. R. (2003). Personality trait of behavioural inhibition is associated with oscillatory systems reciprocal relationships. *International Journal of Psychophysiology, 48*, 247–261.

Knyazev, G. G., Savostyanov, A. N., & Levin, E. A. (2004). Alpha oscillations as a correlate of trait anxiety. *International Journal of Psychophysiology, 53*, 147–160.

Leuchter, A. F., Cook, I. A., Uijtdehaage, S. H., Dunkin, J., Lufkin, R. B., Anderson-Hanley, C., Abrams, M., Rosenberg-Thompson, S., O'Hara, R., Simon, S. L., Osato, S., & Babaie, A. (1997). Brain structure and function and the outcomes of treatment for depression. *Journal of Clinical Psychiatry, 58*, 22–31.

Lorenz, K. (1996). *On aggression.* New York: Harcourt Brace.

Lovelace, L., & Gannon, L. (1999). Psychopathy and depression: Mutually exclusive constructs. *Journal of Behavior Therapy and Experimental Psychiatry, 30*, 169–176.

Lykken, D. T. (1957). A study of anxiety in the sociopathic personality. *Journal of Abnormal Psychology, 55*, 6–10.

Lykken, D. T. (1995). *The antisocial personalities.* Hillsdale, NJ: Erlbaum.

Maia, T. V., & McClelland, J. L. (2004). A reexamination of the evidence for the somatic marker hypothesis: what participants really know in the Iowa gambling task. *Proceedings of the National Academy of Sciences USA, 101*, 16075–16080.

Mayberg, H. S., Liotti, M., Brannan, S. K., McGinnis, S., Mahurin, R. K., & Jerabek, P. A. (1999). Reciprocal limbic-cortical function and negative mood: Converging PET findings in depression and normal sadness. *American Journal of Psychiatry, 156*, 675–682.

McBurnett, K., Lahey, B. B., Frick, P. J., Risch, S. C., Loeber, R., Hart, E. L., Christ, M. A. G., & Hanson, K.S. (1991). Anxiety, inhibition, and conduct disorder in children: II. Relation to salivary cortisol. *Journal of the American. Academy of Child and Adolescent Psychiatry, 30*, 192–196.

McBurnett, K., Lahey, B. B., Rathouz, P. J., & Loeber, R. (2000). Low salivary cortisol and persistent aggression in boys referred for disruptive behavior. *Archives of General Psychiatry, 57*, 38–43.

McEwen, B. C., & Seeman, T (2003). Stress and affects: Applicability to the concepts of allostatis and allostatic load. In R. J. Davidson, K. R. Scherer, & H. H. Goldsmith (Eds.), *Handbook of affective sciences* (pp. 1117–1137). New York: Oxford University Press.

Meisel, R. L., & Sachs, B. D. (1994). The physiology of male sexual behavior. In E. Knobil & J. D. Neil (Eds.), *The physiology of reproduction* (pp. 3–106). New York: Raven.

Mitchell, D. G. V., Colledge, E., Leonard, A., & Blair, R. J. R. (2002). Risky decisions and response reversal: Is there evidence of orbitofrontal cortex dysfunction in psychopathic individuals? *Neuropsychologia, 40*, 2013–2022.

Montagne, B., van Honk J., Kessels, R. P. C., Frigerio E., Burt M., Perrett D. I., & de Haan, E. H. F (2005). Reduced efficiency in recognizing fear in subjects scoring high on psychopathic personality characteristics. *Personality and Individual Differences, 38*, 5–11.

Newman, J. P., Patterson, C. M., Howland, E. W., & Nichols, S. L. (1990). Passive avoidance in psychopaths: The effects of reward. *Personality and Individual Differences, 11*, 1101–1114.

Newman, J. P., & Lorenz, A. R. (2003). Response modulation and emotion processing: Implications for the psychopathy and other dysregulatory psychopathology. In R. J. Davidson, K. R. Scherer, & H. H. Goldsmith (Eds.), *Handbook of affective sciences* (pp. 904–929). New York: Oxford University Press.

Panksepp, J., & Panksepp J. B. (2000). The seven sins of evolutionary psychology. *Evolution and Cognition, 6*, 108–131.

Patrick, C. J. (1994). Emotion and psychopathy: Startling new insights. *Psychophysiology, 31*, 319–330.

Patrick, C. J., Bradley, M. M., & Lang, P. J. (1993). Emotion in the criminal psychopath: Startle reflex modulation. *Journal of Abnormal Psychology, 102*, 82–92.

Patrick, C. J., Cuthbert, B. N., & Lang, P. J. (1994). Emotion in the criminal psychopath: Fear image processing. *Journal of Abnormal Psychology, 103*, 523–534.

Pitchford, I. (2001). The origins of violence: Is psychopathy an adaptation? *The Human Nature Review, 1*, 28–36.

Raine, A. (1996). Autonomic nervous system factors underlying disinhibited, antisocial, and violent behavior: Biosocial perspectives and treatment implications. *Annals of the New York Academy of Sciences, 794*, 46–59.

Raine, A., Lencz, T., Bihrle, S., Lacasse, L., & Colletti, P. (2000). Reduced prefrontal gray matter volume and reduced autonomic activity in antisocial personality disorder. *Archives General Psychiatry, 57*, 119–127.

Raine, A., Stoddard, J., Bihrle, S., & Buchsbaum M. (1998). Prefrontal glucose deficits in murderers lacking psychological deprivation. *Neuropsychiatry Neuropsychology and Behavioral Neurology, 11*, 1–7.

Ressler, N. (2004). Rewards and punishments, goal directed behavior and consciousness. *Neuroscience and Biobehavioral Reviews, 28*, 27–39.

Rosen J. B., & Schulkin, J. (1998). From normal fear to pathological anxiety. *Psychological Review, 105*, 325–350.

Sack, A. T., & Linden, D. E. (2003). Combining transcranial magnetic stimulation and functional imaging in cognitive brain research: Possibilities and limitations. *Brain Research Reviews, 43*, 41–56.

Salekin, R. T. (2002). Psychopathy and therapeutic pessimism clinical lore or clinical reality? *Clinical Psychology Review, 22*, 79–112.

Schulkin, J. (2003a). *Rethinking homeostasis: Allostatic regulation in physiology and pathophysiology.* Cambridge, MA: MIT Press.

Schulkin, J. (2003b). Allostasis: A neural behavioral perspective *Hormones and Behavior, 43*, 21–27.

Schulz, K. P., Halperin, J. M., Newcorn, J. H., Sharma, V., & Gabriel, S. (1997). Plasma cortisol and aggression in boys with ADHD. *Journal of the American Academy of Child and Adolescent Psychiatry, 36*, 605–609.

Schutter, D. J. L. G., De Haan, E., & Van Honk, J. (2004). Anterior asymmetrical alpha activity predicts IOWA gambling performance: distinctly but reversed. *Neuropsychologia, 42*, 939–943.

Schutter, D. J. L. G., & Van Honk, J. (2004). Decoupling of midfrontal delta-beta oscillations after testosterone administration. *International Journal of Psychophysiology, 51*, 71–73.

Schutter, D. J. L. G. & Van Honk, J. (2005). Salivary cortisol levels and the coupling of midfrontal delta-beta oscillations. *International Journal of Psychophysiology, 55*, 127–129.

Schutter, D. J. L. G., Van Honk, J., d'Alfonso, A., Postma, A., & De Haan, E. H. F. (2001). Effects of slow rTMS as the right dorsolateral prefrontal cortex on EEG asymmetry and mood. *Neuroreport, 12*, 345–347.

Stalenheim, E. G., Eriksson, E., Von Knorring, L., & Wide, L. (1998). Testosterone as a biological marker in psychopathy and alcoholism. *Psychiatry Research, 9*, 79–88.

Tops, M., Wijers, A. A., van Staveren, A. S., Bruin, K. J., Den Boer, J. A., Meijman, T. F., & Korf, J. (2005). Acute cortisol administration modulates EEG alpha asymmetry in volunteers. *Biological Psychology, 69*, 181–93.

Tranel, D., Bechara, A., & Damasio, A. R. (2000). Decision making and the somatic marker hypothesis. In M. S. Gazzaniga (Ed.), *The new cognitive neurosciences* (pp. 1115–1131). Cambridge, MAT: MIT Press.

Van Honk, J., & De Haan, E. (2000). Cortical and subcortical routes for conscious and unconscious processing of emotional faces. In B. De Gelder, C. A. Heywood, & E. De Haan (Eds.), *Varieties of unconscious processing* (pp. 222–237). Oxford, UK: Oxford University Press.

Van Honk, J., Hermans, E. J., d'Alfonso, A. A. L., Schutter, D. J. L. G., Van Doornen, L., & De Haan, E. H. F. (2002a). A left-prefrontal lateralized, sympathetic mechanism directs attention towards social threat in humans: Evidence from repetitive transcranial magnetic stimulation. *Neuroscience Letters, 319*, 99–102.

Van Honk, J., Hermans, E. J., Putman, P., Montagne, B., & Schutter, D. J. L. G. (2002b). Defective somatic markers in sub-clinical psychopathy. *Neuroreport, 13*, 1025–1027.

Van Honk, J., Kessels, R. P. C., Putman, P., Jager, G., Koppeschaar, H., & Postma, A. (2003a). Attentionally modulated effects of cortisol and mood on memory for emotional faces in healthy young males. *Psychoneuroendocrinology, 28*, 941–948.

Van Honk, J., Peper, J. S., & Schutter, D. J. L. G. (2005). Testosterone reduces unconscious fear but not consciously experienced anxiety *Biological Psychiatry, 58*, 218–225.

Van Honk, J., & Schutter D. J. L. G. (2004). Transcranial magnetic stimulation and processing of facial threats. *American Journal of Psychiatry, 161*, 928.

Van Honk, J., & Schutter, D. J. L. G. (2005). Dynamic brain systems in quest for emotional homeostasis. *Behavioral and Brain Sciences, 28*, 220–221.

Van Honk, J., Schutter, D. J. L. G., d'Alfonso, A. A. L., Kessels, R. P. C., & De Haan, E. H. F. (2002c). 1Hz rTMS over the right prefrontal cortex reduces vigilant attention to unmasked but not to masked fearful faces. *Biological Psychiatry, 52*, 312–317.

Van Honk, J., Schutter, D. J. L. G., d'Alfonso, A. A. L., Kessels, R. P. C., Postma, A., & De Haan, E. H. F. (2001a). Repetitive transcranial magnetic stimulation at the frontopolar cortex reduces skin conductance but not heart rate: Reduced gray matter excitability in orbitofrontal regions. *Archives of General Psychiatry, 58*, 973–974.

Van Honk, J., Schutter, D. J. L. G., Hermans, E. J., & Putman, P. (2003b). Low cortisol levels and the balance between punishment sensitivity and reward dependency. *Neuroreport, 14*, 1993–1996.

Van Honk, J., Schutter, D. J. L. G., Hermans, E. J., Putman, P., Tuiten, A., & Koppeschaar, H. (2004). Testosterone shifts the balance between sensitivity for punishment and reward in healthy young women. *Psychoneuroendocrinology, 29*, 937–943.

Van Honk, J., Tuiten, A., Hermans, E. J., Putman, P., Koppeschaar, H., Thijssen, J., De Haan, E., Verbaten, R., & Van Doornen, L. (2001b). A single administration of testosterone elevates cardiac defence reflexes to angry faces in healthy young women. *Behavioral Neuroscience, 115,* 238–242.

Vanyukov, M. M., Moss, H. B., Plail, J. A., Blackson, T., Mezzich, A. C., & Tarter, R. E. (1993). Antisocial symptoms in preadolescent boys and in their parents: Associations with cortisol. *Psychiatry Research, 46,* 9–17.

Veit, R., Flor, H., Erb, M., Hermann, C., Lotze, M., Grodd, W., & Birbaumer, N. (2002). Brain circuits involved in emotional learning in antisocial behavior and social phobia in humans. *Neuroscience Letters, 328,* 233–236.

Viau, V. (2002). Functional cross-talk between the hypothalamic-pituitary-gonadal and adrenal axes. *Journal of Neuroendocrinology, 14,* 506–513.

Virkkunen, M. (1985). Urinary free cortisol secretion in habitually violent offenders. *Acta Psychiatrica Scandinavica, 72,* 40–44.

Williams, J. M. G., Mathews, A., and MacLeod, C. (1996). The emotional Stroop task and psychopathology. *Psychological Bulletin, 120,* 3–24.

Wood, R. I. (1996). Functions of the steroid-responsive neural network in the control of male hamster sexual behavior. *Trends in Endocrinology and Metabolism, 7,* 338–344.

COGNITIVE NEUROPSYCHIATRY
2006, 11 (3), 307–331

Toward a framework for defective emotion processing in social phobia

Erno J. Hermans and Jack van Honk

Helmholtz Institute, Utrecht University, The Netherlands

Introduction. This paper explores and outlines an evolutionary approach to understanding social phobia (SP) as a developmental disorder in brain mechanisms that regulate socioemotional behaviour.

Methods. A literature review of cognitive, neuronal, and endocrine correlates of SP is presented using an integrative approach.

Results. Social phobia patients present with a specific and developmentally stable functional neuroanatomical and neuroendocrine profile that can be linked to findings of cognitive attentional abnormalities.

Conclusions. It is argued that SP is the human counterpart to primate subordination stress and develops from clearly identifiable precursors in early childhood, the understanding of which requires fundamental insights into the regulation of socioemotional behaviour. The current state of knowledge speaks strongly in favour of a diathesis model, in which distorted cognitions that are characteristic of SP are secondary to hyperexcitability of fear circuits that set off at least as early as at preverbal ages and ultimately may lead to the development of SP.

The widely varying prevalence estimates (Cuthbert, 2002; Merikangas, Avenevoli, Acharyya, Zhang, & Angst, 2002) of social phobia (SP; also known as social anxiety disorder) can be seen as symptomatic for the not unquestioned status of this disorder in psychiatry today. It can be taken to merely signify a lack of unequivocal diagnostic criteria, but also to indicate that SP is not a discretely definable condition. Indeed, it is reasonable to assume that the extreme social fears endured by diagnosed patients will to some extent overlap with the, perhaps controllable, but sometimes overwhelming stage-fright that the majority of people has had to cope with when confronting a large audience

Correspondence should be addressed to Erno Hermans, Helmholtz Institute, Utrecht University, Heidelberglaan 2, 3584 CS, Utrecht, The Netherlands; e-mail: E.Hermans@fss.uu.nl

This work was supported by an Innovative Research Grant from the Netherlands Organisation for Scientific Research (NWO) to Jack van Honk (No. 016-005-060). We thank Guido van Wingen for his valued assistance and input.

http://www.psypress.com/cogneuropsychiatry   DOI:10.1080/13546800500213993

for the first time. Unlike, for instance, psychotic psychiatric conditions, the symptoms of social phobia seem imaginable, at least, for everyone.

This is not the venue, however, to discuss the question if SP should be considered a "real" disorder. What this observation illustrates is that SP can plausibly be conceived of as the far end of a spectrum of normal fears (Rapee & Spence, 2004), which have adaptive value when within normal range (cf. Rosen & Schulkin, 1998). As a consequence, an understanding of the underlying problems associated with SP requires fundamental knowledge of the mechanisms underlying emotionality as well as social behaviour. If seen as the end of a spectrum, studies on individual differences within the normal range, as well as on the other end of the spectrum (i.e., psychopathy), are indispensable for an understanding of this disorder, while SP is a very interesting subject of fundamental interest in itself because it gives the opportunity to observe a system "at its extreme". Reciprocally, fundamental knowledge gathered from this might foster new avenues in treatment.

Starting from this point of view, research has made considerable progress in recent years in delineating the neuroanatomical and neurochemical mechanisms behind socioemotional functioning. As reviewing all would be beyond the scope of this paper, we put our focus on some of our own work relevant to SP, along with a discussion of relevant findings from patient studies. Our aim will be to provide a link between cognitive, neural, and endocrine correlates of SP. But first, we will address the question what is special about social anxiety.

Are social fears any different from other fears?

A recurrent question in the study of any anxiety disorder is what sets this specific disorder apart from others, in terms of symptomatology, etiology, or biological markers. From the point of view we take in this paper, we argue that this question should be rephrased to ask what sets *social anxiety* apart from other *anxieties*, and even, what sets social behaviour apart from other behaviours. In the following we will argue that social behaviour in humans is highly guided by primordial, dedicated social communication systems that have evolved to serve this purpose.

An interesting starting point in this regard is the observation that the objects of human fears and phobias are not arbitrary (Marks, 1969). Phobic stimuli seem to be largely restricted to certain categories, like animals (snakes, spiders, mice), heights, social interaction, etc. A striking common feature of all these is that even though some of these stimuli may still be associable with adverse events occurring in modern societies, the vast majority of actually threatening objects in the contemporary environment of man seems incapable of becoming the object of phobic fear. Intuitively, it would seem likely that the prevalence of car phobia, for instance, should be much higher than spider phobia, as it is reasonable to suppose that fewer people have suffered traumatic experiences with spiders than in traffic. Similar puzzling but striking observations have been reported in relation to SP: The mean age of onset of this disorder differs substantially from other anxiety disorders, and roughly corresponds to pubertal age, a developmental period when social hierarchies start to emerge (Öhman, 1986). Furthermore, SP also contrasts with other anxiety disorders, such as specific phobias, panic disorder, and generalised anxiety disorder, in the absence of a strong preference for the female sex (although epidemiological data indicate that SP occurs slightly more often in women; Merikangas et al., 2002), which can be taken to suggest a connection to the stronger hierarchical organisation of male social order. However, the possible significance of these observations, if any, remains to be elucidated.

Many have argued that these observations make sense when viewed from a functional evolutionary perspective: Fear serves to motivate behaviour (e.g., fight or flight) that increases chances of survival (Marks & Nesse, 1994) or "makes us want to do what our ancestors had to do in order to survive" (Öhman, Flykt, & Lundqvist, 2000, p. 297). Thus, the evolutionary development of a characteristic, such as fear, can be viewed from within the same framework of evolutionary biology: A certain genetic change that gives one member of a species a slight edge over another in the competition for reproduction, may spread itself fast among the gene pool, especially when this alteration promises a solution to a pending problem for this species. It is this development of a new clearly definable characteristic of a species, an adaptation, that is of primary interest to evolutionary biology, and it is the tenet of evolutionary psychology that the same mechanisms also apply to the psychological domain (Tooby & Cosmides, 1992).

Drawing on ethological studies, Mayr (1974) distinguishes between communicative and noncommunicative animal behaviour. The latter refers to behaviour in relation to the inanimate physical world. According to Mayr, it is this type of behaviour that relies most on open genetic programmes, meaning that there is a less rigid relation between genotype and the phenotypic outcome of the development of this programme. In order to be fully able to exploit natural resources in a dynamic environment, an animal has to be able to learn from its previous experiences.

In communicative behaviour, however, the stakes are higher. This category refers to interactions with other organisms. In interspecific communicative behaviour, especially in dealing with natural predators, every learning experience is potentially fatal. Therefore, Mayr argues, relatively closed genetic programmes probably guide communicative behaviours instead. However, the optimum in terms of survival chances lies in a trade-off between the certainty of rigid closed programs in recurrent situations and adaptability to changing environments of open programmes. The balance between these determines, in the long run, the relative closure of genetic programmes that guide these behaviours.

It is conceivable that relative closure of genetic programmes is even higher when it comes to social behaviour. Communication between primates mostly relies on postures, gestures, and facial expressions. All social animals show dominance hierarchies in which some members gain higher status than others. Formation of these classifications is said to take place at a highly symbolic level. Because of these symbolic acts there is no need to revert to actual violence between individual members of a group. When a subordinate individual reciprocates a gesture of dominance or aggression with the appropriate sign of appeasement, the dominant member has achieved his/her goal as in so doing his/her social status is reinstated. Displays of dominance include, for instance, showing ones teeth or raising the eyebrows. Averting the eyes and appeasing smiles, on the other hand, can be seen as signs of submission. Öhman (1986) hypothesises that human social fears can be traced back to these primordial social systems. Following Mayr's (1974) supposition that intraspecific behaviour bears heavily upon closed genetic programmes, we argue that remnants of these primitive communicative systems are still part of the human behavioural repertoire.

In sum, arguably, the question if social fears are different from other fears should be answered affirmatively from a theoretical point of view. Over the last decade, empirical evidence that converges with these suppositions has accumulated following the advent of in vivo brain imaging techniques, which are especially suitable to investigate localisation and specialisation of functions and brain regions. Thus, we now know that "the social brain" relies on a network of relatively specialised brain areas (Adolphs, 2003). Not surprisingly, many of these regions overlap with those to which affective functions have been ascribed, to such an extent that it is justifiable to refer to this network as the "socioemotional brain". Specific aberrations within this network are thought to underlie specific pathologies, among which autism and SP stand out as the prominent. The latter being the topic of this paper, we will address three different lines of research. In the next section, we will discuss a somewhat older branch of cognitive research that essentially has sought to render a core symptom of SP quantifiable—The attentional focus on social scrutiny—and has done so by pursuing a line of research that aimed at the quantification of information-processing biases in this disorder. As this line of research has subsisted in relative isolation of other research into the biological and neural deficits associated with SP, we aim at providing a direct link between these fields in the subsequent section, just as we have done so in conducting our own research.

Selective attention in SP: Vigilance or avoidance?

One can argue that the term "selective attention" is pleonastic: Because we are incessantly flooded by sensory information, attention is selective by definition. Whereas we can, of course, select information by volition, some information appears to us to break its way into our focus of attention all by itself. It is this latter type of attention that the term selective attention refers to. An appealing example is how within a stream of unattended words coming from multiple surrounding speakers, the sudden mention of one's own name is able to rigorously draw attention to this one speaker. This example makes clear that attention allocation is not only guided by serial, conscious processes that we might use, for instance, to search an area for a specific object. Rather, attention allocation mechanisms work in an automatic, parallel fashion (McNally, 1995), continuously scanning the environment for potentially salient information. It is easy to see how such a mechanism might subserve a fear system: It is too late to flee a predator if you have to stumble upon it. Because of the high stakes involved, *false positives* must outnumber *misses*. But, as too much of anything is not good, excess false positives come at a cost. Hence, such attentional biases have been suggested to play a crucial role in the development, and especially the persistence, of anxiety disorders. The reason for this is that selective attention may become a circular, self-reinforcing mechanism when anxiety is triggered by the detection of threat, and vice versa, response thresholds are lowered by increased anxiety (Mathews & MacLeod, 1985).

These thoughts quickly gained momentum within cognitive psychology, supported by an ever growing body of empirical evidence that supports the notion that attentional mechanisms of patients with various anxiety disorders are specifically tuned to process cues relevant to their disorder (Williams, Mathews, & MacLeod, 1996). The greater part of this research has employed cognitive interference paradigms, in essence based on the original Stroop effect (Stroop, 1935). These paradigms allow assessment of selective processing of certain cues by determining their interference with a very easy, primary task, mostly colour-naming of the stimulus. Thus, most studies presented patients with words relevant to their condition, and required them to name the colour in which this word was printed as rapidly as possible. This procedure rests on the assumption that when subjects' attentional mechanisms automatically allocate processing capacity to the semantic aspects of the stimulus, less capacity is left for the primary task, which is reflected in longer response latencies. Typical data were reported by Mattia, Heimberg, and Hope (1993): SP patients show delayed color-naming to words pertaining to social scrutiny and rejection. In sum, using such cognitive emotional paradigms, one of the core symptoms of SP, rumination on social scrutiny, became quantifiable in the psychological laboratory.

Several problems, however, arise from the use of verbal stimuli in these studies. For instance, an alternative explanation for these findings can be found in the relatively higher frequency of use for these words that patients can be thought to exhibit due to excessive rumination (see e.g., Abbott & Rapee, 2004), even though stimulus words used in these studies are mostly matched on general frequency of use (Williams et al., 1996). Even though these problems might be overcome by a more careful selection, verbal descriptions of threat cues cannot be equated to the threat itself, and can instigate an emotional response only indirectly. It is for this reason that many researchers now opt for pictorial stimuli, often facial expressions, in their research (Clark, 1999; Van Honk, Tuiten, de Haan, van den Hout, & Stam, 2001a; Vuilleumier, 2002).

Early findings using facial expressions emphasise the preferential access of these stimuli to attention allocation mechanisms. For instance, in a visual search paradigm, subjects were quicker to determine the presence of an angry facial expression amidst neutral distractors than conversely (Hansen & Hansen, 1988). Although this study may have been hampered by methodological problems (Purcell, Stewart, & Skov, 1996), the basic finding of this experiment has recently been replicated using carefully selected schematic faces (Öhman, Lundqvist, & Esteves, 2001). Moreover, in a similar paradigm, Byrne and Eysenck (1995) found detection speed to vary with measures of trait anxiety.

In comparable spatially oriented attentional tasks relations were found between personality characteristics and proneness to direct attention toward a significant stimulus. One such task is the facial *dot probe* task. In this paradigm, participants view long runs of trials in which they have to detect a probe, which is presented laterally on to the screen, that replaces either a threat cue (an emotional face) or a control stimulus (mostly a neutral face). Response latencies in this task putatively reflect the degree to which the subjects' spatial attention has been reallocated in response to presentation of the threat stimulus. In a series of experiments, relations between trait anxiety (Bradley, Mogg, Falla, & Hamilton, 1998), levels of dysphoria (Bradley et al., 1997), and levels of social anxiety (Mogg & Bradley, 2002), and the strength of this attentional effect were established. However, results have not always been consistent. Mogg, Philippot, and Bradley (2004) reported that stimulus onsets asynchronies (SOAs) between cue and probe of 500 ms, SP patients are quicker to identify the probe than controls. In contrast, Chen, Ehlers, Clark, and Mansell (2002) found SP patients to be slower at the same SOA. One possible explanation for this discrepancy is a difference in control stimuli between these two reports: The former employed neutral faces, whereas the latter used household objects. Additionally, there is discussion about the question what the dot probe paradigm actually measures: The degree to which a stimulus is capable of drawing attention, as presumed originally, or the difficulty of disengaging attention from a threatening cue, as some have argued recently (Koster, Crombez, Verschuere, & De Houwer, 2004).

Also, it is important to recognise the fact that facial threat may elicit a process that is wholly different from semantic threat. Whereas persistent thoughts of social rejection and negative self-evaluation may play an important role in SP, everyday life of SP patients is characterised by avoidance of social scrutiny rather than excess attention towards it (cf. Clark, 1999), which is manifested in evading eye contact. Results consistent with this view were reported by Horley, Williams, Gonsalvez, and Gordon (2003), which demonstrate, using an eye-tracking device, that SP patients are prone to avoid processing facial features, especially eyes. In our own research, we have sought to capture this phenomenon in a pictorial version of the original Stroop task. In this task, participants have to name the colour of the stimulus, which is either a coloured emotional, or a neutral facial expression. Thus, one is said to exhibit selective attention towards a stimulus when the response latency for the emotional expression is longer than that for the neutral expression.

As demonstrated in the beginning of this paper, submission gesturing, such as gaze aversion, and provocation using angry or contemptuous facial expressions, may subserve peaceful organisation of primate social systems (Öhman, 1986; Sapolsky, 1990). Within this evolutionary framework, facial expressions are viewed as vehicles of communication, each of which has evolved to communicate a specific message (Fridlund, 1994). Thus, one cannot equate the threat that is communicated by the angry face to that signalled by the fearful face (Adams & Kleck, 2003), a fact that has often been overlooked in the past. The fearful face conveys the presence of threat somewhere in the environment (Whalen, 1998). Therefore, the degree to which one exhibits selective attention to fearful faces is related to state anxiety levels (Hermans et al., 1999; Van Honk, Schutter, d'Alfonso, Kessels, & de Haan, 2002b).

In contrast, the angry facial expression signals provocation to the observer. Although this can be viewed as a threat signal as well, it is important to recognise the fact that by means of gaze aversion, the subordinate individual is relieved of this threat. Therefore, selective attention to angry facial expressions may be determined by a different dimension, ranging from socially anxious to socially dominant, in which the former is expected to cause attentional avoidance of this facial threat. A study involving participants selected upon extremely high vs. low trait anger questionnaire scores found support for this hypothesis (Van Honk et al., 2001a). Attentional bias toward angry facial expressions was not found in the low trait anger group, conceptually similar to the subordinate individual, but in the high trait anger group. Subsequently, a second experiment showed that self-reported trait anxiety was not predictive of selective attention to angry faces. Moreover, Putman, Hermans, and Van Honk (2004) recently found a positive relation between attentional bias in the same task and high scores on the behavioral activation scale (Carver & White, 1994), a concept that encompasses a wider range of approach behaviour than mere anger (Carver, 2004). The same data indicated that self-reported *social* anxiety, was predictive of attentional avoidance of angry faces (i.e., shorter reaction times to angry faces). Finally, the most recent data from our laboratory indicate that this avoidance effect extends to SP patients (Hermans et al., 2005).

In conclusion, when compared with other, lexical, studies on attentional biases in SP, our findings with more ecologically valid pictorial stimuli are directly opposite. We argue that this reflects a dissociation between primordial, reflex-like responses to social threat, and cognitively guided attentional responses that occur at a different level of verbal and conscious deliberation.

While a specific pattern of cognitive rumination on social scrutiny may accompany SP, we hypothesise that these cognitions appear as a consequence of aforementioned primitive responses that have their roots in primordial subordination stress (see also Mathew, Coplan, & Gorman, 2001). In the following text we will further explore this dissociation between cognitive and reflex-like responses and their possible connection to subordination stress in our discussion of neural and endocrine correlates of SP.

Central regulation of social anxiety and SP

Amygdala

It is widely recognised that the fear system revolves around the amygdala. The involvement of this small bilateral limbic structure in different aspects of fear has been amply documented (for a review, see Davis & Whalen, 2001). The amygdala is crucially involved in the acquisition and expression of conditioned responses (Bechara et al., 1995), but also in unconditioned fear (Whalen, 1998). For instance, patients who have suffered strokes to this particular structure show impaired recognition of emotional expressions but can still correctly identify familiar faces (Adolphs, Tranel, Damasio, & Damasio, 1995). Although its specific role in social behaviour is the subject of debate (Amaral et al., 2003), consensus is emerging that the function of this structure is best characterised as a protection device that is at least involved in emotional aspects of social behaviour.

Afferent input to the central nucleus of the amygdala arrives from the hippocampus as well as many cortical areas. Moreover, it may receive sensory input through a pathway from the thalamus, through the superior colliculus and pulvinar (Morris, Ohman, & Dolan, 1999), which is suggested to be a remnant of a primordial mechanism for fast, makeshift selection of signals of imminent danger (amply described in LeDoux, 1996). Respectively, these account for activation of the fear system caused by events retrieved from memory or contextual conditioning, by cognitive ruminations or elaborate sensory analysis, and by sudden impending threat (Lang, Davis, & Ohman, 2000). Efferently, the central nucleus of the amygdala is highly involved in modulating the peripheral physical changes associated with emotional responses. Some of the projected sites include the lateral hypothalamus which mediates sympathetic autonomic nervous system responses like heart rate increases and skin conductance responses; the nucleus reticularis pontis caudalis implied in startle potentiation; and the nucleus ambiguus which is involved in parasympathetic control of the heart. Hypothalamic projections also regulate the endocrine system, as will be described in the next section.

Not surprisingly, neuroimaging research in SP has for the greater part focused on functioning of this structure, and has, by-and-large, been successful in supporting the notion of hyperexcitablility of the amygdala in SP. For instance, SP patients exhibit exaggerated amygdalar responses to neutral faces (Birbaumer et al., 1998). Moreover, responses are enhanced in response to angry and contemptuous faces (Stein, Goldin, Sareen, Zorrilla, & Brown, 2002). Less surprisingly, the amygdala hyperresponds to symptom provocation (Tillfors et al., 2001), and during anticipation of public speaking (Tillfors, Furmark, Marteinsdottir, & Fredrikson, 2002). In sum, one can conclude that the conception that SP is characterised by hypervigilance to social threat cues at the level of the amygdala is well supported. This observation, however, begs the question as to what is the nature of this enhanced reactivity: Is it cause or effect? In other words, is this effect a consequence of sensitisation of this structure itself, or is it secondary to malfunctioning of another region that fails to down-regulate it? We will first consider the latter option, before turning to the possible developmental causes of amygdalar sensitisation.

Prefrontal cortex

A wide array of functions has been ascribed to the prefrontal cortex (PFC), not all of which have direct bearing on socioemotional functioning. Roughly, cognitive accounts hold this structure responsible for executive function and working memory, the more dorsal parts corresponding to higher levels of cognition. A more or less comparable hierarchical organisation has been proposed concerning the emotional functions of the PFC, where goal-directed planning functions, including volitional regulation of emotional processes (Ochsner, Bunge, Gross, & Gabrieli, 2002), are attributed to dorsal parts, and lower level processes that subserve this goal-attainment may reside in more ventral areas. For instance, the ventromedial area is thought to participate in assessment of affective consequences of behavioural options by incorporating feedback from the peripheral nervous system (Bechara, Damasio, Damasio, & Anderson, 1994). The more lateral orbitofrontal area has been implicated in a great many functions, including reinforcement detection in terms of punishment and reward (Kringelbach & Rolls, 2004), the dysfunction of which may lead to antisocial acts (Raine, Lencz, Bihrle, LaCasse, & Colletti, 2000). It should be noted, however, that the functional specifics of all subcomponents of the PFC are just beginning to be disentangled.

A fascinating, very robust, phenomenon is the lateralisation effect that is found in electroencephalographic (EEG) activation of the anterior PFC. During a long period of research, the nature of this anterior asymmetry has been refined more and more, from the valence hypothesis of hemispheric specialisation, according to which the left hemisphere is specialised for positive emotion, and the right for negative emotion, to the approach-withdrawal account put forth primarily by Davidson (e.g., 2002), and further detailed to accommodate the emotion anger on the approach side (Harmon-Jones, 2003; Van Honk et al.,

2002a). Evidence for this asymmetry abounds. To name a few, higher scores on the Behavioral Activation Scale (BAS; Carver & White, 1994) predict left dominance (Harmon-Jones & Allen, 1997). In contrast, depression is related to left PFC hypoactivity (Henriques & Davidson, 1991). Importantly, relations to other biological markers of an inclination towards inhibited temperament, such as high levels of the adrenal steroid cortisol (see next section), indicate that positive relations with right anterior dominance may appear at an age of only 6 months (Buss et al., 2003) suggesting firm dispositional roots of this asymmetry.

Several reports have appeared over the last few years that have used neuroimaging to investigate prefrontal functioning in SP. First, EEG was used to assess the prefrontal asymmetry in these patients, and yielded results consistent with the above account (Davidson, Marshall, Tomarken, & Henriques, 2000). They recorded EEG data while patients were anticipating a public speech performance, and found that right hemispheric activity increased.

Neuroimaging techniques other than EEG, such as PET and fMRI, have yielded results that are by-and-large compatible with these ideas, although some inconsistencies remain. For instance, increased regional cerebral blood flow was detected using PET in the right, dorsolateral region of the PFC of SP patients (Tillfors et al., 2002), but this right hemispheric dominance was not found by Stein et al. (2002) and Veit et al. (2002). The latter study did report very remarkable findings in more ventral, orbital areas of the PFC. Social phobia was not only compared to healthy control subjects, but also to psychopathic individuals, and yielded results that are consistent with the functional specialisation of this area as outlined above. Social phobia and psychopathy were characterised by hyper- and hypoactivity, respectively, in this area, suggesting that incorporation of reinforcement contingencies into affective processes is relatively weak in psychopathy, and relatively strong in SP.

On the down side, different studies report many different cortical areas that are less easily linked to contemporary thoughts of brain function. Several reasons may account for this divergence. First, different neuroimaging techniques have different sensitivities. Functional magnetic resonance imaging (fMRI) and positron emission tomography (PET) are superior to EEG in terms of spatial resolution, and may be commonly applied in a manner that is relatively insensitive to the rough anterior asymmetry as measured using EEG. Moreover, "activity" is defined in different ways: For instance, decreased alpha frequency band oscillations in EEG vs. haemodynamic responses to increased local oxygen use in fMRI. If further differences in paradigms, ranging from symptom provocation, and conditioning to passive viewing of pictures, are taken into account, it is hardly surprising that inconsistencies emerge.

Summarising, one can defend the position that SP is accompanied by a specific profile of prefrontal lobe functioning. But again, the question remains to what extent this difference plays a causal role in SP.

Frontolimbic interactions

As has been outlined above, the state of knowledge at this point in time, as far as the evidence is concerned, is that SP is characterised by hyperactivity in the amygdala as well as several frontal sites. Based on these facts, it can be argued that the following course of events takes place when SP patients encounter a social cue: Their amygdala will most likely exhibit an initial hyperreaction to the event. This will bring about peripheral autonomic nervous system reactions, in such a way that peripheral feedback will converge with slower, more cognitively guided assessment of the same event in the orbitofrontal and dorsolateral parts of the PFC, and bring about a distorted reassessment in this area. As a consequence, there is less negative feedback to amygdala, which will result in sustained activation in this area.

Endocrine regulation of social anxiety and SP

The endocrine system can be conceived of being a means of communication by which body and mind can change each other's *modus operandi*. Evidently, it allows the brain to command the peripheral physical changes which it deems necessary to attain its goals. Interestingly, contemporary research indicates that the central nervous system, and especially the circuit involved in motivation and emotion, in its turn, is highly responsive to endocrine feedback. Thus, the body may, in its turn, strategically change the mind's priorities by means of endocrine communication. Hence, it is increasingly recognised that the endocrine system plays an important role in regulation of social behaviour.

The hypothalamic-pituitary-adrenal (HPA) and hypothalamic-pituitary-gonadal (HPG) axes, and their respective end products, the glucocorticoid cortisol and the gonadal steroid testosterone, are important players in these processes. Both have organisational effects during development, as well as activating effects in the short run. Moreover, both are responsive to the social environment (Flinn, Baerwald, Decker, & England, 1998). Interestingly, the roles that these two systems play in regulation of social behaviour appear antagonistic: Whereas HPA activity is associated with withdrawal behaviour, the HPG axis is linked to the approach side. Accordingly, aberrations in both axes have been implicated in the pathophysiology of different psychiatric disorders. In the following text, we will discuss the contribution of each to social behaviour and possible connections to SP.

Hypothalamic-pituitary-adrenal axis

The HPA axis is a complex system that appears to serve as an interface between central fear states and the peripheral resources these recruit. It is implicated in regulating responses to stressful, impending events, as well as maintenance of states of vigilance (Rosen & Schulkin, 1998). The system has three main components. First, corticotropin-releasing hormone (CRH) is released from the paraventricular nucleus (PVN) of the hypothalamus. This peptide, along with, and in interaction with, arginine vasopressin (AVP), triggers the release of adrenocorticotropic hormone (ACTH) in the pituitary, which in turn activates synthesis of glucocorticoids, mainly cortisol, in the adrenal cortex. The mechanisms by which the HPA axis regulates fear have been well delineated in contemporary research. Apart from a host of peripheral effects, including effects on metabolism and immune function, glucocorticoids exert important effects in the brain. For instance, cortisol has been shown to down regulate the HPA axis by inhibiting CRH output of the PVN. This negative feedback is seen as crucial in restricting metabolically costly hyperactivation of the HPA axis. The dexamethasone suppression test (DST) is often used to test this feedback loop: Under normal circumstances, cortisol levels drop after dexamethasone administration as this substance initiates the same inhibitory processes as excess levels of cortisol normally would. In contrast, there is evidence that cortisol increases CRH gene expression in the central nucleus of the amygdala (Rosen & Schulkin, 1998), which results in hyperactivation of this area, presumably to maintain a state of heightened vigilance while at the same time restricting demanding overactivation of the axis. Abnormalities in HPA axis functioning have been documented in several psychiatric disorders. Assessment of HPA functioning has largely relied on measurements of cortisol, as measurements of cortisol can be achieved noninvasively. Results are not consistent across disorders, suggesting specificity of HPA dysfunctions to various disorders. For instance, in (melancholic) depressive disorders, which have a high comorbidity rate with SP and other anxiety disorders, basal levels of cortisol are by-and-large above average. Moreover, dexamethasone administration does not result in suppression of cortisol levels in these patients (Carroll, 1984), suggesting aberrations in feedback control over HPA axis functioning.

Early suggestions concerning the role of the HPA axis in regulation of social behaviour, indicating a possible connection to SP, stem from comparative research on social stress in primates. For instance, Sapolsky (1990) studied wild olive baboons, and observed hypercortisolism in animals low in the dominance hierarchy. Moreover, these animals exhibited decreased feedback inhibition in the DST. Pursuing this line of thought, several investigations have been reported from our own laboratory in which relations between HPA axis functioning and subtle measures of social approach and withdrawal tendencies were investigated in humans, using the emotional Stroop paradigm as outlined above. In one study, high basal salivary measures of cortisol were shown to be related to avoidance of angry facial expressions (Van Honk et al., 1998), an effect that has also been found to be related to socially anxious traits (Van Honk, Tuiten, de Haan et al., 2001a, see above).

As stated earlier, SP has been argued to have its evolutionary roots in subordination stress. Thus, not surprisingly, the hypothesis has been coined that

HPA axis dysregulation (i.e., chronic overactivation) might be an important feature of SP. Results of research into this issue, however, have not been unequivocally affirmative. Hypercortisolemia, as found in socially submissive primates, has not been found in these patients. Several studies have documented a failure to find elevated basal cortisol levels (Condren, O'Neill, Ryan, Barrett, & Thakore, 2002; Martel et al., 1999; Potts, Davidson, Krishnan, Doraiswamy, & Ritchie, 1991; Uhde, Tancer, Gelernter, & Vittone, 1994). In addition, Uhde et al. (1994) reported no differences between post-dexamethasone cortisol levels between patients and the control group.

However, baseline levels of cortisol do not provide a complete account of HPA functioning. First, responsivity of the HPA axis might be a better determinant of dysfunction than basal levels of its end product. Furlan, DeMartinis, Schweizer, Rickels, and Lucki (2001), and Condren et al. (2002) used psychological stressors to induce a cortisol response. These studies were the first to report a significant difference between SP patients and control subjects on HPA axis functioning measures. SP patients proved hyperresponsive, and, importantly, this hyperresponsivity was specific to psychological stress (Furlan et al., 2001).

Second, the HPA axis is a dynamic system that is likely tuned in a very early developmental phase to respond adaptively to challenges posed by its environment. For instance, behavioural reactions of young infants (age 3) to novel events have proved predictive of salivary cortisol levels at ages 5.5 and 7.5 (Kagan, Reznick, & Snidman, 1988). Moreover, children classified as shy by their parents at age 4 exhibit hypercortisolemia (Schmidt et al., 1997). Furthermore, heightened adrenocortical responsivity has been found in 7-year-old children with low social competence as compared to highly competent (Schmidt et al., 1999b), although results have not always been consistent (Schmidt, Fox, Schulkin, & Gold, 1999a). Thus, the link between glucocorticoid exposure and behavioural inhibition and shyness is strongest during early life. These findings are consistent with animal studies that stress the importance of glucocorticoids during the development of the behavioural inhibition system in rats. These studies showed that overexposure to corticosterone has neurotrophic effects on the hippocampus (Takahashi & Kalin, 1999). This structure is highly involved in negative feedback regulation of the HPA axis, but also plays an important role in conditioning. Although the adjacent amygdala is thought to create associations between conditioned stimuli and conditioned responses, the role of the hippocampus seems to be to create a representation of the environment in which the conditioning experience has occurred (Sanders, Wiltgen, & Fanselow, 2003). Thus, deteriorated functioning of the hippocampus can first lead to a hyperactivation of the HPA axis, and second, to overgeneralization of conditioned responses to other, irrelevant, contexts. Note that both increase activation of the amygdala and associated symptoms of fear, and may thus explain the hyperexcitability of the amygdala that has been found to be characteristic of SP in neuroimaging studies (see previous section).

Hypothalamic-pituitary-gonadal axis

Like the HPA axis, effects of the HPG axis originate in the hypothalamus, which commands the release of luteinising hormone (LH) in the pituitary by means of gonadotropin-releasing hormone (GnRH). LH, in turn, causes release of testosterone (T) from the Leydig cells in the testes. Although mostly considered an androgen hormone, T production is not limited to men, although female blood plasma T levels are on average about 10% of male levels. Women produce T in the ovaries and the adrenal cortex in similar amounts, and slight (20–25%) fluctuations occur within the menstrual cycle (Sinha-Hikim et al., 1998), which peak just before the LH surge preceding ovulation. Organisational functions of T include perinatal sex differentiation, and pubertal development of secondary sex characteristics. However, T continues to have activating effects on the brain throughout life.

High basal levels of T have traditionally been linked to aggression, dominance, and competitiveness, or, more generally, approach behaviour. In addition to the fact that basal levels of testosterone are strongly related to social rank in animals (Mazur & Booth, 1998), raising androgen levels by means of administration or otherwise has been shown to induce anxiolytic effects in a variety of species (Aikey, Nyby, Anmuth, & James, 2002; Boissy & Bouissou, 1994; Bouissou & Vandenheede, 1996). Thus, its possible relevance to SP lies in the fact that its effects are opposed to some of the symptoms of SP.

In humans, testosterone levels are higher in individuals with dominating personality styles. Interestingly, T levels prove responsive to social interaction as well. For instance, in anticipation of competitive events, levels of T increase and remain high until after the contest (Bateup, Booth, Shirtcliff, & Granger, 2002). These responses appear greater when competition occurs outside one's own group than inside (Wagner, Flinn, & England, 2002). Intriguingly, it has been observed that men's HPG axes respond to short interactions with women (Roney, Mahler, & Maestripieri, 2003). Thus, increases in T levels occur as a function of, and in support of, approach-related behaviours.

Only in recent years, are studies beginning to be conducted in which behavioural effects of T are tested causally by means of T administration. Many of these studies have investigated the effects of androgen replacement therapy in patients with endocrine dysfunctions. These studies mostly yielded positive effects in terms of restoration of sexual interest (see Apperloo, Van Der Stege, Hoek, & Weijmar Schultz, 2003). It must be noted, however, that none of these studies has addressed other measures than sexual interest. Interesting recent studies, however, are starting to give good indications that T might have therapeutic efficacy in patients suffering from refractory depression, especially those with low T baselines (Pope, Cohane, Kanayama, Siegel, & Hudson, 2003; Seidman & Rabkin, 1998).

The mechanisms by which T has enhancing effects are unclear due to longer periods of treatment that allow for changes to take place at multiple levels. Therefore, in our laboratory, several placebo-controlled experiments in which a single dose of testosterone was administered have been conducted. These studies yielded measurable effects on sexual arousal (Tuiten et al., 2000). Moreover, other experiments showed that not only sexual arousal is influenced: Using a similar procedure, an increased heart rate was found in a reaction to angry faces (Van Honk et al., 2001b). Additionally, participants shifted towards a pattern of more risky choice behaviour in the IOWA gambling task (Van Honk et al., 2004). Results from the last two studies may be summarised as indicating that T is capable of inducing a shift in the balance between punishment and reward sensitivity.

Interactions between HPA and HPG axes

At a functional level, HPA and HPG axes activity seems antagonistic. As mentioned before, end products of the HPG axis have been linked to an increase in types of behaviour that are characterised as approach-related: Increased reproductive activity, competitive and dominant behaviour, and perhaps aggression (Mazur & Booth, 1998), whereas HPA activity is associated with withdrawal behaviour, anxiety, decreased libido, and depression. It may therefore be worthwhile to conceive of the HPA and HPG axes as complementary parts of an integrated system. Indeed, several studies now indicate that both interact at multiple levels.

High plasma levels of circulating glucocorticoids have, for instance, been associated with low basal levels of androgens, a pattern that has been observed in subordinate rodents (Blanchard, Sakai, McEwen, Weiss, & Blanchard, 1993). Correlational studies in humans yield similar results. For instance, high levels of stress, and thus, prolonged exposure to adrenocortical steroids, are detrimental to sexual functioning, presumably as a consequence of inhibition of the HPG axis. This is seen in patients with depression having high cortisol levels (e.g., Michael & O'Keane, 2000), but has also been observed in individuals who endured prolonged exposure to glucocorticoids for other reasons, such as long duration exercise (MacConnie, Barkan, Lampman, Schork, & Beitins, 1986). These examples of HPG suppression by HPA end products raises the important question whether these effects are reciprocal. Indeed, recent experimental work on animals indicate that this is the case. For instance, gonadectomy increases phasic activity of the HPA axis, whereas HPA function is gradually brought back to normal levels as a function of T substitution (Viau & Meaney, 1996). It seems that T exerts these effects centrally through enhancing negative feedback of the HPA axis (Viau, 2002).

In sum, much progress has been made in delineating the neuroendocrine events associated with social functioning. In particular, animal models are increasingly detailed in their account of the influence of various hormones on social behaviour. Human behavioural research lags behind in this regard, but we think the following conclusions may be drawn. Given the complexity of the neuroendocrine system, studying merely baseline activity of a single system is not very informative. A more promising enterprise is the examination of responsivity, as is becoming increasingly common in human behavioural research. Another step further is to not look at a single system in isolation, but to study interactions between them. Thus, we think a thorough understanding of dysfunctioning of the HPA system in a certain patient population will benefit from considering its interactions with other systems.

Regarding endocrine functioning in SP the following conclusions can be drawn. First, although baseline studies of cortisol have not revealed consistent elevations, the HPA axis has been found to be hyperresponsive in these patients. Second, functioning of the HPG axis in SP remains understudied. We hypothesise that SP is characterised by lower tonic HPG activity, and most importantly, decreased HPG axis control over HPA activity during social stress (Viau, 2002). Future studies should address this possibility.

Discussion and conclusions

An evolutionary view on etiology

In this paper we sought to put forth the hypothesis that SP is best conceived of as a dysregulation of a defence mechanism, or as an adaptation *gone awry* (cf. Nesse, 2000). Like other fears, social anxiety is functional as long as it remains within boundaries. It has its specific function in regulating social order and the inhibition of inappropriate behaviour and antisocial acts, it has its specific pathology when out of bounds, and it has its own neural substrate. It should be emphasised, however, that such an adaptationist argument in itself implies no specific claim on the etiology of SP, it merely establishes the theoretical grounds for treating social anxiety as a separable "mental faculty". Grounding the theoretical viability and utility of this concept allows one to infer specific and separable brain mechanisms that regulate social anxiety, which in turn provide a heuristic path for investigating SP. In other words, an adaptationist approach uses ultimate causes to infer proximate design (Tooby & Cosmides, 1992). The question of how such an adaptation can become a disabling condition in a minority thus needs to be addressed separately. The answer to this question cannot be simply framed in terms of a nature-nurture distinction. Inevitably, every organism develops as an interaction between genes and environment, and every genotype develops over evolutionary time in interaction with ever-changing environments, thus incorporating expected environmental invariants into the genotype. There are many paths within this mechanism by which adaptations can be rendered dysfunctional (see Cosmides & Tooby, 1999). Some possibilities relevant to SP are briefly summarised below.

The first option that can be considered is that SP may be best characterised as a simple functional defect in the mechanisms that regulate social anxiety. This option is not very plausible, because a simple defect would likely yield qualitative rather than quantitative differences with the average population. However, most people have experienced some mild form of the symptoms of SP, and diagnosed SP and severe shyness have proven to be hardly separable in several aspects (Turner, Beidel, & Townsley, 1990). An explanation in terms of a functional defect would therefore be contradictory to a spectrum approach that emphasises the utility of social anxiety and treats SP as the far end of a broader dimension (Rapee & Spence, 2004).

Second, a possible reason why an otherwise functioning adaptation may become disabling is a mismatch between the current environment and the recurrent environmental constants to which the adaptation was attuned, often referred to as the *environment of evolutionary adaptedness* (EEA). Examples of this abound in other categories: Humans, for instance, have an unhealthy preference for sweet and fat food presumably because of scarcity of certain nutrients in the EEA. An example more closely related to SP is the aforementioned affinity of the human fear system for small creeping animals that hardly pose any genuine threat in modern environments, which arguably accounts for the excess incidence of this type of specific phobia (Öhman & Mineka, 2001). One may defend that a similar argument holds for SP: Human social behaviour has probably evolved in smaller and more closed communities than the one we live in today. As a consequence, we daily meet a manifold of the number of strangers that our ancestors met, and it can also be speculated that these encounters have become less dangerous because of the way current environments are organised.

The third option that deserves mention here is related to the above. If we assume that selection pressures have calibrated population-wise average social anxiety levels to the average EEA, and that evolution proceeds by generating variance, it can be deduced that such a stochastic process generates dysfunctional extremes at the end of this distribution. These extremes are sometimes referred to as *instance failures* (Cosmides & Tooby, 1999).

In sum, from an evolutionary viewpoint, social anxiety is regarded as an adaptation that, like others, develops during an organisms' lifetime in dynamic interplay between a genetic programme and the environmental conditions it encounters. The more *open* a genetic programme, the more it relies on "learning" mechanisms to fine-tune the adaptation to the current environment (Mayr, 1974). "Learning" in this sense may be taken to mean everything from acquiring cultural values to setting a default level of activity of an endocrine system or an autonomic nervous system. Psychopathology, such as SP, then emerges as a consequence of an all too large discrepancy between the *expected* environment and the *real* environment. Mutations in each may underlie the etiology of SP in an individual, but the question on the relative weight of these contributions is one that needs to be addressed empirically. Although reviewing the entire literature concerning the etiology of SP (e.g., see Rapee & Spence, 2004) is beyond the scope of this paper, we would like to emphasise that the current state of knowledge indicates that there is at least a significant genetic contribution to SP, with heritability estimates reaching up to .5 (Kendler, Karkowski, & Prescott, 1999). Recent years have witnessed the first attempts to link SP, and correlates of SP, to specific genetic polymorphisms. Although these studies have not yielded wholly consistent results, we will briefly touch upon them below because of their possibly considerable impact on future directions of research into SP.

There is a growing body of research on a polymorphism in the promoter region of the serotonin transporter gene, which is implicated in serotonin reuptake. The short allele variant, as opposed to the long variant, is associated with less serotonin transporter expression, causing reduced serotonin reuptake. The presence of at least one short allele has been related to self-reported neuroticism (Lesch et al., 1996), and mood disorders, such as depression (Caspi et al., 2003) and seasonal affective disorder (Rosenthal et al., 1998), although replication failures have also been reported (Flory et al., 1999). It has also been directly linked to brain functioning using an fMRI task that selectively engages the amygdala (Hariri et al., 2002): Carriers of the short variant exhibit a hyperreactivity of these fear circuits that is comparable to individuals with mood and anxiety disorders. In similar vein, Battaglia et al. (2005) reported that short allele-carrying children exhibit a different electrophysiological response to pictures of angry facial expressions. However, attempts to link this polymorphism directly to SP have failed: Stein, Chartier, Kozak, King, and Kennedy (1998) found no evidence of a linkage. Nevertheless, social phobia patients with at least one short allele have been shown to exhibit increased self-reported as well as amygdala response to symptom provocation (Furmark et al., 2004). Speculatively, one may argue that differences between short and long allele carriers surface more readily in the context of heightened emotional arousal. Investigations into other polymorphisms that are related to dopaminergic functioning have as yet remained equally inconclusive. Polymorphisms in the dopamine D2, D3, and D4 receptor gene, and the dopamine transporter do not predict SP (Kennedy et al., 2001). In conclusion, it can be argued that research into specific genetic factors that predispose towards SP is still in its infancy, but holds great promise for the future. In due course, it will likely yield an interacting set of polymorphisms rather than a single genotype of SP.

Concluding remarks

We think the data reviewed in this paper compellingly speak in favour of a diathesis model of SP. Although SP has a characteristic average age of onset in mid-puberty (Marks, 1969), there are many indications that identifiable pre-cursors of shyness and inhibited temperament occur as early as only few months after birth, which implies that there is a stable pattern of a temperament of behavioural inhibition, starting at a preverbal age, leading up to the development of SP (Hirshfeld et al., 1992; Schwartz, Snidman, & Kagan, 1999). For instance, inhibited infants exhibit hypercortisolemia when they reach pubertal age (Kagan et al., 1988; Schmidt et al., 1997), and even show hyperresponsivity of the amygdala to unfamiliar faces as adults (Schwartz, Wright, Shin, Kagan, & Rauch, 2003). At a biological level, an explanation for the maintenance of this pattern has been suggested to lie in the organisational effects of early gluco-corticoid overexposure in young infants, which is thought to cause amygdalar hyperexcitability and overgeneralisation of fear responses as a consequence of decreased hippocampal function (Takahashi & Kalin, 1999). Notwithstanding notable but rare exceptions, such as cases of severe disfigurement (Newell & Marks, 2000), the symptoms of SP generally forge through a pattern of increasing hyperactivity of central fear circuits that dates back to a preverbal age. Consequently, although SP may be characterised by excessive cognitive rumination on social scrutiny and negative self-evaluation, we argue that these cognitions are secondary to the mechanisms that ultimately lead to a hyperactive social anxiety system.

REFERENCES

Abbott, M. J., & Rapee, R. M. (2004). Post-event rumination and negative self-appraisal in social phobia before and after treatment. *Journal of Abnormal Psychology, 113*, 136–144.

Adams, R. B., Jr., & Kleck, R. E. (2003). Perceived gaze direction and the processing of facial displays of emotion. *Psychological Science, 14*, 644–647.

Adolphs, R. (2003). Cognitive neuroscience of human social behaviour. *Nature Reviews Neuro-science, 4*, 165–178.

Adolphs, R., Tranel, D., Damasio, H., & Damasio, A. R. (1995). Fear and the human amygdala. *Journal of Neuroscience, 15*, 5879–5891.

Aikey, J. L., Nyby, J. G., Anmuth, D. M., & James, P. J. (2002). Testosterone rapidly reduces anxiety in male house mice (Mus musculus). *Hormones and Behavior, 42*, 448–460.

Amaral, D. G., Bauman, M. D., Capitanio, J. P., Lavenex, P., Mason, W. A., Mauldin-Jourdain, M. L., et al. (2003). The amygdala: Is it an essential component of the neural network for social cognition? *Neuropsychologia, 41*, 517–522.

Apperloo, M. J., Van Der Stege, J. G., Hoek, A., & Weijmar Schultz, W. C. (2003). In the mood for sex: The value of androgens. *Journal of Sex and Marital Therapy, 29*, 87–102.

Bateup, H. S., Booth, A., Shirtcliff, E. A., & Granger, D. A. (2002). Testosterone, cortisol, and women's competition. *Evolution and Human Behavior, 23*, 181–192.

Battaglia, M., Ogliari, A., Zanoni, A., Citterio, A., Pozzoli, U., Giorda, R., et al. (2005). Influence of the serotonin transporter promoter gene and shyness on children's cerebral responses to facial expressions. *Archives of General Psychiatry*, *62*, 85–94.

Bechara, A., Damasio, A. R., Damasio, H., & Anderson, S. W. (1994). Insensitivity to future consequences following damage to human prefrontal cortex. *Cognition*, *50*, 7–15.

Bechara, A., Tranel, D., Damasio, H., Adolphs, R., Rockland, C., & Damasio, A. R. (1995). Double dissociation of conditioning and declarative knowledge relative to the amygdala and hippocampus in humans. *Science*, *269*, 1115–1118.

Birbaumer, N., Grodd, W., Diedrich, O., Klose, U., Erb, M., Lotze, M., et al. (1998). fMRI reveals amygdala activation to human faces in social phobics. *NeuroReport*, *9*, 1223–1226.

Blanchard, D. C., Sakai, R. R., McEwen, B., Weiss, S. M., & Blanchard, R. J. (1993). Subordination stress: behavioral, brain, and neuroendocrine correlates. *Behavioural Brain Research*, *58*, 113–121.

Boissy, A., & Bouissou, M. F. (1994). Effects of androgen treatment on behavioral and physiological responses of heifers to fear-eliciting situations. *Hormones and Behavior*, *28*, 66–83.

Bouissou, M. F., & Vandenheede, M. (1996). Long-term effects of androgen treatment on fear reactions in ewes. *Hormones and Behavior*, *30*, 93–99.

Bradley, B. P., Mogg, K., Falla, S. J., & Hamilton, L. R. (1998). Attentional bias for threatening facial expressions in anxiety: Manipulation of stimulus duration. *Cognition and Emotion*, *12*, 737–753.

Bradley, B. P., Mogg, K., Millar, N., Bonham Carter, C., Fergusson, E., Jenkins, J., et al. (1997). Attentional biases for emotional faces. *Cognition and Emotion*, *11*, 25–42.

Buss, K. A., Schumacher, J. R., Dolski, I., Kalin, N. H., Goldsmith, H. H., & Davidson, R. J. (2003). Right frontal brain activity, cortisol, and withdrawal behavior in 6-month-old infants. *Behavioral Neuroscience*, *117*, 11–20.

Byrne, A., & Eysenck, M. W. (1995). Trait anxiety, anxious mood, and threat detection. *Cognition and Emotion*, *9*, 549–562.

Carroll, B. J. (1984). Dexamethasone suppression test for depression. *Advances in Biochemical Psychopharmacology*, *39*, 179–188.

Carver, C. S. (2004). Negative affects deriving from the behavioral approach system. *Emotion*, *4*, 3–22.

Carver, C. S., & White, T. L. (1994). Behavioral inhibition, behavioral activation, and affective responses to impending reward and punishment: The BIS/BAS Scales. *Journal of Personality and Social Psychology*, *67*, 319–333.

Caspi, A., Sugden, K., Moffitt, T. E., Taylor, A., Craig, I. W., Harrington, H., et al. (2003). Influence of life stress on depression: moderation by a polymorphism in the 5-HTT gene. *Science*, *301*, 386–389.

Chen, Y. P., Ehlers, A., Clark, D. M., & Mansell, W. (2002). Patients with generalized social phobia direct their attention away from faces. *Behaviour Research and Therapy*, *40*, 677–687.

Clark, D. M. (1999). Anxiety disorders: why they persist and how to treat them. *Behaviour Research and Therapy*, *37*(Suppl 1), S5–S27.

Condren, R. M., O'Neill, A., Ryan, M. C., Barrett, P., & Thakore, J. H. (2002). HPA axis response to a psychological stressor in generalised social phobia. *Psychoneuroendocrinology*, *27*, 693–703.

Cosmides, L., & Tooby, J. (1999). Toward an evolutionary taxonomy of treatable conditions. *Journal of Abnormal Psychology*, *108*, 453–464.

Cuthbert, B. N. (2002). Social anxiety disorder: trends and translational research. *Biological Psychiatry*, *51*, 4–10.

Davidson, R. J. (2002). Anxiety and affective style: role of prefrontal cortex and amygdala. *Biological Psychiatry*, *51*, 68–80.

Davidson, R. J., Marshall, J. R., Tomarken, A. J., & Henriques, J. B. (2000). While a phobic waits: Regional brain electrical and autonomic activity in social phobics during anticipation of public speaking. *Biological Psychiatry*, *47*, 85–95.

Davis, M., & Whalen, P. J. (2001). The amygdala: Vigilance and emotion. *Molecular Psychiatry, 6,* 13–34.

Flinn, M., Baerwald, C., Decker, S., & England, B. (1998). Evolutionary functions of neuroendocrine response to social environment. *Behavioral and Brain Sciences, 21,* 372–374.

Flory, J. D., Manuck, S. B., Ferrell, R. E., Dent, K. M., Peters, D. G., & Muldoon, M. F. (1999). Neuroticism is not associated with the serotonin transporter (5-HTTLPR) polymorphism. *Molecular Psychiatry, 4,* 93–96.

Fridlund, A. J. (1994). *Human facial expression: An evolutionary view.* San Diego, CA: Academic Press.

Furlan, P. M., DeMartinis, N., Schweizer, E., Rickels, K., & Lucki, I. (2001). Abnormal salivary cortisol levels in social phobic patients in response to acute psychological but not physical stress. *Biological Psychiatry, 50,* 254–259.

Furmark, T., Tillfors, M., Garpenstrand, H., Marteinsdottir, I., Langstrom, B., Oreland, L., et al. (2004). Serotonin transporter polymorphism related to amygdala excitability and symptom severity in patients with social phobia. *Neuroscience Letters, 362,* 189–192.

Hansen, C. H., & Hansen, R. D. (1988). Finding the face in the crowd: An anger superiority effect. *Journal of Personality and Social Psychology, 54,* 917–924.

Hariri, A. R., Mattay, V. S., Tessitore, A., Kolachana, B., Fera, F., Goldman, D., et al. (2002). Serotonin transporter genetic variation and the response of the human amygdala. *Science, 297,* 400–403.

Harmon-Jones, E. (2003). Clarifying the emotive functions of asymmetrical frontal cortical activity. *Psychophysiology, 40,* 838–848.

Harmon-Jones, E., & Allen, J. J. (1997). Behavioral activation sensitivity and resting frontal EEG asymmetry: Covariation of putative indicators related to risk for mood disorders. *Journal of Abnormal Psychology, 106,* 159–163.

Henriques, J. B., & Davidson, R. J. (1991). Left frontal hypoactivation in depression. *Journal of Abnormal Psychology, 100,* 535–545.

Hermans, E. J., Montagne, B., Schutters, S., Putman, P., Westenberg, H. G., & Van Honk, J. (2005). *Reduced attentional processing of facial threat in Social Anxiety Disorder.* Manuscript submitted for publication.

Hermans, E. J., Van Honk, J., Putman, P., Tuiten, A., De Haan, E. H., & Van Doornen, L. J. (1999). Anxiety, vagal tone, and selective attention to masked fearful faces. *Psychophysiology, 36*(Suppl. 1), S45.

Hirshfeld, D. R., Rosenbaum, J. F., Biederman, J., Bolduc, E. A., Faraone, S. V., Snidman, N., et al. (1992). Stable behavioral inhibition and its association with anxiety disorder. *Journal of the American Academy of Child and Adolescent Psychiatry, 31,* 103–111.

Horley, K., Williams, L. M., Gonsalvez, C., & Gordon, E. (2003). Social phobics do not see eye to eye: A visual scanpath study of emotional expression processing. *Journal of Anxiety Disorders, 17,* 33–44.

Kagan, J., Reznick, J. S., & Snidman, N. (1988). Biological bases of childhood shyness. *Science, 240,* 167–171.

Kendler, K. S., Karkowski, L. M., & Prescott, C. A. (1999). Fears and phobias: Reliability and heritability. *Psychological Medicine, 29,* 539–553.

Kennedy, J. L., Neves-Pereira, M., King, N., Lizak, M. V., Basile, V. S., Chartier, M. J., et al. (2001). Dopamine system genes not linked to social phobia. *Psychiatric Genetics, 11,* 213–217.

Koster, E. H. W., Crombez, G., Verschuere, B., & De Houwer, J. (2004). Selective attention to threat in the dot probe paradigm: Differentiating vigilance and difficulty to disengage. *Behaviour Research and Therapy, 42,* 1183–1192.

Kringelbach, M. L., & Rolls, E. T. (2004). The functional neuroanatomy of the human orbitofrontal cortex: Evidence from neuroimaging and neuropsychology. *Progress in Neurobiology, 72,* 341–372.

Lang, P. J., Davis, M., & Ohman, A. (2000). Fear and anxiety: Animal models and human cognitive psychophysiology. *Journal of Affective Disorders, 61,* 137–159.

LeDoux, J. E. (1996). *The emotional brain: The mysterious underpinnings of emotional life.* New York: Simon & Schuster.

Lesch, K. P., Bengel, D., Heils, A., Sabol, S. Z., Greenberg, B. D., Petri, S., et al. (1996). Association of anxiety-related traits with a polymorphism in the serotonin transporter gene regulatory region. *Science, 274,* 1527–1531.

MacConnie, S. E., Barkan, A., Lampman, R. M., Schork, M. A., & Beitins, I. Z. (1986). Decreased hypothalamic gonadotropin-releasing hormone secretion in male marathon runners. *New England Journal of Medicine, 315,* 411–417.

Marks, I. M. (1969). *Fears and phobias.* Oxford, UK: Academic Press.

Marks, I. M., & Nesse, R. M. (1994). Fear and fitness: An evolutionary analysis of anxiety disorders. *Ethology and Sociobiology, 15,* 247–261.

Martel, F. L., Hayward, C., Lyons, D. M., Sanborn, K., Varady, S., & Schatzberg, A. F. (1999). Salivary cortisol levels in socially phobic adolescent girls. *Depression and Anxiety, 10,* 25–27.

Mathew, S. J., Coplan, J. D., & Gorman, J. M. (2001). Neurobiological mechanisms of social anxiety disorder. *American Journal of Psychiatry, 158,* 1558–1567.

Mathews, A., & MacLeod, C. (1985). Selective processing of threat cues in anxiety states. *Behaviour Research and Therapy, 23,* 563–569.

Mattia, J. I., Heimberg, R. G., & Hope, D. A. (1993). The revised Stroop color-naming task in social phobics. *Behaviour Research and Therapy, 31,* 305–313.

Mayr, E. (1974). Behavior programs and evolutionary strategies. *American Scientist, 62,* 650–659.

Mazur, A., & Booth, A. (1998). Testosterone and dominance in men. *Behavioral and Brain Sciences, 21,* 353–363.

McNally, R. J. (1995). Automaticity and the anxiety disorders. *Behaviour Research and Therapy, 33,* 747–754.

Merikangas, K. R., Avenevoli, S., Acharyya, S., Zhang, H., & Angst, J. (2002). The spectrum of social phobia in the Zurich cohort study of young adults. *Biological Psychiatry, 51,* 81–91.

Michael, A., & O'Keane, V. (2000). Sexual dysfunction in depression. *Human Psychopharmacology, 15,* 337–345.

Mogg, K., & Bradley, B. P. (2002). Selective orienting of attention to masked threat faces in social anxiety. *Behaviour Research and Therapy, 40,* 1403–1414.

Mogg, K., Philippot, P., & Bradley, B. P. (2004). Selective attention to angry faces in clinical social phobia. *Journal of Abnormal Psychology, 113,* 160–165.

Morris, J. S., Ohman, A., & Dolan, R. J. (1999). A subcortical pathway to the right amygdala mediating "unseen" fear. *Proceedings of the National Academy of Sciences USA, 96,* 1680–1685.

Nesse, R. M. (2000). Is depression an adaptation? *Archives of General Psychiatry, 57,* 14–20.

Newell, R., & Marks, I. (2000). Phobic nature of social difficulty in facially disfigured people. *British Journal of Psychiatry, 176,* 177–181.

Ochsner, K. N., Bunge, S. A., Gross, J. J., & Gabrieli, J. D. (2002). Rethinking feelings: an FMRI study of the cognitive regulation of emotion. *Journal of Cognitive Neuroscience, 14,* 1215–1229.

Öhman, A. (1986). Face the beast and fear the face: animal and social fears as prototypes for evolutionary analyses of emotion. *Psychophysiology, 23,* 123–145.

Öhman, A., Flykt, A., & Lundqvist, D. (2000). Unconscious emotion: Evolutionary perspectives, psychophysiological data, and neuropsychological mechanisms. In R. D. Lane & L. Nadel (Eds.), *The cognitive neuroscience of emotion* (pp. 296–327). New York: Oxford University Press.

Öhman, A., Lundqvist, D., & Esteves, F. (2001). The face in the crowd revisited: A threat advantage with schematic stimuli. *Journal of Personality and Social Psychology, 80,* 381–396.

Öhman, A., & Mineka, S. (2001). Fears, phobias, and preparedness: Toward an evolved module of fear and fear learning. *Psychological Review, 108,* 483–522.

Pope, H. G., Jr., Cohane, G. H., Kanayama, G., Siegel, A. J., & Hudson, J. I. (2003). Testosterone gel supplementation for men with refractory depression: A randomized, placebo-controlled trial. *American Journal of Psychiatry, 160,* 105–111.

Potts, N. L., Davidson, J. R., Krishnan, K. R., Doraiswamy, P. M., & Ritchie, J. C. (1991). Levels of urinary free cortisol in social phobia. *Journal of Clinical Psychiatry, 52*(Suppl.), 41–42.

Purcell, D. G., Stewart, A. L., & Skov, R. B. (1996). It takes a confounded face to pop out of a crowd. *Perception, 25,* 1091–1108.

Putman, P., Hermans, E. J., & Van Honk, J. (2004). Emotional Stroop performance for masked angry faces: It's BAS, not BIS. *Emotion, 4,* 305–311.

Raine, A., Lencz, T., Bihrle, S., LaCasse, L., & Colletti, P. (2000). Reduced prefrontal gray matter volume and reduced autonomic activity in antisocial personality disorder. *Archives of General Psychiatry, 57,* 119–127; discussion 128–119.

Rapee, R. M., & Spence, S. H. (2004). The etiology of social phobia: Empirical evidence and an initial model. *Clinical Psychology Review, 24,* 737–767.

Roney, J. R., Mahler, S. V., & Maestripieri, D. (2003). Behavioral and hormonal responses of men to brief interactions with women. *Evolution and Human Behavior, 24,* 365–375.

Rosen, J. B., & Schulkin, J. (1998). From normal fear to pathological anxiety. *Psychological Review, 105,* 325–350.

Rosenthal, N. E., Mazzanti, C. M., Barnett, R. L., Hardin, T. A., Turner, E. H., Lam, G. K., et al. (1998). Role of serotonin transporter promoter repeat length polymorphism (5-HTTLPR) in seasonality and seasonal affective disorder. *Molecular Psychiatry, 3,* 175–177.

Sanders, M. J., Wiltgen, B. J., & Fanselow, M. S. (2003). The place of the hippocampus in fear conditioning. *European Journal of Pharmacology, 463,* 217–223.

Sapolsky, R. M. (1990). Adrenocortical function, social rank, and personality among wild baboons. *Biological Psychiatry, 28,* 862–878.

Schmidt, L. A., Fox, N. A., Rubin, K. H., Sternberg, E. M., Gold, P. W., Smith, C. C., et al. (1997). Behavioral and neuroendocrine responses in shy children. *Developmental Psychobiology, 30,* 127–140.

Schmidt, L. A., Fox, N. A., Schulkin, J., & Gold, P. W. (1999). Behavioral and psychophysiological correlates of self-presentation in temperamentally shy children. *Developmental Psychobiology, 35,* 119–135.

Schmidt, L. A., Fox, N. A., Sternberg, E. M., Gold, P. W., Smith, C. C., & Schulkin, J. (1999b). Adrenocortical reactivity and social competence in seven year-olds. *Personality and Individual Differences, 26,* 977–985.

Schwartz, C. E., Snidman, N., & Kagan, J. (1999). Adolescent social anxiety as an outcome of inhibited temperament in childhood. *Journal of the American Academy of Child and Adolescent Psychiatry, 38,* 1008–1015.

Schwartz, C. E., Wright, C. I., Shin, L. M., Kagan, J., & Rauch, S. L. (2003). Inhibited and uninhibited infants "grown up": Adult amygdalar response to novelty. *Science, 300,* 1952–1953.

Seidman, S. N., & Rabkin, J. G. (1998). Testosterone replacement therapy for hypogonadal men with SSRI-refractory depression. *Journal of Affective Disorders, 48,* 157–161.

Sinha-Hikim, I., Arver, S., Beall, G., Shen, R., Guerrero, M., Sattler, F., et al. (1998). The use of a sensitive equilibrium dialysis method for the measurement of free testosterone levels in healthy, cycling women and in human immunodeficiency virus-infected women. *Journal of Clinical Endocrinology and Metabolism, 83,* 1312–1318.

Stein, M. B., Chartier, M. J., Kozak, M. V., King, N., & Kennedy, J. L. (1998). Genetic linkage to the serotonin transporter protein and 5HT2A receptor genes excluded in generalized social phobia. *Psychiatry Research, 81,* 283–291.

Stein, M. B., Goldin, P. R., Sareen, J., Zorrilla, L. T., & Brown, G. G. (2002). Increased amygdala activation to angry and contemptuous faces in generalized social phobia. *Archives of General Psychiatry, 59,* 1027–1034.

Stroop, J. R. (1935). Studies of interference in serial verbal reactions. *Journal of Experimental Psychology, 18,* 643–662.

Takahashi, L. K., & Kalin, N. H. (1999). Neural mechanisms and the development of individual differences in behavioral inhibition. In L. A. Schmidt & J. Schulkin (Eds.), *Extreme fear, shyness, and social phobia: Origins, biological mechanisms, and clinical outcomes* (pp. 91–118). London: Oxford University Press.

Tillfors, M., Furmark, T., Marteinsdottir, I., Fischer, H., Pissiota, A., Langstrom, B., et al. (2001). Cerebral blood flow in subjects with social phobia during stressful speaking tasks: a PET study. *American Journal of Psychiatry, 158,* 1220–1226.

Tillfors, M., Furmark, T., Marteinsdottir, I., & Fredrikson, M. (2002). Cerebral blood flow during anticipation of public speaking in social phobia: a PET study. *Biological Psychiatry, 52,* 1113–1119.

Tooby, J., & Cosmides, L. (1992). The psychological foundations of culture. In J. H. Barkow, L. Cosmides & J. Tooby (Eds.), *The adapted mind: Evolutionary psychology and the generation of culture* (pp. 19–136). New York: Oxford University Press.

Tuiten, A., Van Honk, J., Koppeschaar, H., Bernaards, C., Thijssen, J., & Verbaten, R. (2000). Time course of effects of testosterone administration on sexual arousal in women. *Archives of General Psychiatry, 57,* 149–153.

Turner, S. M., Beidel, D. C., & Townsley, R. M. (1990). Social phobia: Relationship to shyness. *Behaviour Research and Therapy, 28,* 497–505.

Uhde, T. W., Tancer, M. E., Gelernter, C. S., & Vittone, B. J. (1994). Normal urinary free cortisol and postdexamethasone cortisol in social phobia: comparison to normal volunteers. *Journal of Affective Disorders, 30,* 155–161.

Van Honk, J., Hermans, E. J., d'Alfonso, A. A., Schutter, D. J., van Doornen, L., & de Haan, E. H. (2002a). A left-prefrontal lateralized, sympathetic mechanism directs attention towards social threat in humans: Evidence from repetitive transcranial magnetic stimulation. *Neuroscience Letters, 319,* 99–102.

Van Honk, J., Schutter, D. J., d'Alfonso, A. A., Kessels, R. P., & de Haan, E. H. (2002b). 1 hz rTMS over the right prefrontal cortex reduces vigilant attention to unmasked but not to masked fearful faces. *Biological Psychiatry, 52,* 312–317.

Van Honk, J., Schutter, D. J. L. G., Hermans, E. J., Putman, P., Tuiten, A., & Koppeschaar, H. (2004). Testosterone shifts the balance between sensitivity for punishment and reward in healthy young women. *Psychoneuroendocrinology, 29,* 937–943.

Van Honk, J., Tuiten, A., de Haan, E., van den Hout, M., & Stam, H. (2001a). Attentional biases for angry faces: Relationships to trait anger and anxiety. *Cognition and Emotion, 15,* 279–297.

Van Honk, J., Tuiten, A., Hermans, E., Putman, P., Koppeschaar, H., Thijssen, J., et al. (2001b). A single administration of testosterone induces cardiac accelerative responses to angry faces in healthy young women. *Behavioral Neuroscience, 115,* 238–242.

Van Honk, J., Tuiten, A., van den Hout, M., Koppeschaar, H., Thijssen, J., de Haan, E., et al. (1998). Baseline salivary cortisol levels and preconscious selective attention for threat. A pilot study. *Psychoneuroendocrinology, 23,* 741–747.

Veit, R., Flor, H., Erb, M., Hermann, C., Lotze, M., Grodd, W., et al. (2002). Brain circuits involved in emotional learning in antisocial behavior and social phobia in humans. *Neuroscience Letters, 328,* 233–236.

Viau, V. (2002). Functional cross-talk between the hypothalamic-pituitary-gonadal and -adrenal axes. *Journal of Neuroendocrinology, 14,* 506–513.

Viau, V., & Meaney, M. J. (1996). The inhibitory effect of testosterone on hypothalamic-pituitary-adrenal responses to stress is mediated by the medial preoptic area. *Journal of Neuroscience, 16,* 1866–1876.

Vuilleumier, P. (2002). Facial expression and selective attention. *Current Opinion in Psychiatry, 15,* 291–300.

Wagner, J. D., Flinn, M. V., & England, B. G. (2002). Hormonal response to competition among male coalitions. *Evolution and Human Behavior, 23,* 437–442.

Whalen, P. J. (1998). Fear, vigilance, and ambiguity: Initial neuroimaging studies of the human amygdala. *Current Directions in Psychological Science, 7,* 177–188.

Williams, J. M., Mathews, A., & MacLeod, C. (1996). The emotional Stroop task and psychopathology. *Psychological Bulletin, 120,* 3–24.

COGNITIVE NEUROPSYCHIATRY
2006, 11 (3), 332–360

Cognitive neuropsychology of alexithymia: Implications for personality typology

Bob Bermond

University of Amsterdam, The Netherlands

Harrie C. M. Vorst

University of Amsterdam, The Netherlands

Peter P. Moormann

University of Leiden, The Netherlands

Introduction. We examine the cognitive neuroscience of the five components of the alexithymia syndrome, and propose a classification of alexithymia types based on psychobiological traits.
Method. Literature review.
Results. The following neural structures have been shown to be prominent in emotional function: right and left hemisphere, corpus callosum, anterior commissure, anterior cingulate, prefrontal cortex, amygdala, and insular cortex. The specific relevance of these structures to alexithymia is discussed.
Conclusions. The following conclusions and/or propositions are presented: The right hemisphere produces a global, nonverbal overview of emotional information; the left hemisphere seems dedicated to analysing emotions and higher explicit emotional cognitions. Both orbitoprefrontal cortices are important in affective aspects of alexithymia, while right temporal cortex is involved in cognitive aspects. Two subparts of anterior cingulate fulfil functions in the affective and cognitive dimensions of alexithymia. The amygdalae are involved in both cognitive and affective aspects. All structures mentioned can modulate one another. The role of interhemispheric information transfer via the corpus callosum and the anterior commissure is also discussed. The evidence that that cognitive processing of emotional information inhibits affective processing of such information is discussed in terms of its implications for a theory of alexithymia subtypes.

Correspondence should be addressed to Bob Bermond, Department of Psychology, University of Amsterdam, Roetersstraat 15, 1018 WB Amsterdam, The Netherlands; e-mail: B.Bermond@uva.nl

We are obliged to Conner Dolan, Hubert Eleonora, and Martin Elton, University of Amsterdam, for their constructive criticism, and improvement of the manuscript.

http://www.psypress.com/cogneuropsychiatry   DOI:10.1080/13546800500368607

In the late 1940s, MacLean (1949) noted that the emotional experience of many patients with psychosomatic complaints remained far below normal levels of conscious symbolic and verbal elaboration. This resulted in problems during psychoanalysis-based therapy (Groen, van der Horst, & Bastiaans, 1951; Ruesch, 1948; Sifneos, 1973b, 1975). Sifneos (1973a) introduced the term "alexithymia" (derived from the Greek *a* = lack, *lexis* = work, *thymos* = mood or emotion) for this phenomenon. Since then, alexithymia has become an established concept (Ahrens & Deffner, 1986). In the accounts of Marty and M'Uzan, (1963), Nemiah and Sifneos (1970), Nemiah (1977, 1996), and Sifneos (1973a, 1991, 2000), five aspects of alexithymia have emerged. These are reduced capacities for emotionalising (the ease by which one experiences an emotional feeling, or becomes emotionally aroused—by external or internal stimuli), fantasising, identifying emotions, verbalising emotions, and thinking about or analysing emotions. This account of alexithymia is comparable to the accounts offered by others (Hendryx, Haviland, & Shaw, 1991; Krystal, 1988; Taylor, Ryan, & Bagby, 1985; Vorst & Bermond 2001). Although genetic factors appear to be involved in alexithymia (Heiberg & Heiberg, 1977; Valera & Berebaum, 2001), it has also been suggested that alexithymia could be the result of severe trauma (Krystal, 1988), sexual assault (Albach, Moormann, & Bermond, 1996; Berenbaum, 1996; Cloitre, Scarvalone, & Difede, 1997; Sher & Twaite, 1999; Zeitlin, McNally, & Cassiday, 1993), or childhood in an emotionally dysfunctional family (Lumley, Mader, Gramzow, & Papineau, 1996; Mallinckrodt, King, & Coble, 1998). It is often assumed—although the literature is far from clear—that emotional physiological regulation systems in alexithymics are characterised by a longer duration to respond, enhanced amplitude, or higher baseline values compared to controls (Bermond, 1997). In addition, it is assumed that alexithymia is associated with an increased probability of a variety of complaints and somatic illnesses. However, here again the literature is not clear. For instance, Lundh and Simonsson-Sarnecki (2001) failed to find the expected association between alexithymia and somatic complaints in a community sample of 137 individuals. The consensus is, however, that alexithymia and somatic complaints are correlated, albeit possibly weakly (de Gucht & Heiser, 2003; Gündel, Ceballos-Baumann, & von Rad, 2000; Taylor, Bagby & Parker, 1997). The exact interpretation of this correlation also remains unclear, as it may be due to an increased tendency to seek professional help, rather than an actual increase in somatic complaints (Lumley & Norman, 1996). This would be consistent with the notion that alexithymics suffer from hypochondria, rather than from psychosomatic disorders (Papciak, Feuerstein, Belar, & Pistone, 1987; Shipko, 1982; Wise, Mann, Hryvriak, Mitchell, & Hill, 1990).

So far, two English review articles about the neuropsychology of alexithymia have appeared (Bermond 1997; Larsen et al., 2003). The aim of the present paper is to elaborate on these reviews by relating alexithymia to more neural structures, and by discussing more recent developments.

NEUROPSYCHOLOGICAL EXPLANATIONS
OF ALEXITHYMIA

Alexithymia and left hemisphere preference or right hemisphere deficiencies

Processing emotional information has been shown to take place mainly in the right hemisphere (Adolphs, Damasio, Tranel, Cooper, & Damarsis, 2000; Banich, 1997; Bear 1983; Fricchione & Howanitz, 1985; Gainotti, 1972; Gainotti, Caltagirone, & Zoccolotti, 1993; Heilman, Scholes, & Wilson, 1975; Joseph 1982, 1992a, 1992b; Kolb & Whishaw, 1990; Làdavas, Cimatti, del Pesce, & Tuozzi, 1993; Malloy & Duffy, 1994; Lane, Kivley, du Bois, Shamasundaru, & Schwarz, 1995; Ross & Rush, 1981; Tucker 1981). The right hemisphere has been implicated in regulation of the subjective emotional experience, memorising emotions, in the communication of emotions to others, and in emotional physiological responses (Dimond & Farrington, 1977; Dimond, Farrington, & Johnson, 1976; Fricchione, & Howanitz, 1985; Gainotti, 1972, 2001; Ross & Rush, 1981; Wechsler, 1973). Blair, Morris, Frith, Perrett, & Dolan (1999) demonstrated right temporal lobe activation in reaction to sad facial expressions. These results suggest that alexithymia could involve: (a) a malfunctioning of the right hemisphere: or (b) a hyperactive left hemisphere (Bear, 1983; Berenbaum & Prince, 1994; Taylor, 1984a, 1984b; Voeller, 1986; Weintraub & Mesulam, 1983). Both positions have been supported (Aftanas, Varlamov, Reva, & Pavlov, 2003; Bermond, Bleys, & Stoffels, 2004; Kano et al., 2003; Parker, Taylor & Bagby, 1992; Spalletta et al., 2001).

Conjugate lateral eye movements (CLEMs) are considered to be indicative of relative hemispheric activations. Movements to the left are considered to indicate higher right hemisphere activation, whereas movements to the right indicate a relative higher activation of the left hemisphere. Cole and Bakan (1985) and Parker et al. (1992) both registered CLEMs in alexithymics and non-alexithymics, and produced opposite results. However, Cole and Bakan measured alexithymia using the Schalling Sifneos Personality Scale (SSPS), which is considered to be lacking in reliability (Morrison & Phil, 1989; Norton, 1989; Taylor, et al., 1997). Parker et al. (1992) used both the Toronto Alexithymia Scale (TAS) and the SSPS. They found a relationship between right CLEMs (higher left hemisphere activation) and alexithymia as measured by the TAS. No such relationship was observed using the SSPS. Jessimer and Markham (1997) showed alexithymic and nonalexithymic subjects chimeric pictures of faces composed of conjoined emotive and nonemotive halves. Their results indicated that alexithymic subjects showed less leftward perceptual bias (indicating reduced right hemisphere responding) and poorer recognition of the facial expressions than nonalexithymic subjects. Lane et al. (1995), using the Levy Chimeric Faces Test (LCFT), demonstrated that greater right hemisphere dominance in processing emotional information was related to higher "emotional awareness" as measured by the Levels of Emotional Awareness Scale (LEAS). The authors' description of the scale suggests that the construct "emotional awareness" may be equivalent to "Identifying" and "Verbalising", which are subscales in the TAS and Bermond Vorst Alexithymia Questionnaire (BVAQ). This implies that scores on LEAS are correlated negatively with scores on alexithymia. Thus, the results of Lane and co-workers are consistent with the results of Jessimer and Markham (1997). Spalletta et al. (2001) measured alexithymia in stroke patients with unilateral lesions. Lesions were located in various regions: neocortical areas, subcortical areas, brainstem, and cerebellum. Despite the variety in localisation, right hemisphere lesions were found to be more strongly associated with higher TAS scores, compared to left hemisphere lesions. Kano et al. (2003) measured brain activity, using positron electron tomography (PET), in alexithymic and nonalexithymic subjects, while they were shown angry, sad, happy, and neutral faces. Compared to nonalexithymics, areas of significantly lower cerebral blood flow (rCBF) in alexithymics were located in the neocortex of the right hemisphere, while areas of higher rCBF were generally located in the neocortex of the left hemisphere. Lumley and Sielky (2000), using a finger localisation task, demonstrated that individuals, who scored high on alexithymia as measured by the TAS, made more errors in localising fingers in the left hand (right hemisphere) compared to localisation of fingers of the right hand. Finally, Bermond et al. (2004) studied alexithymic and nonalexithymic subjects, using a visual-matching task paradigm with lateralised stimuli. They demonstrated that alexithymic subjects with severe reductions in "identifying" and "verbalising" emotions process emotional words—which are presented to the right hemisphere—in their left hemisphere. In contrast, nonalexithymic subjects process such information in the right hemisphere. This effect was independent of scores on emotionalising.

A magnetic resonance imaging (MRI) study conducted by Gündel et al. (2004) found a positive correlation between alexithymia scores and the size of the right anterior cingulate (see below) in healthy (nonalexithymic) men.

In conclusion, these results, while not completely unequivocal, do support the notion that alexithymia could be associated with: (a) underfunctioning of the right hemisphere; or (b) a hyperactive left hemisphere.

Alexithymia and the corpus callosum

Various studies have indicated that verbal conscious and analytical information processing occurs predominantly in the left hemisphere, while unconscious, nonverbal and parallel holistic information processing generally takes place in the right hemisphere (Galin, 1974; Gazzaniga, 1989, 1995; Joseph, 1982, 1992a; Kalat, 1992; Kolb & Whishaw, 1990; Kupfermann, 1991; Miller, 1986; Tucker, Roth, & Bair, 1986). These findings, together with those stressing the importance of the right hemisphere for emotions, suggest that alexithymia could be related to dysfunction of the corpus callosum (Galin, 1974; Krystal, 1988; Làdavas et al., 1993; Miller, 1986). This hypothesis has been supported in research (Buchanan, Waterhouse, & West, 1980; Dewaraja & Sasaki, 1990; Ernst, Key, & Koval, 1999; Hoppe & Bogan, 1977; Houtveen, Bermond, & Elton, 1997; Lumley & Sielky, 2000; Parker, Keightley, Smith, & Taylor, 1999; TenHouten, Hoppe, & Walter 1985, 1986; Zeitlin, Lane, O'Leary, & Schrift, 1989). The corpus callosum agenesis case study of Buchanan et al. (1980) provides a clear description of all alexithymia features in a patient who received maximum score on the Beth Israel Hospital Psychosomatic Questionnaire (BIHPQ; an 8-item therapist-evaluation alexithymia scale) from three independent raters. The study of Ernst et al. (1999) is also a corpus callosum agenesis case study. Their patient showed flat affect and scored in the alexithymic range on the TAS-20. However, this patient displayed many comorbid problems [spina bifida, hydrocephalus, central sleep apnea, and hypothalamic, pituitary, pineal gland dysfunction (requiring hormone replacement therapies), and chronic pain], so that the results regarding alexithymia should be interpreted with care. The studies of Hoppe, and Bogen, and TenHouten and co-workers all concern either a group of 8 patients with corpus callosum transections, or a group of 12 such patients and their matched controls. Patients were shown a 3 minute film about the death of a baby and of a boy. The combined results clearly indicate that, compared to their matched controls, commissurotomised patients used fewer affect-laden words, and fewer adjectives in their descriptions of the film. In addition, their descriptions of the film content were more concrete, and contained more nonemotional utilitarian details. These patients also demonstrated less creativity and fantasy. Finally, all scored as alexithymic on 6 of the 8 BIHPQ items.

A role for the corpus callosum is also supported by the studies of Zeitlin et al. (1989), and Parker et al. (1999). They demonstrated that male alexithymic subjects make more mistakes in finger localisation tasks requiring callosal transfer of information. Lumley and Sielky (2000) have replicated these results, although they only found a significant relationship with "identifying emotions". Furthermore, these authors failed to find this relationship in females. Huber et al. (2002) demonstrated in a PET study that alexithymic subjects showed less activation in the corpus callosum in response to emotional stimuli compared to nonalexithymics. However, Kano et al. (2003), who also measured brain activity using PET, reported the opposite result. Although there are various methodological differences in the experiments by Kano et al. and Huber et al., the main differences concern the technique of emotion induction. Huber et al. asked their patients to remember emotional experiences (happiness, sadness, and neutral), whereas Kano et al. presented to their patients pictures of faces with emotional expressions (anger, sadness, happiness, and neutral). In essence, individuals in the latter study were passively watching, while individuals in the former were actively remembering. It is possible that passively watching requires little transfer of information from the right hemisphere to the left hemisphere (a strategy is expected in alexithymic subjects), whereas actively remembering would require more information exchange between the verbal left and emotional right hemisphere.

Some indirect support is provided by an EEG study of Aftanas et al. (2003). These authors observed in alexithymics, but not in nonalexithymics, deficient left hemisphere synchronisation in the upper theta band in response to emotional stimuli, along with excessive event-related synchronisation to emotional stimuli in the right hemisphere. Using Poffenberger's (1912) paradigm for estimating the corpus callosum transmission times, Dewaraja and Sasaki (1990) observed longer right-to-left hemisphere transfer times in alexithymic persons than in nonalexithymic subjects. Although this is remarkable, it does not explain the alexithymic features. After all, alexithymia is defined by severe reductions in the experience of various components of emotions, and the results of Dewaraja and Sasaki do not indicate that less or incorrect information is sent to the left hemisphere. Moreover, the implicit assumption in the experimental design of Dewaraja and Sasaki, namely, that the information is processed in the hemisphere where it arrives, is dubious (Bermond et al., 2004). Contralateral processing, according to the relay model of Springer and Deutsch (1993) has to be expected if the opposite hemisphere is better suited for the cognitive task involved (Banich & Karol, 1992; Gazzaniga, Ivry, & Mangun, 1998). This could explain why Grabe et al. (2004) found more or less the opposite results; shorter transcallosal conduction times in male alexithymics compared to nonalexithymic males. However, the neural coherence results of Houtveen et al. (1997) implied less information transfer from the right frontal cortex to the left hemisphere in alexithymics. In conclusion, the idea that alexithymia could be related to a "functional commissurectomy" seems fairly well supported by experimental data, although the results are not unequivocal.

Alexithymia and the anterior commissure

Bermond (1997), referring to the work of Gazzaniga and LeDoux (1978), stressed the relation between the anterior commissure and alexithymia. Gazzaniga and LeDoux (1978) elaborated on earlier work of Roger W. Sperry, in which emotion-inducing pictures were presented to the right hemisphere of split-brain (commissurectomy) patients. Although these patients could not verbalise the content of these pictures, the pictures induced emotional feelings, and the patients could verbalise the emotional significance correctly. In the study of Gazzaniga and LeDoux (1978), words were presented either to the left or the right hemisphere of subjects with corpus callosum transections. These subjects could verbalise the words, if presented to the left hemisphere, but claimed that nothing was presented if the same words were presented to the right hemisphere.

However, when asked to evaluate the emotional valence of this "nothingness", they evaluated the "unseen" words exactly like the same words if presented to the left hemisphere. According to Gazzaniga and LeDoux this indicates that the emotional-cognitive information is sent from the right to the left hemisphere by the corpus callosum, whereas the emotional value is sent to the left hemisphere over the anterior commissure. These authors further substantiated their conclusion by referring to a study by Sperry, in which emotion-inducing pictures were presented to the right hemisphere of a patient in whom both the corpus callosum and the anterior commissure were transected. Although such pictures induced emotional behavioural responses in the patient, these responses were not accompanied by concomitant affect. The explanation of Gazzaniga and LeDoux fits with results showing that the anterior commissure connects the amygdala and the paleocortical parts in both hemispheres, as well as the anterior temporal lobes, a part of the temporal lobe to which the corpus callosum does not project (Kolb & Whishaw, 1990).

Thus, alexithymia, characterised by the presence of conscious emotional cognitions, together with severe reductions in affect (emotionalising), is expected as a result of dysfunctions in the anterior commissure. To date, no studies have related the anterior commissure directly to alexithymia. The fact that most research has been done with the TAS, which does not measure emotionalising, may explain this dearth of studies.

Alexithymia and the anterior cingulate

In 1937, Papez proposed that the anterior cingulate cortex (ACC) fulfils functions in the regulation of emotions. Specifically, he proposed that emotional experience emerges in this structure. More recently, Lane and co-workers (1998) related ACC activity to conscious awareness of emotions. Paus (2001) ascribes three main functions to the ACC: motor control, cognition, and arousal/drive regulation (related to conditioned emotional learning, vocalisations associated with the expression of internal states, assessment of motivational interactions, assignment of emotional valences to internal and external stimuli, and mother-infant interactions). Referring to the "emotional" functions, Paus underlined the dopaminergic, serotonergic, and noradrenergic innervations of the ACC. Further, Paus distinguishes two subparts of the ACC: a ventral tier covering Brodmann's areas 24a and b and 25, and a dorsal tier covering 24c and 32. The ventral tier receives direct projections from the limbic system (amygdala and ventral striatum), whereas the dorsal tier receives direct projections from the hypothalamus (mediodorsal-and anterior nuclei, and midline nuclei), and indirect limbic projections via the ventral tier. Devinsky, Morrell, and Vogt (1995) and Bush, Luu, and Posner (2000) also distinguish two subparts in the anterior cingulate: an "affect" and a "cognition" component. Although they differ slightly in the assigned locations of the comparable subparts of the ACC, their descriptions overlap: ''Affect division'' [Brodmann's areas; 25, 33, and 24; (Devinsky et al., 1995); 24 a–c, 32 & 25 (Bush et al., 2000)]; 'cognition division' [caudal areas 24 and 32, (Devinsky et al., 1995) 24 b–c and 32 (Bush et al., 2000)]. The cognitive subdivision maintains strong reciprocal interconnections with lateral prefrontal cortex, parietal cortex, and premotor and supplementary motor areas. The affective subdivision, by contrast, is connected to the amygdala, periaquaductal gray, nucleus accumbens, hypothalamus, anterior insula, hippocampus, and orbitofrontal cortex, and has outflow to autonomic, visceromotor and endocrine systems. Regarding alexithymia, it is of particular importance that these two subparts of the anterior cingulate show reciprocal suppression, and that cognitive and emotional information is processed separately (Bush et al., 2000).

ACC activity has been related to mood changes, and ACC lesions have consistently been associated with change in affect (Luu & Posner, 2003). Emotional lability has been related to reduced cerebral blood flow in the ACC (Lopez et al., 2001). Changes in subjective emotional experiences and deficits in the recognition of emotional expressions have been described in patients with lesions in the anterior cingulate (Hornak et al., 2003). In a PET study, Lane et al. (1998) observed significantly increased ACC activation in response to watching emotion inducing films. Blair et al. (1999), again in a PET study, demonstrated that activation in the ACC was positively correlated to the intensity of images of faces expressing anger. Phillips et al. (2004), in a fMRI study, obtained similar results with fearful expressions. Finally, Sanfey et al. (2003) demonstrated increased cingulate activations in subjects who were angered by unfair offers made by others.

There is thus ample reason to think that the anterior cingulate plays a role in the regulation of emotions, both emotional cognitions and emotionalising. Thus, dysfunction of the ACC could be related to various features of alexithymia. Lane et al. (1998) reported positive associations between LEAS scores and cerebral blood flow in the ACC during film-induced negative emotions. As argued above, the LEAS might measure the opposite of important alexithymia features. Thus, their results suggest that alexithymia is related to less ACC activation. In line with this, Huber et al. (2002) and Kano et al. (2003), using PET, both demonstrated that alexithymics showed less activation in the anterior cingulate cortex than nonalexithymics, while looking at angry faces or during autobiographical recall of emotional situations. Berthoz et al. (2002) obtained results that are more complicated. In a functional magnetic resonance imaging (fMRI) study, they observed higher activation in alexithymics, compared to nonalexithymics, in the anterior cingulate in reactions to positive emotional pictures, and lower activation in the left anterior cingulate in alexithymics in reaction to negative emotional pictures. As Kano et al. (2003) used angry face stimuli, this suggests that reduced cingulate activation in alexithymics is limited to negative emotions. However, it is also possible that the anterior cingulate reacts specifically to angry faces, since Blair et al. (1999) registered an increase in cingulate activity in reaction to angry faces, but not in reaction to sad faces (using PET in a group of normal subjects). However, another explanation is possible. Phan, Wager, Taylor, and Liberzon (2002) published a meta-analysis on 55 PET or fMRI studies regarding emotions. The results indicated that positive emotions (happiness) result in activation in the basal ganglia, not in activation of the ACC. It is thus possible that the alexithymic subjects, in the study of Berthoz and co-workers, had difficulties in appraising the positive pictures as positive stimuli. Gündel et al. (2004) reported conflicting results. In a MRI study, they found a positive correlation between the volume of the right anterior cingulate and TAS scores. The authors explained their results by supposing that the anterior cingulate might be involved in a suppression mechanism that pushes unwanted associations out of awareness. This notion is consistent with the finding that the cognitive and emotional parts of the ACC show reciprocal inhibition (Bush et al., 2000). Given this otherwise reasonable hypothesis, one would expect an increase in ACC activation in alexithymic subjects, when they process emotional information. The studies by Huber et al. (2002), Kano et al. (2003) and Lane et al. (1998) indicated just the opposite.

In conclusion, although the literature is unequivocal regarding a role of the anterior cingulate in the regulation of emotions, the literature is far less clear concerning the relationship between the anterior cingulate and alexithymia.

Alexithymia and the prefrontal cortex

In 1947, Freeman and Watts concluded on basis of the literature that frontal lobotomy was particularly successful in patients with strong emotional complaints (Kucharski, 1984). This was unsurprising, as the intervention was originally meant to reduce emotions (Kolb & Whishaw, 1990). In 1946, Freeman introduced the transorbital method, in which mainly the medial orbitofrontal parts of the prefrontal cortex (O-PFC) were isolated from the rest of the brain. Restriction to this part of the brain turned out to be clinically more effective and also resulted in fewer adverse effects (Freeman, 1971; Livingston, 1969). Trigg (1970), who reviewed the literature, cited a great number of similar case studies. Generally before surgery, patients were preoccupied with their emotional feeling, which they experienced as overwhelming. Following the operation, the patients experienced flatness of affect and absence of spontaneous emotional reflection (Damasio, 1994; Damasio, Tranel, & Damasio, 1990; Trigg, 1970). However, the emotional cognitions remained unchanged (Trigg, 1970). Such prefrontal lesions, however, also induce a disinhibition of emotional behaviour, resulting in short periods of violent emotional behaviour (Fuster, 1989; Jarvie, 1954; Malloy & Duffy, 1994; Valenstein, 1990). Violent emotional behaviour in absence of accompanying affect has also been described in alexithymic patients (Krystal, 1988; Nemiah, Fryberger, & Sifneos, 1976). Furthermore, other work has suggested that patients with prefrontal lesions also show a reduction in facial expression and an impoverished imagination, features which have also been described in alexithymic patients (Kolb & Whishaw, 1990; Krystal, 1988; Levine & Alberts, 1948; McDonald & Prkachin, 1990; Sifneos, 1975; Taylor, Ryan, & Bagby, 1985). Moreover, deficits in the recognition of emotional expressions have been described in patients with orbitofrontal lesions (Hornak et al., 2003), and reduction in empathy has been observed in patients with ventromedial prefrontal lesions (M-PFC; covering both the O-PFC and ACC, Bechara, 2004) (Shamay-Tsoory, Tomer, Berger, & Aharon-Peretz, 2003). Furthermore, the orbitofrontal cortex has been implicated in the decoding of negative as well as positive reinforcers (Rolls, 2000), and specific O-PFC activations in reaction to emotional stimuli have also been demonstrated (Taylor, Liberzon, Decker, & Koeppe, 2002). The O-PFC has been implicated in the regulation of facial expression and emotional learning (Angrilli, Palomba, Cantagallo, Maletti, & Stegagno, 1999; O'Doherty, Kringelbach, Rolls, Hornak, & Andrews, 2001). Finally, the functional presence of PFC is not only required for emotionalising, but also for various forms of fantasising (creativity, originality, imaginative powers, mental imagery, and divergent thinking) (Damasio, 1994; Damasio & Anderson. 1993; Kolb & Whishaw, 1996).

The O-PFC projects to the hypothalamus, where orbitofrontal neurons connect with neurons projecting to the brainstem and spinal autonomic centres. It is by these connections that the O-PFC has control over primitive emotional autonomic responses (Barbas, Saha, Rempel-Clower, & Ghashghaei, 2003; Simpson et al., 2001). Further the O-PFC and the amygdala, another important neural structure in the regulation of emotions (Davidson, Jackson, & Kalin, 2000), have strong reciprocal connections (Barbas, Saha, Rempel-Clower, & Ghashghaei, 2003; Compton, 2003; Ghashghaei & Barbas, 2002), so can modulate one another.

Damasio and co-workers have also underlined the importance of the O-PFC/ M-PFC cortex in emotion regulation (e.g., Bechara, 2004; Bechara, Damasio, & Damasio 2000; Damasio, 1994, 1999; Tranel, Bechara, & Denburg, 2002). These studies stress both the reduction in emotionalising due to such lesions, and deficiencies in emotional decision making. It seems that emotional decision making is more related to emotional cognitions than emotionalising itself. This seems to conflict with older literature, which stresses that destruction of the O-PFC does not affect emotional cognitions. However, as argued above, such lesions impair spontaneous emotional reflection. This is consistent with the idea that the emotional experience forces people to reflect upon their emotions (Laird & Bressler, 1992). In other words, a dysfunctioning of the O-PFC could result in a severe reduction in emotionalising together with the presence of emotional cognitions. Such patients lack the internal drive to reflect upon their emotional cognitions. However, they will do so if stimulated by others (Damasio et al., 1990). This lack of spontaneous reflection, together with the fact that most of the patients studied by Damasio and co-workers had M-PFC lesions, could explain disrupted emotion decision making. Thus, PFC dysfunction could be related to the features "emotionalising", "fantasising", and "analysing" of alexithymia.

A few recent studies have directly addressed the relationship between the PFC and alexithymia. Aftanas et al. (2003) demonstrated that in response to emotional stimuli, alexithymics manifest a decrease in frontal left hemisphere event related potentials (ERPs) in the upper theta band in the early test period of 0–200 ms. According to the authors, this indicates a dysregulation of the appraisal of emotional stimuli. The PET study of Kano et al. (2003), demonstrated lower activations in the right O-PFC in alexithymics, compared to nonalexithymics, in reaction to negative emotional stimuli. Huber et al. (2002), also using PET, reported in alexithymics lower activations in the right frontal cortex and higher activations in the left frontal cortex during recall of autobiographic emotional experiences, results that may seem contradictory. However, there are indications that activation in one hemisphere inhibits activation in the other hemisphere, no matter the cause of the activations (Kolb & Whishaw, 1990, 1996; Sperry, Zaidel, & Zaidel, 1979). Thus, left hemisphere to right hemisphere inhibitions have occurred in the processing of emotional information, resulting in lower subjective emotional experiences and lower emotional physiological responses (Dimond & Farrington, 1977; Dimond et al., 1976). The fMRI results of Berthoz et al. (2002) are complex. They report in alexithymics less activation in the left mediofrontal cortex in reaction to highly negative emotional stimuli, but more bilateral activation in the mediofrontal cortex in reaction to positive stimuli.

In sum, although there is general agreement about the function of the PFC, especially the O-PFC/ M-PFC, in emotional experience, literature that directly relates alexithymia to the prefrontal cortex is limited and equivocal.

Alexithymia and the amygdala

Both the amygdala and the PFC receive massive projections from sensory cortices, and from higher order temporal lobe association areas specialised in processing features of stimuli and their memory. Both structures appear to have a global overview of the environment, which is probably necessary in processing and remembering emotional significance (Ghashghaei & Barbas, 2002). The amygdala also receives direct projections from the accessory olfactory bulb and thalamus. The amygdala projects to neocortical structures, and directly or indirectly to various subcortical structures involved in emotional physiological responses and emotional behaviours (hypothalamus, hippocampus, bed nucleus of the stria terminalis, preoptic area and central grey) (Baum, 2002; LeDoux, 1996, 2000; McCarthy & Becker, 2002; Young & Insel, 2002). This subcortical network may be viewed as a phylogenetically older emotion regulation system.

Various studies indicate that the amygdala is involved in detection of emotional significance of stimuli (Adams, Gordon, Baird, Ambady, & Kleck, 2003; Breiter et al., 1996; Compton, 2003; Davidson & Irwin, 1999; Gainotti et al., 1993; Ono, Nishijo, & Nishino, 2000; Phillips et al., 2003), and in recognition of emotion facial expressions (Alphonse et al., 1999; Alphonse & Tranel, 2003). Gainotti (2001) argues that external stimuli are appraised in the amygdala. In line with this, Morris, Öhman, and Dolan (1998) demonstrated that subliminally projected images of angry faces, which were not consciously perceived, resulted in a selective activation of the right amygdala. Likewise, de Gelder et al. (1999) demonstrated in a "blind-sight study" that emotional expressions of faces presented in the "blind" part of the visual field were identified correctly well above chance. These authors explained their results by stating that the "unseen" stimuli activate the amygdala via the colliculopulvinar pathway. Furthermore, Morris et al. (1996, 1998b) presented PET results indicating that amygdala activation is emotion specific, and that activations of other neural structures by the amygdala are also emotion-specific. The studies of Bar-On, Tranel, Denburg, and Bechara (2003) and Bechara, Damasio, and Damasio (2003), indicate that patients with amygdala lesions show very low levels of "emotional intelligence", and are poor in emotional decision making. In contradistinction to this, Anderson and Phelps (2002) presented results indicating that patients with unilateral and bilateral amygdala lesions report emotional feelings of normal intensities. Furthermore, Keightley et al. (2003) reported results based on fMRI-data, which indicated that the amygdala is more active during emotional processing. Taylor et al. (2002) reported similar results based on PET data. Whalen et al. (1998) reported significant fMRI modulations in the amygdala in response to emotional stimuli that were not consciously apperceived. The modulations involved increases in reaction to negative, and decreases in reaction to positive, emotional stimuli. Recently Williams, McGlone, Abbott, and Mattingley (2005) reported results indicating that the amygdala response is modulated by attention. Amygdala activation was found to increase given positive stimuli (happy faces) when subjects were asked to attend to these stimuli. The increase in amygdala activation to negative stimuli (fearful faces) was enhanced when subject did not attend to such stimuli. Finally, Phan et al. (2002) stated that glucose metabolism in the M-PFC is strongly inversely associated with metabolic rate of the amygdala. In addition, they reported that amygdala activation is attenuated during cognitive appraisal and tasks demanding higher cognitive processing, whereas the activity of the M-PFC is increased during cognitive appraisal. More complicated, but still comparable fMRI results are reported by Ochsner, Bunge, Gross, and Gabrieli (2002). Their results indicated that reappraisal of negative emotion-inducing pictures as emotionally neutral pictures results in increased activation of the lateral as well as medial PFC and decreased activation in the amygydala and orbito-PFC. Opposite results in M-PFC and O-PFC suggest that successful reappraisal-induced increase in M-PFC activity is attributable to an increase in anterior cingulate activation, whereas such reappraisal simulta-neously results in decreased activation of the orbito-PFC. As argued above, this subpart of the medial-PFC is directly linked to emotionalising or emotional feelings.

Taken together, these results are comprehensible. The amygdala mediates both emotional physiological and inborn and acquired behavioural responses (Iversen, Kupfermann, & Kandel, 2000), whereas the prefrontal cortex (O-PFC/M-PFC) is related to emotional feeling. Emotional feeling, further-more, is in some way related to emotional reflection (Buck, 1993; Dama-sio, 1999; Laird & Bressler, 1992). If the M-FPC did not inhibit the amygdala, then this phylogenetically older structure would initiate pre-programmed emotional behaviour. This would render emotional feeling and reflection purposeless. Conversely, if the emotional stimuli are of such inten-sity that an immediate behavioural response is required, emotional feeling and reflection are diversions, which should be blocked. Although reciprocal facilitations of the amygdala and medial-PFC cannot be ruled out, the main function of the connections between these structures seems to be inhibitory. Thus, very strong activations of the amygdala can result in auto-execution of preprogrammed emotional behaviour. Because the PFC is bypassed, this behaviour is accompanied neither by emotional feelings, nor by emotional reflection.

The combination of these results, furthermore, suggests that with respect to emotional experience, the amygdala is primarily involved in "implicit identi-fying emotions", and, through connections to cortical areas, also involved in "explicit identifying emotions". However, Iversen et al. (2000) stress the idea that the "emotion-identifying" modules for visual stimuli in the inferior tem-poral cortex can make the appropriate responses autonomously, and forward this information to the amygdala. This suggests that explicit (neocortical) emotional cognitions do not depend on implicit (amygdala) emotional cognitions. Fur-thermore, the amygdala is, through projections to the PFC, involved in "emo-tionalising". Thus, amygdala dysfunction could also have an effect on emotionalising, while hardly affecting explicit emotional cognitions (Alphonse & Tranel, 2003).

Surprisingly, there are almost no studies relating the amygdala directly with alexithymia. Berthoz, Ouhayoun, Perez-Diaz, Consoli, and Jouvent (2000) reported that they failed to find differences between alexithymics and nonalexithymics in amygdala activation. Likewise, Kano et al. (2003) reported the absence of such differences in subcortical structures. We pre-dict that subjects with extremely low capacities to emotionalise will show, in response to innate or conditioned emotional stimuli, strong activations in the amygdala, while subjects with extremely high capacities to emotionalise and reflect upon their emotions, will show low amygdala activations in reac-tion to such stimuli.

Insular cortex and alexithymia

Gainotti (2001) related the insula to the regulation of autonomic components of emotions. Although the exact function of the insula in emotional experience remains unclear, various studies have implicated the insular cortex in the regulation of negative emotional experiences, such as pain, distress, hunger, thirst, fear, anger, sadness, and disgust (Hennenlotter et al., 2004; Ishai, Pessoa, Bikle, & Ungernleider, 2004; Phan et al., 2002; Phillips et al., 2003; Reiman et al., 1997; Sanfey, Rilling, Aronson, Nystrom, & Cohen, 2003; Taylor, Phan, Deeker, & Koeppe, 2003), emotional decision making (Ernst et al., 2003), and the production of facial emotional expressions (Carr, Iocoboni, Dubeau, Maziotta, & Lenzi, 2003). To our knowledge, only one study has directly addressed the role of the insula in alexithymia. Kano et al. (2003) demonstrated reduced insula activations in alexithymics compared to nonalexithymics in response to angry faces.

Other neural areas and alexithymia

The two PET studies cited above (Huber et al., 2002; Kano et al., 2003) also related alexithymia to other neural structures. Kano et al. reported that alexithymics, compared to nonalexithymics, show less activation in the right inferior parietal and occipital cortices, and more activation in the left inferior parietal cortex and cerebellum (all in response to angry and sad facial expressions). Huber et al. asked subjects to recall autobiographic emotional situations. They report higher activations in alexithymics, compared to nonalexithymics, in cuneus and precuneus, thalamus (pulvinar), right inferior temporal and left superior temporal regions, and the cerebellum.

The lower activations in the right inferior parietal cortex and right occipital cortex, and higher activations in the left superior temporal regions, and left inferior parietal cortex are consistent with the idea of a left hemisphere preference in alexithymics. Further, the lower activation in the occipital cortex may be explained by assuming that alexithymics show less top-down facilitation, from higher brain centres to more primary sensory nuclei. This could be of interest for the field of alexithymia, since there are indications that feedback of sensory information from higher brain centres to more primary sensory areas is a prerequisite for conscious perception (Lamme & Roelfsema, 2000). The increased activation of the thalamus in alexithymics may indicate an increased activation of a phylogenetically older emotion regulation system, since the thalamus projects directly upon the amygdala (LeDoux, 1996). However, if this were the case, one might also expect increased activations in the amygdala, and such results have not been published. The increased activation in the right inferior cortex (Huber et al., 2002) is hard to explain in the framework of alexithymia. One could argue that right inferior temporal cortex modules involved in aspects of emotional experience (Iversen et al., 2000) are, in alexithymic subjects, not well suited for this function and, therefore, demand more neural activity and, thus, more oxygen and glucose utilisation, in order to fulfil this function properly. This is conceivable because Huber et al. forced their subjects to actively remember autobiographical emotional experiences. The cuneus, precuneus, and cerebellum have been implicated in various emotional functions in other research (concerning the (pre-)cuneus, see Fernandez et al., 2001; Gardner, Martin, & Jessel, 2000; Hennenlotter et al., 2004; Juengling et al., 2003; Kilts, Egan, Gideon, Ely, & Holtman, 2003; concerning the cerebellum, see Critchley, Elliott, Mathias, & Dolan, 2000a; Fernandez et al., 2001; Leroi et al., 2002; Paravizi, Anderson, Martin, Damasio, & Damasio, 2001; Parsons et al., 2000). Increased activation in the cuneus is of interest, as ascending pain fibres synapse here (Gardner et al., 2000). These results therefore suggest that alexithymics might experience more pain than nonalexithymics, which might relate to the increased proclivity to seek help (Lumely & Norman, 1996) and hypochondria seen in alexithymics (Papciak et al., 1987; Shipko, 1982; Wise et al. 1990). Decreased cerebellum activations have been implicated in autism and Asperger syndrome (Critchley et al., 2000b; Frith, 2004), suggesting that the cerebellum may be involved in mentalising. However, its exact function in emotional experience remains unclear.

DISCUSSION

The mass of neuropsychological work presented above leads to the following suggestions. Both orbito-prefrontal/medial-prefrontal cortices, although the right more than the left, are important in emotionalising and fantasising. Modules in the right temporal cortex (Frith, 2004) are involved in emotional cognitions, and, mainly by their connections to the O-PFC, marginally involved in emotionalizing. With respect to emotional cognitions, these neural structures, as well as the right O-PFC/M-PFC contact modules, related to consciousness and language, in the left hemisphere by the corpus callosum. With respect to "emotionalising", these structures contact modules related to consciousness and language in the left hemisphere via the anterior commissure. The two subparts of anterior cingulate have a role in emotionalising and emotional cognitions, respectively. The amygdalae are directly involved in implicit emotional cognitions. By their projections to neocortical structures, they are involved in explicit emotional cognitions. By their connections with the prefrontal cortex, they are involved in emotionalising. All structures mentioned are interconnected, so can modulate one another (Frith, 2004; Ghashghaei & Barbas, 2002; Iversen et al., 2000; Phan et al., 2002; Phillips et al., 2004). The affective subpart of the anterior cingulate is strongly connected to the O-PFC. It is therefore possible that this structure derives its role in emotionalising from its projections to the O-PFC.

In the mature brain, both the amygdala and PFC receive information on various levels of processing. Both structures control structures involved in emotional physiological responses and in emotional behavior (Barbas et al., 2003; Iversen et al., 2000), but they differ in their function in the regulation of emotions. The amygdalae can induce auto-executing of preprogrammed emotional behaviour, accompanied neither by emotional feelings, nor by emotional reflection.

With respect to emotional cognitions, the right hemisphere is strikingly incapable of making even the simplest deductions, although this hemisphere does produce a global, nonverbal overview of the emotional information. As Gazzaniga (1995) demonstrated, this hemisphere fails to make the simplest of inferences (e.g., the combination of firewood and matches may give rise to a campfire). According to Gazzaniga (1995) the human inferential system is limited to the left hemisphere: "The left hemisphere, on the other hand, is constantly, almost reflexively, labeling experiences, making inferences as to cause, and carrying out a host of other cognitive activities". Thus the left hemisphere is required in analyzing emotions, and for explicit emotional cognitions.

As argued above, there are clear indications that activation of structures involved in emotional cognition inhibit activations in structures involved in affective aspects of emotions. Reciprocal inhibitions have been demonstrated between the two hemispheres, between the two subregions of the anterior cingulate, and between amygdala and PFC. Furthermore, Keightley et al. (2003) reported increased activity in various parts of the left hemisphere (dorsal portion of the frontal lobe and parietal lobe) in subjects who were asked to indicate whether presented facial expressions were positive or negative. No such increased activity was found, when the subjects were asked to passively look at these expressions. Taylor et al. (2003) demonstrated in a PET study that the activation of brain structures involved in processing emotional information was reduced in subjects who were asked to rate of the intensities of aversive stimuli. Again, this reduction was absent when subjects were asked to passively look at the stimuli. Taylor et al. concluded: "This finding is consistent with reports showing that detached analytical appraisal of emotional stimuli can reduce both subjective and psychophysiological responses". Pessoa, Kastner, and Ungerleider (2003), in a review of the attention literature, arrived at two interesting conclusions. First, they presented results indicating that there is a ventral system, strongly lateralised to the right hemisphere, which detects behaviourally relevant stimuli and works as an alerting mechanism for the dorsal frontal attention system. This right hemisphere system is also important in emotions, because this system is involved in drawing attention to emotionally salient stimuli. Second, in the light of recent fMRI investigations, they concluded that the stimulus-evoked fMRI response is essentially absent in individuals who engage in a competing task with high attentional load.

Kolb and Whishaw (1996) described two very different personality styles in cognitive problem solving, one with a left hemisphere preference, and the other with a right hemisphere preference. The left-hemisphere-preference-type is viewed as analytical, logical, neat and tidy, interested in details, and directed to cognitive control. The right-hemisphere-preference-type is viewed as a synthesiser, interested in generalisations, with a facility to perceive a gestalt quickly, and to integrate diverse concepts into a meaningful whole.

In line with Kolb and Whishaw, and given the neuropsychological data presented above, the following four different personality types are conceivable within the broader framework of the alexithymia concept. (1) Persons characterised by a strong proclivity to activate neural modules involved in the cognitive processing of nonemotional information will inhibit the neural modules involved in "emotionalising" and the modules involved in cognitive aspects of the emotional experience. Such persons will ignore their emotions and direct their attention to other things. (2) Persons characterised by a strong proclivity to activate neural modules involved in the cognitive processing of emotional information, will inhibit the neural modules involved in "emotionalising". Such persons will mainly experience emotionally detached emotion-related cognitions. (3) Persons, with a strong proclivity to activate neural modules involved in emotionalising, will inhibit the neural modules involved in cognitive aspects of the emotional experience. Such persons will go with the flow of the emotion, and not analyse their emotions. (4) Persons, who activate modules involved in emotionalising first, and subsequently activate the cognitive-emotion-modules. Such persons will go with the flow of the emotion, and thereafter analyse their emotions.

It is conceivable that these very different ways of handling emotions develop into more or less stable personality traits, due to childhood experiences. However, genetic predispositions to one of the four types may not be ruled out (Heiberg & Heiberg, 1977; Valera & Berebaum, 2001).

Most research in the field of alexithymia has been done with the Toronto Alexithymia Scale (TAS), or later versions of TAS, the TAS-R, and TAS-20 (Bagby, Parker, & Taylor, 1994; Taylor et al., 1992, 1985). None of these scales measure "emotionalising". In addition, the TAS-R and TAS-20 do not measure "fantasising". The Bermond-Vorst Alexithymia Questionnaire (BVAQ) was developed to measures all five alexithymia features. The BVAQ has also good psychometric properties (Berthoz et al., 2000; Müller, Bühner, & Elligring, 2004; Vorst & Bermond, 2001; Zech, Luminet, Rime, & Wagner, 1999). Principal component analysis of the BVAQ subscale scores produced two uncorrelated factors: an affective dimension (involving the features emotionalising and fantasising), and a cognitive dimension (involving identifying, and verbalising emotions). The feature analysing loaded on both factors (Vorst & Bermond, 2001). These two orthogonal dimensions have now been replicated in confirmatory factor analyses in seven countries and six different languages

(Bermond et al., in press). Given the fact that the two alexithymia dimensions are orthogonal to one another, four extreme groups are conceivable. Three of these show clear, but distinct, deficits in their experience of emotions, and are designated alexithymia types 1 through 3. Type 1 is characterised by low affective and low (emotion related) cognitive capacities, Type 2 by high affective and low cognitive capacities, and type 3 by low affective and high cognitive capacities. The fourth group, characterised by high affective and high cognitive capacities, has been dubbed the lexithymic group (Vorst & Bermond, 2001; Bermond et al., in press). The characteristics of these four groups fit with those described above. It has further been demonstrated that each of these four extreme groups are clearly linked to specific other personality traits (Niessen, 2001).

The fact that the two alexithymia dimensions are orthogonal may explain the unexpected lack of correlation, observed by Lane et al. (1998), between scores on the LEAS ("identifying" and "verbalising" emotions) and the intensity of self-reported affect ("emotionalising").

Lumley et al. (1996), Mallinckrodt et al. (1998), and Fitzgerald (2003) proposed that a childhood in an emotionally dysfunctional family could result in alexithymia. This calls for an ontogenetic explanation of alexithymia. The amygdala and anterior commissure are functional very early in life, the neocortex matures later, while the prefrontal cortex and corpus callosum are fully matured only towards the end of adolescence, as is the case for the higher socio-emotional-cognitive capacities (Kolb & Whishaw, 1990, 1996). Thus, in the infant brain emotions are regulated only by the amygdalae and other subcortical structures that receive direct or indirect amygdala projections. Subsequent emotional development depends mainly upon the maturation rate of the functions of the PFC and the corpus callosum. However, our knowledge of the maturation rates of these structures with regard to emotional functions is very limited. Given the principle of fixation, it is possible that, due to childhood experiences, the two components of the system regulating the emotional experience become fixated at various stages of maturity, resulting in the four extreme groups mentioned above, and in various intermediate personality types. This idea is supported by studies concerning brain plasticity during early childhood. Davidson, Jackson, and Kalin (2000) state: "Some of the most impressive evidence for brain plasticity is emotional learning (LeDoux, 1996). Plasticity in the neural circuitry underlying emotion is also likely to play an important role in understanding the impact of early environmental factors in influencing later individual differences and risk for psychopathology". These authors refer to studies in Long Evans rats, which can show two styles of maternal care, which are denoted high licking/grooming and low licking/grooming. These maternal styles are not genetically preprogrammed, but transmitted to the next generation on the basis of the received amount of licking during childhood (Francis, Dorio, Liu, & Meaney, 1999). Pups that have received low levels of licking are more fearful and more stress-responsive in adulthood. As adults they also show neurobiological changes, which explain the increased stress responsiveness. This includes higher levels of ACTH and glucocorticoids in response to acute stress, decreased glucocorticoid feedback sensitivity and increased levels of hypothalamic ACTH-RH mRNA expression (Liu & Dirio, 1997), fewer benzodiazepine receptors in various subnuclei of the amygdala and the locus coeruleus, increased ACTH-RH receptor densities in the locus coeruleus, (suggesting enhanced hormonal stress responses), and less GABA inhibition of emotions (especially fear; Caldji et al., 1988). Comparable effects, including unstable physiological stress mechanisms (high variability in heart and respiratory rates, high blood pressure, and high cortisol levels in response to stress), have been reported in adult male rhesus monkeys of low-ranking mothers. This also suggests that these males experience more stress during their lives (Nelson, 1995). Finally, the combination of high levels of ACTH-RH and adrenal androgens with low levels of cortisol during development, as in humans with congenital adrenal hyperplasia, has been shown to result in significantly smaller amygdalae (Merke et al., 2003). It is of interest here that enhanced glucocorticoid levels have been shown to result in enhanced right hemisphere frontal activity, and greater negative affect (Schmidt, Fox, Goldberg, Smith, & Schulkin, 1999). This suggests that subjects with highly responsive adrenal cortices (as described above) will, in their reaction to emotional stimuli, show more emotionalising, more right hemisphere activation, and thus less left hemisphere activation.

These results illustrate that differences in early childhood experiences may have far-reaching consequences, leading to life long changes in the functioning of the central nervous system, and the formation of stable, neurologically based, personality traits. This idea is shared by other authors, including Joseph (1999), who states: "Deprived or abnormal rearing conditions induce severe disturbance in all aspects of social and emotional functioning, and effect the growth and survival of dendrites, axons, synapses, interneurons, neurons, and glia". The study of the influences of early (neurophysiological) stress responses upon the ontogeny of the affective and cognitive alexithymia dimensions will advance our understanding of alexithymia greatly.

In summary, neuropsychological data suggest that modules involved in emotionalising and modules involved in emotional cognitions tend to inhibit one another. Furthermore, modules involved in processing nonemotional information tend to inhibit both these emotion modules. On the basis of this, four extreme ways of managing emotions are conceivable. (1) Activating only neural modules involved in the cognitive processing of nonemotional information, which would result in negation of the emotions. (2) Activating only neural modules involved in the cognitive processing of emotional information, which would result in emotionally detached emotion-related cognitions. (3) Activating only neural modules involved in emotionalising, which would result in intense emotional feelings that are not accompanied by emotional cognitions. (4) Full-blown activation of neural modules involved in emotionalising, followed by a full-blown activation of neural modules involved in the cognitive processing of emotional information. Persons characterised by this fourth strategy, will first go with the flow of the emotion, and only thereafter analyse their emotions. Recently, it was demonstrated that second order factor analyses of BVAQ scores resulted in two independent factors: an affective alexithymia dimension and a cognitive alexithymia dimension. This is thus compatible with the notion of four extreme groups. The characteristics of the four extreme groups based upon the two alexithymia dimensions (low affective + low cognitive; low affective + high cognitive; high affective + low cognitive; high affective + high cognitive) are consistent with the groups described above. Finally, it has also been demonstrated that these four extreme groups are each clearly linked to specific other personality traits. We therefore believe that the two alexithymia dimensions may form the foundation of other personality traits.

REFERENCES

Adams, R. B., Gordon, H. L., Baird, A. A., Ambady, N., & Kleck, R. E. (2003). Effects of gaze on amygdala sensitivity to anger and fear faces. *Science, 300,* 1536.

Adolphs, R., Damasio, H., Tranel, D., Cooper, G., & Damasio, A. R. (2000). A role for somatosensory cortices in the visual recognition of emotion as revealed by three-dimensional lesion mapping. *Journal of Neuroscience, 20,* 2683–2690.

Aftanas, L. I., Varlamov, A. A., Reva, N. V., & Pavlov, S. V. (2003). Disruption of early event-related theta synchronization of human EEG in alexithymics viewing affective pictures. *Neuroscience Letters, 340,* 57–60.

Ahrens, S., & Deffner, G. (1986). Empirical study of alexithymia: Methodology and results. *American Journal of Psychotherapy, 40,* 430–447.

Albach, F. Moormann, P. P., & Bermond, B. (1996). Memory recovery of childhood sexual abuse. *Dissociation, IX,* 258–269.

Alphonse, R., & Tranel, D. (2003). Amygdala damage impairs emotion recognition from scenes only when they contain facial expressions. *Neuropsychologia, 41,* 1281–1289.

Alphonse, R., Tranel, D., Hamann, S., Young, A. W., Calder, A. J. Phelps, et al. (1999). Recognition of facial emotion in nine individuals with bilateral amygdala damage. *Neuropsychologia, 37,* 1111–1117.

Anderson, A. K., and Phelps, E. A. (2002). Is the human amygdala critical for the subjective experience of emotion? Evidence of intact dispositional affect in patients with amygdala lesions. *Journal of Cognitive Neuroscience, 14,* 709–720.

Angrilli, A., Palomba, D., Cantagallo, A., Maietti, A. & Stegagno, L. (1999). Emotional impairment after right orbitofrontal lesion in a patient without cognitive deficits. *Neuroreport, 10,* 1741–1746.

Bagby, R. M., Parker, J. D. A., & Taylor, G. J. (1994). The twenty-item Toronto Alexithymia Scale-I. Item selection and cross-validation of the factor structure. *Journal of Psychosomatic Research, 38,* 23–32.

Banich, M. T. (1997). *Neuropsychology: The neural bases of mental functioning.* Boston: Houghton Mifflin.

Banich, M. T., & Karol, D. L. (1992). The sum of the parts does not equal the whole: Evidence from bihemispheric processing. *Journal of Experimental Psychology: Human Perception and Performance, 18,* 763–784.

Barbas, H., Saha, S., Rempel-Clower, N., & Ghashghaei, T. (2003). Serial pathways from primate prefrontal cortex to autonomic areas may influence emotional expression. MBC *Neuroscience, 4,* 25–35.

Bar-On, R., Tranel, D., Denburg, N. L., & Bechara, A. (2003). Exploring the neurological substrate of emotional and social intelligence. *Brain, 1261, 190–800.*

Baum, M. (2002). Neuroendocrinology of sexual behavior in the male. In J. B. Becker, M. Breedlove, C. Crews, & M. M. McCarthy (Eds.), *Behavioral endoctrinology* (2nd ed.). Cambridge, MA: MIT Press.

Bear, D. M. (1983). Hemispheric specialization and the neurology of emotion. *Archives of Neurology, 40,* 195–202.

Bechara, A. (2004). The role of emotion in decision-making: Evidence from neurological patients with orbitofrontal damage. *Brain and Cognition, 55,* 30–40.

Bechara, A., Damasio, H., & Damasio, A. R. (2000). Emotion, decision making and the orbitofrontal cortex. *Cerebral Cortex, 10,* 295–307.

Bechara, A., Damasio, H.., & Damasio, A. R. (2003). Role of the amygdala in decision-making. *Annals of the New York Academy of Sciences, 985,* 356–369.

Berenbaum, H. (1996). Childhood abuse, alexithymia and personality disorder. *Journal of Psychosomatic Research, 41,* 585–595.

Berenbaum, H., & Prince, J. D. (1994). Alexithymia and the interpretation of emotion-relevant information. *Cognition and Emotion, 8,* 231–244.

Bermond, B. (1997). Brain and alexithymia. In A. Vingerhoets, F. van Bussen, & J. Boelhouwers (Eds.). *The (non) expression of emotion in health and disease.* Tilburg, The Netherlands: Tilburg University Press.

Bermond, B., Bleys, J. W., & Stoffels, E. J. (2004). Left hemispheric preference and alexithymia: A neuropsychological investigation. *Cognition and Emotion, 19,* 151–160.

Bermond, B., Clayton, K., Liberova, A., Luminet, O., Maruszewski, T., Ricci Bitti, et al. (in press). A cognitive and an affective dimension of alexithymia in six languages and seven populations. *Cognition and Emotion.*

Berthoz , E., Artiges, P. F., van de Moortele, P. F., Poline, J. B., Rouquette, S., Consoli, S. M., et al. (2002). Effect of impaired recognition and expression of emotions on frontocingulate cortices: An fMRI study of men with alexithymia. *American Journal of Psychiatry, 159,* 961–967.

Berthoz, S., Ouhayoun, B., Perez-Dias, F., Consoli, S. M., & Jouvent, R. (2000). Comparison of the psychometric properties of two self-report questionnaires measuring alexithymia: Confirmation of the 20-item Toronto Alexithymia Scale and the Bermond-Vorst-Alexithymia Questionnaire. *Revue Européenne de Psychologie Appliquée, 50,* 359–368.

Blair, R. J. R., Moris, J. S., Frith, C. D., Perrett, D. I., & Dolan, R. J. (1999). Dissociable neural responses to facial expressions of sadness and anger. *Brain, 122,* 883–893.

Breiter, H. C. Etcoff, N. L., Whalen, P. J., Kennedy, W. A., Rauch, H. C., Buckner, R. L., et al. (1996). Response and habituation of the human amygdala during visual processing of facial expression. *Neuron, 17,* 875–887.

Buchanan, D. C., Waterhouse, G. J., & West, S. Jr. (1980). A proposed physiological basis of alexithymia. *Psychotherapy and Psychosomatics, 34,* 48–255.

Buck, R. (1993). What is this thing called subjective experience? Reflections on the neuropsychology of qualia. *Neuropsychology, 7,* 490–499.

Bush, G., Luu, P., & Posner, M. (2000). Cognitive and emotional influences in anterior cingulate cortex. *Trends in Cognitive Neurosciences, 4,* 215–222.

Caldji, C., Tannenbaum, B., Sharma, S., Francis, D., Plotsky, P. M., & Meaney, M. J. (1998). Maternal care during infancy regulates the development of neural systems mediating the expression of fearfulness in the rat. *Proceedings of the National Academy of Sciences of the USA, 95*, 5335–5340.

Carr, L., Iacoboni, M., Dubeau, M. C., Maziotta, J. C., & Lenzi, G. L. (2003). Neural mechanisms of empathy in humans: A relay from neural systems for imitation to limbic areas. *Proceedings of the National Academy of Sciences of the USA, 100*, 5497–5502.

Cloitre, M., Scarvalone, P., & Difede, J. (1997). Posttraumatic stress disorder, self-and interpersonal dysfunction among sexually retraumatized women. *Journal of Traumatic Stress, 10*, 437–425.

Cole, G., & Bakan, P. (1985). Alexithymia, hemispericity, and conjugate lateral eye movements. *Psychotherapy and Psychosomatics, 44*, 139–143.

Compton, R. J. (2003). The interface between emotion and attention: A review of evidence from psychology and neuroscience. *Behavioral and Cognitive Neuroscience Reviews, 2*, 115–129.

Critchley, H. D., Daly, E. M., Bullmore, E. D., Williams, S. C. R. van Amelsvoort, T., Robertson, D. M. et al. (2000b). The functional neuroanatomy of social behavior: Changes in cerebral blood flow in people with autistic disorder process facial expression. *Brain, 123*, 2203–2212.

Critchley, H. D., Elliott, R., Mathias, C. J., & Dolan, R. J. (2000a). Neural activity relating to generation and representation of galvanic skin conductance responses: A functional magnetic resonance imaging study. *Journal of Neuroscience, 20*, 3033–3040.

Damasio, A. R. (1994). *Descartes error*. New York: Putnams.

Damasio, A. R. (1999). *The feeling of what happens: Body, emotion and the making of consciousness*. London: Heinemann.

Damasio, A. R., & Anderson, S. W. (1993). The frontal lobes. In K. Heilman & E. Valenstein (Eds.), *Clinical neuropsychology* (3rd ed., pp. 410–460). New York: Oxford University Press.

Damasio, A. R., Tranel, D., & Damasio, H. (1990). Individuals with sociopathic behavior caused by frontal damage fail to respond autonomically to social stimuli. *Behavioural Brain Research, 41*, 81–94.

Davidson, R. J., & Irwin, W. (1999). The functional neuroanatomy of emotion and affective style. *Trends in Cognitive Science, 3*, 11–21.

Davidson, R. J., Jackson, D. C., & Kalin, N. H. (2000). Emotion, plasticity, context, and regulation: Perspectives from affective neuroscience. *Psychological Bulletin, 126*, 890–809.

de Gelder, B., Vroomen, J., Pourtois, G., & Weiskrantz, L. (1999). Non-conscious recognition of affect in the absence of striate cortex. *Neuroreport, 10*, 3759–63.

De Gucht, V., & Heiser, W. (2003). Alexithymia and somatisation. A quantitative review of the literature. *Journal of Psychosomatic Research, 54*, 425–434.

Devinsky, O., Morrell, M. J., & Vogt, B. A. (1995). Contributions of anterior cingulated cortex to behaviour. *Brain, 118*, 279–306.

Dewaraja, R., & Sasaki, Y. (1990). A left to right hemisphere callosal transfer deficit of nonlinguistic information in alexithymia. *Psychotherapy and Psychosomatics, 54*, 201–207.

Dimond, S. J., & Farrington, L. (1977). Emotional response to films shown to the right or left hemisphere of the brain measured by heart rate. *Acta Psychologia, 41*, 255–260.

Dimond, S. J., Farrington, L., & Johnson, P. (1976). Differing emotional response from right and left hemispheres. *Nature, 261*, 690–692.

Ernst, H., Key, J. D., & Koval. M. S. (1999). Alexithymia in an adolescent with agenesis of the corpus callosum and chronic pain. *Journal of the American Academy of Child and Adolescence Psychiatry, 38*, 1212–1213.

Ernst, M., Kimes, A. S., London, E. D., Matochik, J. A., Eldreth, D., Tata, S., et al. (2003). Neural substrates of decision making in adults with attention deficit hyperactivity disorder. *American Journal of Psychiatry, 160*, 1061–1070.

Fernandez, M., Pissota, A., Frans, Ö., von Knorring, L., Fischer, H., & Fredrikson, M. (2001). Brain function in a patient with torture related post-traumatic stress disorder before and after fluoxetine treatment: A positron emission tomography provocation study. *Neuroscience Letters, 297*, 101–104.

Fitzgerald, M. (2003). Responses to "features of alexithymia or features of Asperger's syndrome?" by M. Corcos. *European Child and Adolescent Psychiatry*, *12*(Suppl. 2), 15–16.

Francis, D., Diorio, J., Liu, D., & Meaney, M. J. (1999). Nongenomic transmission across generations of maternal behavior and stress responses in the rat. *Science*, *286*, 1155–1158.

Freeman, W. (1971), Frontal lobotomy in early schizophrenia. *British Journal of Psychiatry*, *119*, 621–624.

Fricchione, G., & Howanitz, E. (1985), Aprosodia and alexithymia: A case report. *Psychotherapy and Psychosomatics*, *43*, 156–160.

Frith, U. (2004). Emanuel Miller lecture: Confusions and controversies about Asperger syndrome. *Journal of Child Psychology and Psychiatry*, *45*, 672–688.

Fuster, J. M. (1989). *The prefrontal cortex: Anatomy, physiology and neuropsychology of the prefrontal lobe*. Raven.

Gainotti, G. (1972). Emotional behavior and hemispheric side of the lesion. *Cortex*, *8*, 51–55.

Gainotti G. (2001). Disorders of emotional behaviour. *Journal of Neurology*, *248*, 743–749.

Gainotti, G., Caltagirone, C., & Zoccolotti, P. (1993). Left/right and cortical/subcortical dichotomies in the neuropsychological study of human emotions. *Cognition and Emotion*, *7*, 71–93.

Galin, D. (1974). Implications for psychiatry of left and right cerebral specialization: A neurophysiological context for unconscious processes. *Archives of General Psychiatry*, *31*, 572–583.

Gardner, P. Martin, J. H., & Jessel, T. M. (2000). The bodily senses. In R. Kandel, J. H. Schwartz, & T. M. Jessel (Eds.). *Principles of neural science* (4th ed.). New York: McGraw-Hill.

Gazzaniga, M. S. (1989). Organization of the human brain. *Science*, *245*, 947–952.

Gazzaniga, M. S. (1995). Consciousness and the cerebral hemispheres. In M. S. Gazzaniga (Ed.), *The cognitive neurosciences* (pp. 1391–1401). Cambridge, MA: MIT Press.

Gazzaniga, M. S., Ivry, R. B., & Mangun, G. R. (1998). *Cognitive neuroscience: The biology of the mind*. New York: Norton.

Gazzaniga, M., & LeDoux, J. E. (1978). *The integrated mind*. New York: Plenum.

Ghashghaei, H. T., & Barbas, H. (2002). Pathways for emotion: Interactions of prefrontal and anterior temporal pathways in the amygdala of the rhesus monkey. *Neuroscience*, *115*, 1261–1279.

Grabe, H. J., Moller, B., Willert, C., Spitzer, C., Rizos, T., & Freyberger, H. J. (2004). Interhemispheric transfer in alexithymia: A transcallosal inhibition study. *Psychotherapy and Psychosomatics*, *73*, 117–123.

Groen, J. .J., van der Horst, L., & Bastiaans, J. (1951*). Grondslagen der Klinische Psychosomatiek*. Haarlem, The Netherlands: De Erven F. Bohn.

Gündel, H., Ceballos-Baumann, A. O., & von Rad, M. (2000). Aktuelle Perspektiven der Alexithymie. *Nervenarzt*, *71*, 151–163.

Gündel, H., Lopez-Sala, A., Ceballos-Baumann, A. O., Deus, J., Cardoner, N., Marten-Mittag, B., et al. (2004). Alexithymia correlates with the size of the right anterior cingulate. *Psychosomatic Medicine*, *66*, 132–140.

Heiberg, A., & Heiberg, A. (1977). Alexithymia: An inherited trait? *Psychotherapy and Psychosomatics*, *28*, 221–225.

Heilman, K. L., Scholes, R., & Wilson, R. T. (1975). Auditory affective agnosia: Disturbed comprehension of affective speech. *Journal of Neurology Neurosurgery and Psychiatry*, *38*, 69–72.

Hendryx, M. S., Haviland, M. G., & Shaw, D. G. (1991). Dimensions of alexithymia and their relationships to anxiety and depression. *Journal of Personality Assessment*, *56*, 227–237.

Hennenlotter, A., Schroeder, U., Erhard, P., Haslinger, B., Stahl, R., Weindl, A., et al. (2004). Neural correlate associated with impaired disgust processing in pre-symptomatic Huntington's disease. *Brain*, *127*, 1446–1453.

Hoppe, K. D., & Bogen, J. E. (1977). Alexithymia in twelve commisurotomized patients. *Psychotherapy and Psychosomatics*, *28*, 148–155.

Hornak, J., Bramham, J., Rolls, E. T., Morris, R. G., O'Doherty, J., Bullock, P. R., et al. (2003). Changes in emotion after circumscribed surgical lesions of the orbitofrontal and cingulate cortices. *Brain, 126*, 1691–1712.

Houtveen, J. H., Bermond, B., & Elton, M. R. (1997). Alexithymia: A disruption in a cortical network? An EEG power and coherence analysis. *Journal of Psychophysiology, 11*, 147–157.

Huber, M., Herholz, K., Habedank, B., Thiel, A., Muller-Kuppers, M., Ebel, H., et al. (2002). Differente Muster regionaler Hirnaktivität nach emotionaler Stimulation bei alexithymen Patienten im Vergleich zu Normalpersonen: Eine positronenemissionstomographische (PET-) Studie mit ^{15}O-H$_2$-O und emotionaler Stimulierung durch autobiografische Erinnerung. *Psychotherapie Psychosomatik und Medizinische Psychologie, 52*, 469–478.

Ishai, A., Pessoa, L., Bikle, P. C., & Ungernleider, L. G. (2004). Repetition suppression of faces is modulated by emotion. *Proceedings of the National Academy of Sciences of the USA, 101*, 9827–9832.

Iversen, S., Kupfermann, I., & Kandel, E. R. (2000). Emotional states and feelings. In E. R. Kandel, J. H. Schwartz, & T. M. Jessel (Eds.), *Principles of neural science* (4th ed., pp. 982–998). McGraw-Hill: New York.

Jarvie, H. F. (1954). Frontal lobe wounds causing disinhibition. *Journal of Neurology Neurosurgery and Psychiatry, 17*, 14–32.

Jessimer, M., & Markham, R. (1997). Alexithymia: A right hemisphere dysfunction specific to recognition of certain facial expressions? *Brain and Cognition, 34*, 246–258.

Joseph, R. (1982). The neuropsychology of development: Hemispheric laterality, limbic language, and the origin of thought. *Journal of Clinical Psychology, 38*, 4–33.

Joseph, R. (1992a). *The right brain and the unconscious: Discovering the stranger within.* Plenum: New York.

Joseph, R. (1992b). The limbic system: Emotion, laterality, and unconscious mind. *Psychoanalytic Review, 79*, 405–456.

Joseph, R. (1999). Environmental influences on neural plasticity, the limbic system, emotional development and attachment: A review. *Child Psychiatry Human Development, 29*, 189–208.

Juengling, F. D., Schmahl, C., Hesslinger, B., Ebert, D., Bremner, J. D., Gostomzyk, J., et al. (2003). Positron emission tomography in female patients with borderline personality disorder. *Journal of Psychiatric Research, 37*, 109–115.

Kalat, J. W. (1992), *Biological psychology.* Belmont, CA: Wadsworth.

Kano, M., Fukudo, S., Gyoba, J., Kamachi, M., Tagawa, M., Mochizuki, H., et al. (2003). Specific brain processing of facial expressions in people with alexithymia: An H$_2$ ^{15}O-PET study. *Brain, 126*, 1474–84.

Keightley, M. L. Winocur, G., Graham, S. J., Mayberg, H. S., Hevenor, S. J., & Grady, C. L. (2003). An fMRI study investigating cognitive modulation of brain regions associated with emotional processing of visual stimuli. *Neuropsychologia, 41*, 585–596.

Kilts, C., Egan, G., Gideon, D. A., Ely, T. D., & Hoffman, J. M. (2003). Dissociable neural pathways are involved in the recognition of emotion in static and dynamic facial expressions. *NeuroImage, 18*, 156–168.

Kolb, B., & Whishaw, I. Q. (1990). *Fundamentals of human neuropsychology* (3rd ed.). New York: Freeman.

Kolb, B., & Whishaw, I. Q. (1996). *Fundamentals of human neuropsychology* (4th ed.), New York: Freeman.

Krystal, H. (1988). Alexithymia. In H. Krystal, (Ed.), *Integration and self-healing: Affect – trauma – alexithymia* (pp. 242–286). Mahwah, NJ: Analytic Press.

Kucharski, A. (1984). History of frontal lobotomy in the U.S., 1935–1955. *Neurosurgery, 14*, 765–772.

Kupfermann, I. (1991). Localization of higher cognitive and affective functions: The association cortices. In E. R. Kandel, J. H. Schwartz & T. M. Jessell (Eds.), *Principles of neural science* (3rd ed., pp. 823–839). Amsterdam: Elsevier.

Làdavas, E., Cimatti, D., del Pesce, M., & Tuozzi, G. (1993). Emotional evaluation with and without conscious stimulus identification: Evidence from a split-brain patient. *Cognition and Emotion, 7,* 95–114.

Laird, J. D., & Bresler, C. (1992). The process of emotional experience: A self-perception theory. In (M. S. Clarke (ed.), *Emotion review of personality and social psychology* (Vol. 13, pp. 213–234. Sage.

Lamme, V. A. F., & Roelfsema, P. R. (2000). The distinct modes of vision offered by feed forward and recurrent processing. *Trends in Neuroscience, 23,* 571–579.

Lane, R. D., Kivley, L. S., du Bois, A., Shamasundara, P., & Schwartz, G. E. (1995). Levels of emotional awareness and the degree of right hemisphere dominance in the perception of facial emotion. *Neurospychologia, 33,* 525–538.

Lane, R. D., Reiman, E. M., Axelrod, B., Lang-Sheng, Y., Holmes, A., & Schwartz, G. E. (1998). Neural correlates of levels of emotional awareness: Evidence of an interaction between emotion and attention in the anterior cingulate cortex. *Journal of Cognitive Neuroscience, 10,* 525–535.

Larsen, J. K., Brand, N., Bermond, B., & Hijman, R. (2003). Cognitive and emotional characteristics of alexithymia: A review of neurobiological studies. *Journal of Psychosomatic Research, 54,* 533–41.

LeDoux, J. (1996). *The emotional brain: The mysterious underpinnings of emotional life.* New York: Simon & Schuster.

LeDoux, J. (2000). Emotion circuits in the brain. *Annual Review of Neuroscience, 23,* 155–184.

Leroi, I., O'Hearn, E., Marsh, L., Lyketsos, C. G., Rosenblatt, A., Ross, C. A., et al. (2002). Psychopathology in patients with degenerative cerebellar disease: A comparison to Huntington's disease. *American Journal of Psychiatry, 159,* 1306–1314.

Levine, J., & Albert, H. (1948). Sexual behavior after lobotomy. *Society Proceedings of the Boston Society of Psychiatry and Neurology,* 18 November 1948, pp. 166–168.

Liu, D., & Diorio, J. (1997). Maternal care, hippocampal glucocorticoïd receptors, and Hypothalamic-pituitary-adrenal responses to stress. *Science, 277,* 1659–1663.

Livingston, K. F. (1969). The frontal lobes revisited. *Archives of Neurology, 20,* 90–95.

Lopez, O. L., Zivkovic, S., Smith, G., Becker, J. T., Meltzer, C. C., & DeKosky, S. T. (2001). Psychiatric symptoms associated with cortical-subcortical dysfunction in Alzheimer's disease. *Journal of Neuropsychiatry and Clinical Neuroscience, 13,* 56–60.

Lumley, M., Mader, C., Gramzow, J., & Papineau, K. (1996). Family factors related to alexithymia characteristics. *Psychosomatic Medicine, 58,* 211–216.

Lumley, M., & Norman, S. (1996). Alexithymia and health care utilization. *Psychosomatic Medicine, 58,* 197–202.

Lumley, M. A., & Sielky, K. (2000). Alexithymia, gender, and hemispheric functioning. *Comprehensive Psychiatry, 41,* 352–359.

Lundh, L. G., & Simonsson-Sarnecki, M. (2001). Alexithymia, emotion, and somatic complaints. *Journal of Personality, 69,* 483–510.

Luu, P., & Posner, M. I. (2003). Anterior cingulate cortex regulation of sympathetic activity. *Brain, 126,* 2119–2120.

MacLean, P. D. (1949). Psychosomatic disease and the "visceral brain". *Psychosomatic Medicine, 11,* 338–353.

Mallinckrodt, B., King, J. L., & Coble, H. M. (1998). Family dysfunction, alexithymia, and client attachment to therapist. *Journal of Counseling Psychology, 45,* 497–504.

Malloy, P., & Duffy, J. (1994). The frontal lobes in neuropsychiatric disorders. In F. Boller & J. Grafman (Eds.), *Handbook of neuropsychology* (Vol. 9, pp. 203–232). Amsterdam: Elsevier.

Marty, P., & M'Uzan, M. (1963). La pensé opératoire. *Revue Française de Psychanalyse, 27* (Suppl. XXIIIe Congrès des psychanalystes de langues romanes, Barcelone, Juni 1962), 345–356.

McCarthy, M. M., & Becker, J. (2002). Neuroendorinology of sexual behavior in the female. In J. B. Becker, M. Breedlove, C. Crews, & M. M. McCarthy (Eds.). *Behavioral endocrinology* (2nd ed., pp. 117–153). Cambridge, MA: MIT Press.

McDonald, P. W., & Prkachin, K. M. (1990), The expression and perception of facial emotion in alexithymia: A pilot study. *Psychosomatic Medicine, 52*, 199–210.

Merke, D. P., Fields, J. D., Keil, M. F., Vaituzis, A. C., Chrousos, G. P., & Giedd, J. N. (2003). Children with classic congenital adrenal hyperplasia have decreased amygdala volume: Potential prenatal and postnatal hormonal effects. *Journal of Clinical Endocrinology and Metabolism, 88*, 1760–1765.

Miller, L. (1986). Is alexithymia a disconnection syndrome? A neuropsychological perspective. *International Journal of Psychiatry in Medicine, 16*, 199–209.

Morris, J. S. Friston, K. J. Büchel, C. Frith, C. D. Young, A. W. Calder, A. J., et al. (1998b). A neuromodulatory role for the human amygdala in processing emotional facial expressions. *Brain, 121*, 47–57.

Morris, J. S., Frith, C. D., Perrett, D. I., Young, A. W., Calder. A. J., & Dolan, R. J. (1996). A differential response in human amygdala to fearful and happy facial expressions. *Nature, 383*, 812–815.

Morris, J. S., Öhman, A., & Dolan, R. J. (1998). Conscious and nonconscious emotion learning in the human amygdala. *Nature, 393*, 467–470.

Morrison, S. L., & Phil, R. O. (1989). Psychometrics of the Schalling-Sifneos and Toronto alexithymia scales. *Psychotherapy and Psychosomatics, 51*, 83–90.

Müller, J., Bühner, M., & Elligring, H. (2004). The assessment of alexithymia: Psychometric properties and validity of the Bermond-Vorst Alexithymia questionnaire. *Personality and Individual Differences, 37*, 373–391.

Nelson, R. J. (1995). *An introduction to behavioral endocrinology*. Sunderland, MA: Sinauer Associates.

Nemiah, J. C. (1977). Alexithymia: Theoretical considerations. *Psychotherapy and Psychosomatics, 28*, 199–206.

Nemiah, J. C. (1996). Alexithymia: Present, past and future? *Psychosomatic Medicine, 58*, 217–218.

Nemiah, J. C., Fryberger, H., & Sifneos, P. E. (1976). Alexithymia: A view of the psychosomatic process. In O. W. Hill (Ed.), *Modern trends in medicine* (Vol. 3, pp. 430–440). London: Butterworth.

Nemiah, J. C., & Sifneos, P. E. (1970). Psychosomatic illness: A problem in communication. *Psychotherapy and Psychosomatics, 18*, 154–160.

Niessen, M. A. J. (2001). *Emotionaliteit en cognitieve gevoelscontrole als invloedrijke factoren in persoonlijkheid; Het alexithymia construct nader onderzocht.* [Emotionalizing and cognitive control over feelings as important factors in personality traits: The alexithymia construct revisited.] Unpublished master's thesis University of Amsterdam, The Netherlands.

Norton, N. C. (1989). Three scales of alexithymia: Do they measure the same thing? *Journal of Personality Assessment, 53*, 621–637.

Ochsner, K. N., Bunge, S. A., Gross, J. J., & Gabrieli, J. D. E. (2002). Rethinking feelings: An fMRI study of the cognitive regulation of emotion. *Journal of Cognitive Neuroscience, 14*, 1215–1229.

O'Doherty, J., Kringelbach, M. L., Rolls, E. T., Hornak, J., & Andrews, C. (2001). Reward and punishment representations in the human orbitofrontal cortex. *Nature Neuroscience, 4*, 95–12.

Ono, T., Nishijo, H., & Nishino, H. (2000). Functional role of the limbic system and basal ganglia in motivated behaviors. *Journal of Neurology, 247*(Suppl. 5), V23–32.

Papciak, A. S., Feuerstein, M., Belar, C. D., & Pistone, L. (1987). Alexithymia and pain in an outpatient behavioral medicine clinic. *International Journal of Psychiatry in Medicine, 16*, 347–357.

Papez, J. W. (1937). A proposed mechanism of emotion. *Archives of Neurological Psychiatry, 38,* 725–743.

Paravizi, J., Anderson, S. W., Martin, C. O., Damasio, H., & Damasio, A. R. (2001). Pathological laughter and crying. *Brain, 124,* 1708–1719.

Parker, J. D., Taylor, G. J., & Bagby, R. M. (1992). Relationship between conjugate lateral eye movements and alexithymia. *Psychotherapy and Psychosomatics, 57,* 94–101.

Parker, J. D., Keightley, M. L., Smith, C. T., & Taylor, G. J. (1999). Interhemispheric transfer deficit in alexithymia: an experimental study. *Psychosomatic Medicine, 61,* 464–468.

Parsons, L. M., Denton, D., Egan, G., McKinley, M., Shade, R., Lancaster, J., et al. (2000). Neuroimaging evidence implicating cerebellum in support of sensory/cognitive processes associated with thirst. *Proceedings of the National Academy of Sciences of the USA, 97,* 2332–2336.

Paus, T. (2001). Primate anterior cingulate cortex: Where motor control drive cognition interface. *Nature Reviews Neuroscience, 2,* 417–424.

Pessoa, L., Kastner, S., & Ungerleider, L. G. (2003). Neuroimaging studies of attention: From modulation of sensory processing to top down control. *Journal of Neuroscience, 23,* 3990–3998.

Phan, K. L., Wager, T., Taylor, S. T., & Liberzon, I. (2002). Functional neuroanatomy of motion: A meta-analysis of emotion activation studies in PET and fMRI. *NeuroImage, 16,* 331–348.

Phillips, M. L. Gregory, L. J., Cullen, S., Cohen, S. N. V., Andrew, C., Giampietro, V., et al. (2003). The effect of negative emotional context on neural and behavioural responses to oesophageal stimulation. *Brain, 126,* 669–684.

Phillips, M. L., Williams, L. M., Heining, M., Herba, C. M., Russell, T., Andrew, C., et al. (2004). Differential neural responses to overt and covert presentations of facial expressions of fear and disgust. *NeuroImage, 21,* 1484–1496.

Poffenberger, A. T. (1912). Reaction time to retinal stimulation with special reference to the time lost in conduction through nerve centers. *Archives of Psychology, 13,* 1–73.

Reiman, E. M., Lane, R. D., Ahern, G. L., Schwartz, G. E., Davidson, R. J., Friston, K. J., et al. (1997). Neuroanatomical correlates of externally and internally generated human emotion. *American Journal of Psychiatry, 154,* 918–25.

Rolls, E. (2000). The orbitofrontal cortex and reward. *Cerebral Cortex, 10,* 284–294.

Ross, E. D., & Rush, A. J. (1981). Diagnosis and neuroanatomical correlates of depression in brain-damaged patients: Implications for a neurology of depression. *Archives of General Psychiatry, 38,* 1344–1354.

Ruesch, J. E. (1948). The infantile personality. *Psychosomatic Medicine, 10,* 134–144.

Sanfey, A. G., Rilling, J. K., Aronson, J. A., Nystrom, L. E., & Cohen, J. D. (2003). Neural basis of economic decision making in the ultimatum game. *Science, 300,* 1755–1758.

Schmidt, L. A., Fox, N. A., Goldberg, M. C., Smith, G. C., & Schulkin, J. (1999). Effects of acute prednisone administration on memory, attention and emotion in healthy human adults. *Psychoneuroendocrinology, 24,* 461–483.

Shamay-Tsoory, S. G., Tomer, R., Berger, B. D., & Aharon-Peretz, J. (2003). Characterization of empathy deficits following prefrontal brain damage: The role of the right ventromedial prefrontal cortex. *Journal of Cognitive Neuroscience, 15,* 324–337.

Sher, D., & Twaite, J. A. (1999). Relationship between child sexual abuse and alexithymic symptoms in a population of recovering adult substance abusers. *Journal of Childhood Sexual Abuse, 8,* 25–102.

Shipko, S. (1982). Further reflections on psychosomatic theory: Alexithymia and interhemispheric specialization. *Psychotherapy and Psychosomatics, 37,* 83–86.

Sifneos, P. E. (1973a). The prevalence of ''alexithymic'' characteristics in psychosomatic patients. *Psychotherapy and Psychosomatics, 22,* 255–262.

Sifneos, P. E. (1973b). Is dynamic psychotherapy contraindicated for a large number of patients with psychosomatic diseases? *Psychotherapy and Psychosomatics, 21,* 133–136.

Sifneos, P. E. (1975). Problems of psychotherapy of patients with alexithymic characteristics and physical disease. *Psychotherapy and Psychosomatics, 26*, 65–70.

Sifneos, P. E. (1991). Emotional conflict and deficit: An overview. *Psychotherapy and Psychosomatics, 56*, 116–122.

Sifneos, P. E. (2000). Alexithymia, clinical issues, politics and crime. *Psychotherapy and Psychosomatics, 69*, 113–116.

Simpson, J. S., Snyder, A. Z., Gusnard, D. A., & Raichle, M. E. (2001). Emotion induced changes in human medial prefrontal cortex: I. During cognitive task performance. *Neurobiology, 98*, 683–687.

Spalletta, G., Pasini, A., Costa, A., de Angelis, D., Ramundo, N., Paolucci, S., et al. (2001). Alexithymic features in stroke: Effects of laterality and gender. *Psychosomatic Medicine, 63*, 944–50.

Sperry, R. W., Zaidel, E., & Zaidel, D. (1979). Self recognition and social awareness in the deconnected minor hemisphere. *Neuropsychologia, 17*, 153–166.

Springer, S. P., & Deutsch, G. (1993), *Left brain, right brain*. New York: Freeman.

Taylor, G. J. (1984a). Alexithymia: Concept measurement, and implications for treatment. *American Journal of Psychiatry, 141*, 725–732.

Taylor, G. J. (1984b). Dr Taylor replies. *American Journal of Psychiatry, 141*, 1637–1638.

Taylor, G. J., Bagby, R. M., & Parker, J. D. A. (1992). The revised Toronto alexithymia scale: Some reliability, validity, and normative data. *Psychotherapy and Psychosomatics, 57*, 34–41.

Taylor, G. J., Bagby, R. M., & Parker, J. D. A. (1997). *Disorders of affect regulation: Alexithymia in medical and psychiatric illness*. Cambridge, UK: Cambridge University Press.

Taylor, G. J., Ryan, D., & Bagby, R. M. (1985). Toward the development of a new self-report alexithymia scale. *Psychotherapy and Psychosomatics, 44*, 191–199.

Taylor, S. T., Liberzon, I., Decker, L. R., & Koeppe, R. A. (2002). A functional anatomic study of emotion in schizophrenia. *Schizophrenia Research, 58*, 159–172.

Taylor, S. T., Phan, K. L., Decker, L. R., & Liberzon, U. (2003). Subjective rating of emotionally salient stimuli modulates neural activity. *NeuroImage, 18*, 650–659.

TenHouten, W. D., Hoppe, K. D., Bogen, J. E., & Walter, D. O. (1985). Alexithymia and the split brain: I. Lexical-level content analysis. *Psychotherapy and Psychosomatics, 43*, 202–208.

TenHouten, W. D., Hoppe, K. D., Bogen, J. E., & Walter, D. O. (1986). Alexithymia: An experimental study of cerebral commisurotomy patients and normal control subjects. *American Journal of Psychiatry, 143*, 312–315.

Tranel, D., Bechara, A., & Denburg, N. L. (2002). Asymmetric functional roles of right and left ventromedial prefrontal cortices in social conduct, decision-making, and emotional processing. *Cortex, 38*, 589–612.

Trigg, R. (1970). *Pain and emotion*. Oxford: Clarendon Press.

Tucker, D. M. (1981). Lateral brain function, emotion, and conceptualization. *Psychological Bulletin, 89*, 19–46.

Tucker, D. M., Roth, D. I., & Bair, T. B. (1986). Functional connections among cortical regions: Topography of EEG coherence. *Electroencephalography and Clinical Neurophysiology, 63*, 242–250.

Valera, E. M., & Berenbaum, H. (2001). A twin study of alexithymia. *Psychotherapy and Psychosomatics, 70*, 239–246.

Valenstein, E. S. (1990). The prefrontal area and psychosurgery. *Progress in Brain Research, 85*, 539–554.

Voeller, K. S. (1986). Right hemisphere deficit syndrome in children. *American Journal of Psychiatry, 143*, 1004–1009.

Vorst, H. C. M., & Bermond, B. (2001). Validity and reliability of the Bermond-Vorst Alexithymia Questionnaire. *Personality and Individual Differences, 30*, 413–434.

Whalen, P. J., Rauch, S. L., Etcoff, N. L., McInerney, S. C., Lee, M. B., & Jenike, M. A. (1998). Masked presentations of emotional facial expressions modulate amygdala activity without explicit knowledge. *Journal of Neuroscience, 18*, 411–418.

Wechsler, A. F. (1973). The effect of organic brain disease on recall of emotionally charged versus neutral narrative texts. *Neurology, 23*, 130–135.

Weintraub, S., & Mesulam, M. M. (1983). Developmental learning disabilities of the right hemisphere. *Archives of Neurology, 40*, 463–468.

Williams, M. A., McGlone, F., Abbott, D. F., & Mattingley, J. B. (2005). Differential amygdala responses to happy and fearful facial expressions depended on selective attention. *NeuroImage, 24*, 417–425.

Wise, T. N., Mann, L. S., Hryvniak, M., Mitchell, J. D., & Hill, B. (1990). The relationship between alexithymia and abnormal illness behavior. *Psychotherapy and Psychosomatics, 54*, 18–25.

Young, L. J., & Insel, T. R. (2002). Hormones and parental behavior. In J. B. Becker, M. Breedlove, C. Crews, & M. M. McCarthy (Eds.), *Behavioral endocrinology* (2nd ed., pp. 331–371). Cambridge, MA: MIT Press.

Zech, E., Luminet, O., Rime, B., & Wagner, H. (1999). Alexithymia and its measurement: Confirmatory factor analyses of the 20-item Toronto Alexithymia Scale and the Bermond-Vorst Alexithymia Questionnaire. *European Journal of Personality, 13*, 511–532.

Zeitlin, S. B., Lane, R. D., O'Leary, D. S., & Schrift, M. J. (1989). Interhemispheric transfer deficit and alexithymia. *American Journal of Psychiatry, 146*, 1434–439.

Zeitlin, S. B., McNally, R. J., & Cassiday, K. L. (1993). Alexithymia in victims of sexual assault: An effect of repeated traumatization? *American Journal of Psychiatry, 150*, 661–663.

SUBJECT INDEX

Acoustic startle, 211
Adrenergic-dependent memory, 203–205
Adrenocorticotropic hormone, 318
Affective go/no-go task, 237
Aggression, testosterone, 295
Akinetic depression, 254
Alerting, 208
Alexithymia, 332–360
   amygdala, 342–344
   anterior cingulate, 335, 338–340
   anterior commisure, 337–338
   cerebellum, 345, 346
   conjugate lateral eye movements, 334
   corpus callosum, 335–337
   cuneus, 345, 346
   emotional dysfunctional families, 333, 349–350
   emotionalising, 333
   genetics, 333
   hypochondria, 333, 346
   insular cortex, 345
   introduction of term, 333
   left hemisphere preference, 334–335, 345
   occipital cortex, 345
   pain sensitivity, 346
   parietal cortex, 345
   personality types, 348
   precuneus, 345, 346
   prefrontal cortex, 340–342
   professional help-seeking, 333, 346
   pulvinar, 345
   right hemisphere deficit, 334–335
   sexual assault, 333
   somatic illness, 333
   temporal lobe, 345
   thalamus, 345
   trauma, 333
Alzheimer's disease, facial emotion recognition, 261

Amnesic syndrome, 199
Amygdala, 203–209
   adrenergic receptors, 203–205
   alexithymia, 342–344
   anatomical connectivity with hippocampus, 205, 207, 210, 211
   autonomic nervous system, 211–212
   basolateral nucleus, 211
   bilateral destruction, 219–232
   bipolar disorder, 239
   central nucleus, 211–212
   cortisol, 296
   declarative memory, 205
   emotion experience, 227, 228
   emotion processing, 252
   emotional behaviour, 220
   emotional learning, 203
   emotionalising, 344
   facial expressions, 220, 234, 236, 292
   fear conditioning, 203
   fear processing, 252, 314
   functional dependence on hippocampus, 205
   functional similarity with hippocampus, 207
   HPA axis, 212
   interoceptive information, 199
   memory enhancement, 199, 203, 212
   modulation of memory, 203
   negative emotion, 225–226
   novelty, 207–208, 213
   OMPFC network, 291, 293
   perception modulation, 212
   phobias, 203
   psychopathy, 291, 292, 296
   schizophrenia, 236, 261, 274, 280
   social behaviour, 220, 226–227
   social phobia, 314–315, 319–320
   steroid hormones, 295–296
   testosterone, 296

Batch number: 08159237

Printed by Printforce, the Netherlands